PENGUIN BUSINESS

MONEY, MYTHS AND MANTRAS

Devina Mehra is founder, chairperson and managing director at First Global. She ran an investment banking and stockbroking business that has metamorphosed into an India and global fund management outfit. Hers was the first Indian investment firm to globalize twenty-five years ago. Devina's work has appeared in several publications, including the *Wall Street Journal, Financial Times, Forbes, Fortune, Business Week*, Bloomberg, Barron's, etc. She frequently appears on business channels such as CNBC, ET Now, NDTV Profit and CNBC Awaaz, among others. Devina was a gold medallist both at the Indian Institute of Management-Ahmedabad and Lucknow University. She was the only woman from the field of investing to appear on the *Fortune India* 2022 list of the '50 Most Powerful Women' along with Nirmala Sitharaman and Nita Ambani, among others.

ADVANCE PRAISE FOR THE BOOK

'Devina Mehra, a truly first-generation brilliant professional mind, shares her experience of going from zero to busting global investing myths. Emphasizing that the era of data-based investing is here, she explains that when the playing field changes, the game changes. *Money, Myths and Mantras* is an authentic read for anyone who wants to take the plunge in the world of ambiguity and probability called the stock market'
—**Ramdeo Agrawal, chairman and co-founder, Motilal Oswal Financial Services**

'Devina Mehra's "itch" to share her insights, as she mentions right at the outset, has resulted in a book that is nothing short of a gem. *Money, Myths and Mantras: The Ultimate Investment Guide* is an engaging, easy-to-read resource packed with practical wisdom. Devina's ability to break down complex ideas into clear, digestible lessons speaks of her deep expertise and roots in a family of educators. As someone with several years of experience navigating the ups and downs of the investment world, I can confidently say this book is a refreshing addition to any investor's bookshelf. Whether you're just starting out or have been in the game for years, it's got something for everyone. For beginners, it lays a solid educational foundation, and for seasoned investors, it serves as a friendly nudge to revisit the basics that often slip through the cracks—like a gentle reminder to not overcomplicate things when you think you know it all. What really sets this book apart is how Devina effortlessly combines the latest technologies—such as artificial intelligence, machine learning and quantitative analysis—with the timeless value of human intuition in investing. She demonstrates how these modern tools can enhance decision-making, while reminding us that, in the end, the human touch is often what makes the difference. It is a perfect blend of forward-thinking and traditional wisdom, offering something valuable to both the tech-savvy and those who trust their instincts. Whether you're already an expert or just beginning, this book is a refreshing and indispensable guide, with a little humour thrown in for an introduction'—**Safir R. Anand, investor; senior partner and head of trademarks, contractual and commercial IP, Anand and Anand**

'You now have no excuse. In one book, you can learn the importance of building a robust investment portfolio, starting with asset allocation and diversification across geographies and assets, and then understand how to value companies and what are the behavioural and analytical mistakes you must avoid. While stressing that she does not want to storify her investments, relying more on numbers and data, Devina tells great stories about Buffett and Lynch and many others, which effectively convey the different messages she is trying to drive home'—**Samir Arora, founder and CIO, Helios Capital**

PENGUIN BUSINESS

Penguin Business is an imprint of the Penguin Random House group of companies
whose addresses can be found at global.penguinrandomhouse.com

Published by Penguin Random House India Pvt. Ltd
4th Floor, Capital Tower 1, MG Road,
Gurugram 122 002, Haryana, India

First published in Penguin Business by Penguin Random House India 2025

10 9 8 7 6 5 4 3

ISBN 9780143466512

Typeset in Bembo Std by MAP Systems, Bengaluru, India
Printed at Replika Press Pvt. Ltd, India

www.penguin.co.in

MONEY, MYTHS AND MANTRAS

THE ULTIMATE INVESTMENT GUIDE

DEVINA MEHRA

PENGUIN
BUSINESS

An imprint of Penguin Random House

To my parents (Late) Dr Amarnath Mehra and Swaraj Mehra, who taught me to think for myself and not be afraid of having opinions, even if they did not 'fit in'

Contents

SECTION II
MYTHS AND MANTRAS

SECTION III
HUMAN BEHAVIOUR AND INVESTING

SECTION IV
THE FUTURE IS HERE: THE CHANGING
NATURE OF INVESTING

Foreword

Dustin Hoffman was an unemployed, anonymous, struggling stage actor in 1960s New York when *The Graduate*, a movie he starred in, was released. In a preview showing before the release, he noticed a woman with a limp and a cane on the way out. She was Rudie Harris, famous New York gossip columnist. She recognized him and, pointing her cane towards him, said, 'Your life will never be the same.'

Devina's debut book, *Money, Myths and Mantras: The Ultimate Investment Guide* may or may not change your life forever, but it will certainly change the way you think in financial markets.

In 1992, when Devina and I were practically financial newbies. The so-called Harshad Mehta bull run, the first of the modern Indian finance era, was drawing to a close.

The Sensex had gone from below 1000 points to touch the then lofty levels of 4500. Associated Cement Company or ACC, as it was popularly known, was the market darling and had become a 100-bagger in three years. Yes, 100x. Fortunes had been made by many an old timer. You can understand that we felt left out of the greatest bull run in finance. I remember thinking, 'God, I missed the bus. All the money has been made. I came to the party, but the party was ending.' Here I was, a well-read MBA graduate, and yet I could not name a global cement company. Yet all my firm's jobbers, traders and even punters on the street, knew the exact price of a cement bag in Coimbatore every evening.

To borrow from Churchill, in retrospect, it was not the beginning or the end, but just the end of the beginning. As is well documented, the Sensex rose over the next thirty years to an eye-popping level of 85000 plus (Thursday, 26 September 2024). That is an astounding gain of 1811 per cent or a CAGR (compound annual growth rate) of 14.35 per cent without dividends.

When I joined Dalal Street in the late 1980s, information was scarce and insights were scarcer. CNBC India had not yet been launched. Buffett meant the gourmet lunch spread at the Taj Hotel in Colaba and Munger might have been a district in Bihar, for all we knew. We flew in the dark with no flight instruments to ease our path. Gradually, the cloud cover improved and we got our bearings. Dalal Street became Main Street.

I've asked a few veterans of that 1990s era, what has the best decade for investing? Was it the 1990s when Dr Manmohan Singh started the liberalization process? Was it in 2000, as India basked in the new tech and millennium? Or was it in 2014 when Narendra Modi first came to power? The answer— almost unanimously is—the coming decade. There will be more opportunities to make more money. India will grow richer and more prosperous. The next bull market will dwarf the current one in gains, time and magnitude. This time, thankfully, I'm neither confused nor puzzled. I am a believer.

To help you navigate the treacherous waters, it would help to have a manual. A 'what works, what doesn't' tome that has distilled the experience of the last thirty years in India and the wisdom from the last few hundred years of global boom and busts. A book that has already separated the wheat from the chaff for us—the myths and the mantras!

Well, worry no more. Devina has done just that! She is the Muriel Siebert of Indian Finance. Muriel was of course a trailblazer, pioneer and the first lady of finance on Wall Street.

She became the first women member of the NYSE (New York Stock Exchange), shattering the glass ceiling. Every door that opened was one she kicked down for herself. True for Muriel, true for Devina.

Hundreds of books have been written about investing. However, cliché as it may sound, this book provides an original perspective on the discipline. It not only talks about investing in equities but also underlines the significance of other, often overlooked, asset classes like gold, real estate and debt. It also looks beyond India for investment opportunities.

The book is engrossing and myth-busting, written (mostly) in an accessible manner. I feel it does a great service to investors by simplifying seemingly complex but critical themes such as asset allocation, diversification, valuation, business growth drivers, global economy, impact of interest rates, among others.

What I like about Devina's approach to investing is her ability to identify and expound on the issues that matter the most but are seldom explained clearly.

From DCF (discounted cash flow) to investing in your circle of competence, she picks up each investment dictum, holds it up to light and gives you all possible angles on it. She goes deep to understand the rules of investing but also uses what she calls her first principles approach to point out how and where they do not work.

It is her attitude to investing and life that makes this book different from the usual books on investing. Almost every book on investing, for instance, talks about buying stocks but very little is written about when to sell them. Devina lucidly, with examples, explains the art and science of selling stocks. This book busts many a myth surrounding investing and explains how to cut through the clutter of often confusing advice.

Devina's unwavering focus on numbers, data and logic pervades the book and it includes some great stories and analogies to explain how you will benefit more by listening to numbers, rather than stories, but also how your own brain can sabotage your investment journey.

Devina brings not only business chops, but also analytical chops. Her research is read, not only by a domestic audience, but a global one. (I know, because I have seen her quoted in the global press.) She looks at a page of numbers and they light up like a Diwali firecracker, illuminating the path and offering that rarest of commodity—unique insights. Peter Lynch made Wall Street accessible to Main Street. What Devina's book promises to do is to take Dalal Steet to Bharat. To return to Dustin Hoffman, he is quoted as saying, 'Stardom equals freedom. It's the only equation that matters.' Equity markets done properly help you achieve financial freedom. That is where this book helps!

Enjoy the collected wisdom, lessons and learnings of a pro. Happy investing.

Ramesh S. Damani
Member, BSE
Mumbai, 25 October 2024

Introduction

The book is finally ready!

It has been a decades-long journey—at least in the head.

Vaguely, over many years, I have thought about writing a book. But it was never more than a background thought.

Then, somehow, at the beginning of 2022, I thought maybe this was going to be the year when I finally got around to writing my book. And this, when I had never been the sort to make New Year resolutions. Maybe the universe was listening, because this was the year several of my friends prodded me towards it. And then Manish of Penguin Random House India got in touch with me and started chasing me for a book. Finally, the book was on its way to becoming a real project.

The year 2022 was a rather hectic one on many fronts, so it was almost October before I could really put my mind to the book and begin to structure it in my head. Most of the first draft was written through 2023, even as work and life happened all around me. The editing happened in 2024.

It took longer than expected—but of course. As there were weeks in a row when I wrote nothing at all, partly because I may have been writing something on the contemporary markets, which would not go into the book. Or, as Daniel Kahneman explains in his writings, almost all projects have time and cost overruns, but we still go on thinking that ours won't—one of the many quirks of being a human being.

As for the topic/content of what to write in my first book, that was clear to me from the very beginning. Several people had been asking for an autobiography or life journey kind of book, but I was always sure that the first one had to be about investing principles—a distillation of what I had learnt over three decades of analysing portfolios, companies, securities, economies and more.

It has been a long journey, and the most rewarding part of it has been the learning along the way, and that still continues. As I often say, the most remarkable, and to me the most exciting, even endearing, part of this profession, is that after more than thirty years in it there is always something new to be learnt every single day. There has never come and there will never come a day when I can say that I know it all.

For me, personally, half the fun of learning is also in sharing. In telling someone else, '*Isn't it wonderful that this is the way XYZ happens? Let me tell you about it.*' The bigger the insight, the more you are itching to explain it to someone else.

Maybe it comes from the genes of my teacher parents! Both were professors.

My father was always disappointed that I did not follow in his footsteps because teaching was the love of his life. But I think, ultimately, without the formal robes of an academic, a lot of what I have done has had to do with teaching and research. My parents' legacy lives on in me.

I have been at least partly a teacher, and as every teacher knows, when you teach you also learn.

Coming back to the book, I thought about the conventional pattern of having chapters of predetermined length and following a certain format throughout, but I realized that there were topics that could be explained well in maybe 800 words, whereas there were others for which even 2500 words would not suffice.

Trying to shoehorn one type into the other did not make sense to me. There were topics that required charts and tables, and those that did not. There were also topics that I have covered in videos, for which I could provide QR code links to.

As a very avid reader, I have an aversion to non-fiction books where a few ideas are stretched out to book length. I did not want to torture my reader in that fashion, just to meet a pre-determined chapter length.

In short, I let the subject matter decide the length and the format of the chapters, which makes this book rather unconventional.

I have tried to keep tables, formulas and equations to a minimum, in spite of temptations to the contrary. I wanted to make the book simple and understandable for everyone with an interest in the markets and in their own investments, which is just about everybody, of course. Because if you are not investing, you certainly should be.

Barring a couple of chapters on PE ratios, DuPont analysis, cash flows, etc., most of the book is fairly straightforward. If you, dear reader, find those chapters heavy going, you may skip them on your first reading.

I have tried to make each topic as simple as possible, but no simpler.

I have tried to convey my sense of wonder about this world, where when you tilt it this way or that, the picture, like in a kaleidoscope, changes, and where conventional wisdom is often wrong.

Of course, if you want to really become a consummate investor, there is no way around numbers, calculations and financial statements. You should educate yourself with at least the basics to make sense of this world. But this book is not a finance or investing or valuation textbook meant to guide you through the very first steps of your investment journey. I have later talked about the kind of books you can read to explore these topics further.

The idea here is to make you look at the world of investing through a fresh lens, to think of concepts you may not have thought of, to have a framework for analysing securities and investments, and of course to enjoy the joy of discovery when something just clicks into place.

My path, learnings and principles in investing have not been the same as anyone else's, which is as it should be. But none of this happens in a vacuum either. Many ideas come from all over, react, ferment, combine and separate till something new and unique emerges.

As Newton said about science, we all stand on the shoulders of giants who have gone before us. It is equally true of the investing business. Except that in investing, absolute truths are far harder to come by, experiments cannot be in controlled conditions, enough data points may not be available for a rigorous statistical analysis, and so on. It is the real world with a messy, unknowable future, and that is what makes it fun too.

On a related note, there has also been a niggling thought in my mind that there may be concepts that have their roots in some books or other reading that I have done in the past, maybe decades ago, and where I have forgotten their source. I have, obviously, tried to acknowledge the sources where I am aware of them, but I apologize in advance if something has been overlooked.

One conundrum has been that the theme of my song is that one should look at data, and not stories. But, paradoxically, I have had to think of examples, or rather stories, to explain why one should do that!

Cliched but true: hope you enjoy reading the book as much as I enjoyed writing it. Because it HAS been fun to write it, mainly because I have written only what I felt like writing.

My Journey

'*A journey of a thousand miles begins with a single step.*'

For me, the first step was a little over thirty years ago. I resigned from Citibank on 23 August 1993. And, post the inevitable notice period, got started on my entrepreneurial journey on 1 October 1993.

I know that this book is not about my life journey, but a little background may be necessary.

It's been a long journey since that day when I quit the bank; from getting the coveted Bombay Stock Exchange (BSE) membership to making it as the only investment professional in the 'Most Powerful Women' listing in *Fortune*.[1]

As they say, '*Mauka bhi hai Dastoor bhi.*' Meaning, it is both the (right) occasion and the convention. Hence, allow me the indulgence of going back down memory lane and revisiting some of the landmarks and turning points in my life, starting with the memory of that long-ago August day when almost everybody I met in the corridors of Citibank asked me, '*Devina, what happened? You are looking so happy.*'

Step one was getting membership of the BSE, then the largest stock exchange in the country. And suddenly the proverbial connecting of the dots in hindsight happened—to make my goal manifest against all odds!

Of course, the old-time BSE brokers didn't want outsiders, but some things from my past working and academic life came together to make it happen:

- the five years I reluctantly spent in investment banking (at the time called 'merchant banking'), which gave me the required capital market experience. No other department in a bank would have given me that.
- the two extra marks for my IIM gold medal, which pushed me over the cut-off.
- and then my experience as a credit analyst, which became the launch pad for my becoming a pioneer in securities research.

How long back that was can be seen from the famous HDFC Bank report which came out in 1996, just a year after the bank's IPO and predicted that this baby would become Arnold Schwarzenegger, the then Mr Universe. That report has my name as member, BSE, because in those days only proprietorships or partnerships were allowed as brokers . . . not companies.

A couple of years after I started my business, the National Stock Exchange (NSE) came into being. And companies were allowed to become stockbrokers. So First Global formally came into being.

Then came the heady 1990s, when First Global was one of the top stockbrokers to institutions, especially foreign institutional investors (FIIs). First Global made a name for itself with its original, hard-hitting and well-analysed research reports. We did not like sitting in the comfortable consensus and always called things as we saw it.

As I have said before, learning is my prime motivation and thrill in life. Hence, when the scope for new learnings began to fade towards the end of the 1990s, I decided to go global.

And let me tell you, no person endorsed this move.

All people experienced in the global markets said it could not be done; that one could not research securities sitting remotely. And that even if I did, no one would listen to me on global companies when they had all these old, established Wall Street firms to choose from.

But I had faith in my craft and in my analysis, and that's how First Global became not just the first Indian but also the first Asian firm (excluding Japan) to go global, with membership of the London Stock Exchange (LSE) in 1999 and the National Association of Securities Dealers, USA (NASD) in 2001.

A new experience of understanding more complex companies, geographies and economies followed. Most gratifyingly, First Global was recognized for its quality research by every single major publication in the world. First Global's research was covered by *Forbes*, *Fortune*, *Business Week*, *Wall Street Journal*, *Barron's* and many other publications.

Yes, it could be done.

What next, was the question. Till then, what I and First Global had been doing is called sell-side work. In investing/finance, the buy side consists of those who actually manage funds or assets—for example, those who run mutual funds or Portfolio Management Services (PMS).

Sell side is industry jargon for broking, investment banking, etc., where you are 'selling' your services to fund managers or asset managers who are making the final decisions on investments. Sell-side participants are those who support asset managers with research, stockbroking services, etc. They also help companies raise money via public offerings, institutional placements and the like.

Doing sell-side work, providing research to even the largest funds in the world, became a bit frustrating, as even after all your analysis and conviction, the fund manager may not take the decision you have advised for reasons of their own.

The next logical step was to move to direct fund management.

We started that with global assets in 2015. We then had to decide on the best way to move forward as the investment landscape itself changed.

The challenge was whether you adapt to the changes or become a fossil still chanting the mantras of the 1980s and 1990s, even when the world had totally transformed and required a new set of skills.

It was the equivalent of the dilemma now faced by automakers: Do they continue to sell combustion engine cars forever, or move to electric/eco-friendly vehicles?

Consequently, the next big transformation was to move to a Human-plus-Machine system, driven at the core by artificial intelligence and machine learning, where all the expertise we had gathered over the decades was coded into a rigorous machine system, which could then be applied on a bias-free, noise-free basis on the entire universe of securities available.

But of course, my life started a lot before my entrepreneurial journey did, and maybe I should start at the very beginning to put all this in context.

I need to tell the story of how I, a person who did not even know what an equity share was till the relatively ripe age of nineteen and had a near-zero understanding or knowledge of business, got into this space. Also how, when the business of securities research started in India, happened to enter it right at the beginning, and how the ride has been since, with its myriad twists and turns.

It has been quite a journey from the City of Nawabs, Lucknow, to the City of Gold, Bombay/Mumbai—from my *janmabhoomi* to my *karmabhoomi*.

Did I know that I would end up in the business of investing or even finance when growing up? Not at all.

It all happened through a series of twists and turns, and the story unfolds only in hindsight.

The things in my life that drew me, albeit indirectly, into his journey have been two—one, my love for learning. And two, at least being clear about what I did not want in life or in my work. There was little clarity as to what I wanted to do though.

As it turned out, the profession I ended up in did not even exist, at least in India, when I was growing up.

Here's just a quick sketch of how I ended up here.

There is nothing more thrilling for me than learning a new fact or a new way of looking at something or gaining a new angle of understanding something familiar. This has been the theme of my life, from the time I was a kid to now.

However, the other aspect of this has been that I have always liked to learn a whole variety of things rather than go deeper and deeper into a single matter or subject, which is the reason why I did not do a doctorate. Yes, growing up in an academic household like I did, completing your education meant doing a PhD.

I have also always had a deep desire to understand things in depth to the best of my abilities, till they make sense from first principles, rather than accept something simply because 'that is the way it has always been done' or 'this is what the authorities on the subject say'.

So, while I was never a rebel for the sake of it, if something made logical sense to me I never really cared about being in the minority of one.

The benchmark for me all along has been whether I am doing the best I can—it has had very little to do with what others around me are doing or not doing. This has held, through my student days and till date. While both in the university and at the Indian Institute of Management Ahmedabad (IIM-A), many kept track of their competitors' grades, I never bothered to.

As I said, I grew up in Lucknow, and up till my undergraduate degree, that's where I was. In terms of knowing what I did not want, I was the only person in my maths class who did not even attempt the engineering entrance exams after class 12. This was despite the fact that I had never lost a single mark in a maths test throughout my two years in classes 11 and 12. I was very clear that I did not want to become an engineer.

For my BA, the subjects I chose were maths, statistics and English literature, and I was the only person in the university with this combination. Of course, to varying degrees, these have been of use in my subsequent career. Not surprising, as they are kind of basic building blocks. But even in college I had no knowledge of finance or even economics.

When I went to IIM-A, I had never encountered accounts of any kind. In fact, during my two years there, almost everything was completely new to me, and there were many novel things to be learnt, which I loved.

When I graduated from IIM in 1986, there was nothing like a securities industry in India. There were no professional brokers or fund managers beyond a handful in organizations like Unit Trust of India.

For all practical purposes, this career option did not exist. By a process of elimination, I applied to banks and consultancies, got selected at Citibank and started off in investment banking, which was then known as merchant banking, as I have mentioned earlier. Its function was to raise funds for companies via public issues (the fancier 'Initial Public Offering', or IPO, had not come into usage), rights issues, issues of non-convertible or convertible debentures, etc.

It was very different from how things are now. The Securities and Exchange Board of India (SEBI) did not exist. The pricing of public issues was decided by a department in the Ministry of Finance, called the Controller of Capital Issues, or CCI.

The prospects for innovation were limited, although I did do some novel things. One was to buy the non-convertible part of convertible debentures from retail investors and then package them to sell to institutions.

This was an example of first principles thinking, as I realized that most small investors were buying the debentures for the equity part and were saddled with the debt, which they did not want. On the other hand, the likes of UTI, LIC, etc., were looking for corporate debt to buy.

I ended up spending over seven years in Citibank, first in merchant banking and then in corporate credit, which was the credit and risk assessment department for the bank.

In hindsight, both these stints helped me—the first by giving me exposure to the capital markets, and the second by providing me with an understanding of many industries and companies.

Mind you, a professional security or fund management industry had still not come into existence. The share market consisted of only old-style brokers, and the only stock exchange of note was the BSE. Then there were the smaller, regional exchanges. It was still physical trading with an open outcry system. The NSE had not yet come into being. Yes, it was a very different era.

Then, in 1992, the BSE announced that it was going to give out memberships to seventy-one professionals, at a membership price of Rs 55 lakh each. At that time, BSE membership, or the BSE card as it was called, was trading at around Rs 2 crore in the market. BSE allowed only proprietorships and partnerships as members as they wanted brokers to have unlimited liability. No corporate membership was allowed.

I applied, even though I was a complete outsider. The meandering story of my membership is something I will talk about another time. For now, suffice it to say that the whole process took a long time, and in the midst of that there was another big change. In the 1992-93 Union budget, then finance minister Dr Manmohan Singh announced that the Indian stock market was being opened to FIIs.

This was the immediate trigger for me to start my own firm. With this opening up I thought that professional research would become valuable in the market, where it hitherto did not exist. That was when I resigned from Citibank and started off as an entrepreneur on 1 October 1993.

A few months later, I also got membership to the BSE. The year after that, NSE was formed. After a written test and interview, I got corporate membership there too.

That is how the journey began, hands-on in the stock market.

I was one of the pioneers of equity research, at a time when the term itself was not understood. Time and time again I would call up companies, and especially the old-time, conservative companies would say things like, '*Why should we meet you? You can read the annual report and come to our AGM.*' No one, obviously, had heard of anything like an investor relations department. It was truly uncharted territory.

In terms of concepts, securities research had been barely taught at all in our MBA course, and I had to learn it on the job by reading books. At times I would even ask the institutional investor clients to recommend books to help me understand valuation and cash flows more deeply than I did at the time.

On the ground, it was a fun time going around the country through the heat and dust of the outskirts of the National Capital Region (NCR), Chennai, Hyderabad and other cities, meeting companies. Plus, there was visiting of plants, many literally in the middle of nowhere—something that I had really enjoyed since my Citibank days.

In terms of business, we were dealing with the who's who of the investing world—every large institutional investor in the world investing in India was a First Global client.

Along with these foreign institutional investors entering India came the foreign brokerage houses too. In the beginning I thought that these companies had been doing research for decades whereas we were just starting out, so there must be a lot I could learn from their reports. But once I actually went through them, I was usually disappointed at their quality, both in terms of the content and the presentation. The analysis was pedestrian or compromised and the presentation was extremely boring and soporific. It was a sea of mediocrity at best, and actively misleading at worst. Thereafter, I never bothered to see what the competition was doing and decided to learn this business from first principles—yes, that phrase comes up again.

First Global even did a lot of pioneering work in terms of devising new ratios, new ways of looking at things and making many adjustments to financials that made things clear or more accurately pinpointed what was happening in a business.

The research team and I, personally, spent a lot of time refining estimates and ways of looking at companies, and delving deep into the art and science of investing. I personally went through every assumption in every spreadsheet.

We also spent a lot of effort on making our research reports readable and not just a boring collection of bullet points, charts and graphs.

What we call clickbait now did not exist as a term, but that is what we aimed for with the covers of our research reports—to have catchy headlines to make you open the report, which was itself backed up with solid research. We became one of the leading institutional brokers through the nineties, dealing almost exclusively with foreign institutional investors, who are now called foreign portfolio investors (FPIs).

We pulled no punches, no matter which company we were talking about. We always called it the way we saw it. That became our brand and our reputation as First Global.

Towards the end of the nineties, First Global truly went global. There were two triggers for it.

One was the 1998 Asian crisis, which saw crashes in all the Southeast Asian markets including Taiwan, South Korea, Thailand and Indonesia. Each of these markets fell between 50 per cent and 90 per cent in dollar terms in a single year.[2]

And these were not just any markets, these were the Asian Tigers. They were the poster children of great growth economies: Even India wanted to be an Asian Tiger.

This brought home to me the danger of being exposed to a single market—that in a matter of a single year, an Indonesian investor could be down 90 per cent . . . the thought itself was scary.

Combined with that was the fact that I was getting bored of covering the same old companies, from Bajaj Auto and SBI to Infosys, HDFC, etc. It had been the same list for a while, so that is when I started exploring global options, which was something no one else in India had dreamt of doing.

As I said, our clients were all the major institutions and funds of the world, and by that time one had become friends with fairly senior people there, so I decided to bounce off this idea of globalizing. The feedback I got was that I should try adding one or two more emerging markets, like maybe a Thailand or a Philippines, and since I already knew fund managers looking after those regions, maybe I would get some business there.

But to me it did not make sense. My take was—what was the point of adding a couple of small markets? I wanted to go to the largest markets in the world, like the USA and Europe.

Everyone told me that it could not be done, that nobody would listen to someone coming from India and writing research on American and European companies. Remember, this is well before any outsourcing or off-shoring of research was thought of, I was also told by all the industry veterans that if I wanted to go to the West at all, then I should cover those stocks in the US and Europe which did not have much coverage—basically the smaller stocks.

I disregarded all advice and decided to go head-to-head with the largest firms in the world by covering all large global stocks, which at that time meant stocks like IBM, Cisco, Procter and Gamble, Walmart, Microsoft, etc., in the US, and also stocks across the world, from UK banks to European pharmaceutical stocks to even Chinese and Japanese companies. My logic was that if I knew how to analyse companies and securities, I should be able to analyse them anywhere.

The same first principles of thinking, of delving deep, understanding and estimating things step by step, and having the courage of one's convictions, meant that we, at First Global, found ourselves putting out reports on the largest names in the world. And our work stood out enough to be featured in every major business publication, some of which I have listed earlier. It was one of the most satisfying points in my career.

My stand—that if you knew how to analyse companies, or for that matter, industries or economies, you could do it anywhere—was vindicated.

It was an exciting time because companies in the West are far more complex than Indian companies. The business scenarios are fast changing, and what is a better example of this than to tell you that tech majors in the early 2000s meant Nokia, Dell, Motorola, IBM, Cisco, etc., and now when you talk of technology it is a whole different list.

First Global became the first Asian member (excluding Japan) of the London Stock Exchange in 1999 and of the NASD in 2001, as I have mentioned before. We really were trailblazers.

As in India, we never held back from calling it the way we saw it—this included being the only firm on Wall Street to have a buy on Amazon in early 2001 at a price of $12 (split-adjusted $0.75) and calling out the scams in Enron and Worldcom much before they became public—all coming out of cold, objective analysis of the numbers and other facts available.

All this while we were on the 'sell' side, i.e., a securities/ brokerage house providing research and advice to fund/asset managers. After a while, we started to get a little fed up of trying to persuade fund managers to pursue our ideas; they appeared to be stuck, each in their own unique groove.

Hence began a slow move towards asset management. However, even there I felt that while we had worked on understanding investments with a lot of study and analysis, made alterations to conventional wisdom and even created fresh formulas to understand financials and markets, there was still something missing.

I started to add on other bits and pieces—like understanding that even when one identified a buy or sell trade, sometimes the market continued to move in the reverse direction for some more time and that the entry or exit could be timed better. This led to a system which became more refined over time and added some performance to the fundamental analysis.

Even so, what held me back from jumping with both feet into the asset management business was cognizance of the fact that managing someone's hard-earned wealth could not be taken lightly. While one could take higher risks with one's own money, when taking on the responsibility of someone else's money, you had to have a system that had some consistency, replicability and predictability.

And honest assessment through the decades showed me that we were not quite there yet.

That is the reason why, in spite of having a portfolio management services (PMS) licence since the year 2000, we did not launch an India PMS product till 2020. The global advisory and asset management product was launched about five years before that.

Eventually the final piece in the puzzle got fitted in. We could feed our expertise into an artificial intelligence and machine learning system, which could then objectively and systematically apply the criteria to the entire universe of securities, much more consistently than a human being could. And once we had that system in place, our asset management journey began in earnest.

Personally speaking, I did not mind being the first to go global or the 'last' to launch a PMS. The criterion as always was whether I could do a good job, especially for the client, rather than what everyone else was doing.

The proof of the pudding is in the eating. In the four years since we started, our India PMS schemes have been the top-performing large-cap, multi-cap and flexi-cap schemes. On a risk-adjusted basis, the gap between us and our competitors is even larger. In simple terms, not only have we given the highest returns, but these returns have also come with minimum volatility and drawdowns or losses.

While much has changed in this whole journey, including the business First Global does, certain parts of our DNA have remained the same.

A sample of some of the things I've always told my team:

- Never use a formula whose derivation you do not know.
- Never use a model unless you can explain its limitations and assumptions.
- Nothing is sacrosanct or written in stone: not what I tell you, not what is written in a textbook, not what is said by the greatest investor or professor!
- Test everything against what is happening in the real markets and see what the data shows.
- Let the numbers emerge, whether it is company margins or macroeconomic predictions, rather than start with a view and torture the data to make it say what you want to say.

All this and more lies ahead in the book you hold in your hands.

SECTION I

Getting Started:
The Basics

This is the section that gives you the starting framework telling you how to view your investments and portfolio.

This is also the section where I have discussed some investment basics. A few chapters may seem difficult or 'heavy', especially for those without a background in finance or investment. If that is the case, you can skip them and come back to them sometime later.

However, a top-down look is required, in addition to a map, to navigate the field of investments. So that is where I begin.

Getting the Basics Right: The Four Thumb Rules for Your Financial Health

Let us start at the very beginning . . . a very good place to start—as the song goes. Let us start with a broad, top-down look at your investments.

What do you think of when you think of the term 'investments'?

Most people think of investments in the stock market, mutual funds, etc. But what about the Public Provident Fund (PPF) you bought for tax-saving? The bank fixed deposits? The plot of land you bought or inherited? The apartment you are waiting to get possession of? Each of these is an investment. All of them have to be considered to get an overall picture of your finances before you decide on what you want your financial future to look like.

Plus, as is known, during the course of your investing journey, you have no option but to live through bull markets and bear markets, at times ferocious ones. How do you ensure that your financial investments get a clean bill of health and not end up in the ICU?

What are the basic tenets to keep in mind while investing?

To my mind, they are four in number, and these make up the framework with which you need to view your investments. Of course, there are overlaps between the four.

Each of these concepts will be dealt with in more detail later in the book. The following descriptions of these only provide you a starting framework.

Lesson 1: *Asset allocation* sahi hai

Asset allocation is not just the best thing, it's the only thing.

If you are just going to be a single-asset (say, equity only) player, then you are not going to last very long in this game.

Sometime back, I got a question on social media asking me, 'I am a young person in a good job—so should I have 100 per cent investment in equities?'

And my answer was no, because there are all kinds of demands that may come on your finances: you may lose your job, you may have a family emergency, you may want to buy a house, you may want to study further after a few years, and so on.

Basically, you may have unexpected financial demands in the future, which you may not be factoring in just now.

Equity returns have low predictability, not just on a one- or two-year basis, but sometimes even over a longer time frame. For example, during the entire decade from 2010 to 2020, Indian equity markets compounded at just about 8.5 per cent when fixed deposit rates were also around 8 per cent. So you saw a lot of volatility, with practically no additional return for taking equity risk at all, for a whole decade.[3]

Asset allocation basically means your investment pie chart is strategically diversified across various available asset classes.

Why does asset allocation work? Because different assets give disparate returns at various points in time.

To give a recent example: In 2019, government treasury instruments in India were up 9.5 per cent. Gold prices rose 24.6 per cent. In contrast, the Nifty500 delivered a mere 7.7 per cent return.[4]

But did you ever hear any fund manager or your financial adviser tell you that you were better off investing, or at least diversifying, into government paper and gold, instead of focusing on equities, if you wanted the best returns? I suspect not.

The reason for this is simple: nobody in the business of fund management or financial advice makes much or any money by recommending investments in government securities or gold. The maximum fees are for recommending equity.

All behaviour, good or bad, is always driven by incentives, and sellers of equities incentivize their salespeople far more than sellers of any other asset class, even if they do not deliver returns.

That is part of the reason for this '100 per cent in equity if you are young' recommendations you often see.

Don't ever forget this!

Lesson 2: Take a portfolio approach to investing

Most investors believe that taking individual stock advice, or 'tips' from friends, brokers, talking heads on TV—that is, almost anyone—and then implementing them on their own is the way to making big money.

Wrong. This is a one-way ticket to financial ruin. The correct way to do it is to take a portfolio approach to determine your asset and equity selection.

One part of this is, of course, asset allocation, which is discussed in more detail later in the book.

But even within your equity portfolio, be mindful of the weightage of each of your stocks and each sector.

For every stock you buy, be absolutely clear about the allocation for that stock and how much it changes the weightage of its industry in your portfolio, and how it alters the risk profile of your equity pie.

Concentration in a particular sector or couple of sectors may give you market–beating returns for a couple of quarters, possibly even a couple of years, but that kind of concentrated portfolio always comes to grief.

Just making random stock purchases without a clear portfolio plan will lead you to a point of no return in your investing life.

A case in point are the professional fund managers who put 40 per cent to 60 per cent of their clients' money in financial stocks and saw portfolio values erode dramatically during the COVID-occasioned crash in February–March 2020.

Lesson 3: If there is one God in investing, it is risk management

Prevention is always better than cure. You have heard this many times. This applies equally to wealth as it does to health.

Strong risk management is that preventive measure that can ensure you never need to go into a financial hospital.

Avoiding big losses is about the closest to golden advice you can ever get.

To illustrate this, if your Rs 100 becomes Rs 65 in a market fall, you need a 50+ per cent rise in the market to just come back to Rs 100! That's usually a two to three-year journey.

Falls and rises in the market are not symmetrical. A 50 per cent fall requires a 100 per cent rise in the portfolio value to come back to where you started out from. Therefore, always first concentrate on minimizing big losses (called drawdowns by professionals, to soften the blow) rather than maximizing returns.

As human beings, we are not accustomed to making decisions that recognize pain or crystallize losses. We are happier taking pills to mask pain.

Recognizing and booking a loss becomes an ego game: 'How could I be wrong?' The loss-aversion bias is hard-coded into our psyche. It does not help that we are conditioned to be pained by losses and to avoid them.

This translates into unwillingness to accept a mistake.

Unfortunately, this approach can bring a permanent end to your investing career.

It is marketed by selectively cherry-picking data.

In reality, it is always better to ruthlessly accept a loss and look for better places to deploy the remaining capital.

Unless you are prepared to be brutally clinical about surgically removing losses from your portfolio, you are destined to see them grow into terminally festering wounds.

> Some of the most misleading advice that you hear is to keep averaging on the way down.

Stop losses are, of course, only one part of the risk management process—but an important one.

Lesson 4: Diversify globally if you want to avoid SCCARS

SCCARS stands for single country, single currency, single asset risks. The history of markets around the world shows that this is not a theoretical risk. The Asian crisis of 1997–98 saw the stock markets of all Southeast Asian nations fall by 50 per cent to 90 per cent in dollar terms. Investors in Indonesia saw their net worth erode by 90 per cent in a single year, and even in fast-growing Taiwan the loss was a hefty 50 per cent.[5]

The Southeast Asian crisis is not an isolated example. As we all know, the Japanese stock market did not see the levels it reached in the 1980s for over three decades.

Market falls may not even be related to how great your economy or country looks. The crisis of 1997–98 happened in what were known as the Asian Tigers, the fastest-growing economies in the world at that point!

As I write this in 2023, the Chinese market is still way below its 2007 levels, even as the Chinese economy has gone up six to seven times from that year.

In India itself, the ten-year data for returns from the Indian stock market from 2010 to 2020 in dollar terms was a shocker: it was negative 3 per cent.

> There has been a depreciation of over 85 per cent in the value of the Indian rupee over the course of less than a full career.

What it means is that the average Indian's wealth was eroding in US dollar terms for a whole decade. India was an underperformer almost every year relative to most other global markets.

Therefore, contrary to what is constantly told to you, India was a very poor-performing market for several years compared with its global peers. Of course, that has changed since . . . because, as I've said elsewhere, no theme runs forever.

> If you strip investing of all its jargon, it is a pretty simple game: avoid big losses, stay with the winners and diversify investments across asset classes, sectors and markets.

Let me give you another statistic: when I started my career in the 1980s, the US dollar was worth Rs 12. In 2023, as I write this, it is around Rs 83. So there has been a depreciation of over 85 per cent in the value of the Indian rupee over the course of less than a full career. This is what you have to also take into account when you are planning for your long-term goals, including your retirement. You have to ensure that your hard-earned money retains its value, and global diversification is a key means to this.

Just as in the case of health, doing the basics right is key!

The basic framework

- Make a deliberate decision on asset allocation for your total investments (split among equity, fixed income, gold, real estate, etc.) depending on your age, goals and requirements. Also make provision for the unexpected.
- In the equity portfolio, avoid concentration in only two or three industries.
- Risk management is paramount. In order to win, you have to avoid the big losses.
- Global diversification is a must for your long-term financial health.

Scan the QR code to learn more

What Is Asset Allocation?

'Remember the XYZ stock I told you about three months ago? It is up 80 per cent since then'; '*ABC ekdum solid hai.* Just jump in'; '*PQR kya lagta hai?*" Sounds like familiar party conversation . . . or something that you watch the financial TV channels for?

If your end game is to have fun discussions at parties, this kind of conversation is fine. But if your purpose is to protect and multiply your wealth, or to optimize your portfolio, you are frankly approaching the problem from the wrong end!

Why? The answer takes you to Investing Basics 101. And it is to do with asset allocation, or allocation of your money across asset classes.

Just in case there is any confusion on what an asset class is, the textbook definition is: 'A group of financial instruments that have similar financial characteristics and behave similarly in the marketplace.'

It sounds like it is something very complex, but it isn't really.

Assets can be both financial assets (like shares or bonds) or real assets (like land or gold).

Thus, equity will include your direct stock holdings plus equity holdings via equity mutual funds or PMS schemes. Fixed income will include fixed deposits, bonds, fixed income mutual funds, etc. Then there are assets like gold, silver (held directly or indirectly), other commodities, real estate, alternative assets that can range from cryptoassets to art, and so on.

Depending on the study you read (and there have been many, conducted over the decades), you will find that as much as **85 to 92 per cent of the returns of a portfolio come from asset allocation!**

You got that right!

What this means is that the proportion you invest in equities, fixed deposits/other debt, gold, etc., matters more than which specific stocks you pick. Within equities, it matters more whether you are in banks and consumer stocks against, say, steel and industrial machinery, at any point in time—rather than which specific stocks you have picked in each sector.

> Specific stock selection, which eats up most of your or your adviser's waking hours, contributes only 10 to 15 per cent of the returns.

Moral of the story: it does not make sense to concentrate your resources and time on security or stock selection. Especially since you probably have a day job and are not spending 100 per cent of your working hours on investing.

But all the talk you will hear from portfolio managers will be about how good they are at picking stocks and great bottom-up winners.

The uncomfortable point is: bottom-up stock picking is an extremely difficult art, and nobody in the history of investing has been able to do it successfully for decades. Yes, not even Warren Buffett.

Just look at his record of the past fifteen or twenty years and you will see an investor who has under-performed to just about market-performed versus the S&P 500. Even worse, the volatility of Berkshire Hathway returns has been more than that of the index. Contrary to popular opinion, Buffett's strategy has not worked—either for risk management or higher returns, even when we take a period as long as two decades.

Plus, he missed practically every single multibagger that the US market has given in this period: Amazon, Domino's, Google,

Apple (he bought the stock way too late), Microsoft, etc., and now may be making the reverse mistake by having nearly half of his portfolio in Apple. More on that in a later chapter.

The point? This is PRECISELY the problem with the 'sexy', bottom-up stock-picking approach. Everybody is relevant during a particular period of time. And one fine day, the market changes and one's picks don't do so well any more.

The golden key to investing

Most investors fall in the very familiar trap of getting over-exposed to the hot asset class of their era.

But the key point to always keep in mind is that markets change, sometimes they become easy, sometimes very tough. Sometimes you can swing for the sixes, at other times you have to concentrate on remaining at the crease and not getting out.

Thus, in 2021 everyone wanted to be in Nasdaq and the tech stocks, but when many of those stocks declined between 40 per cent and 90 per cent in the following year, the same people headed for the exit—only to see many of the same stocks top the charts in 2023 again.

In 2021, very many new Nasdaq ETFs and funds were launched, even in India. In addition, laypeople, including school and college students, were opening accounts in US brokerages, especially Robin Hood I had warned at the time that just because the Nasdaq had done well for two or three years didn't mean that it would continue to do well.

> Recency bias always misleads. We extrapolate what has happened in the recent past and expect it to continue, but that isn't how markets, or life, work.

The other common trap is the home country bias.

Let us say you are a British citizen. Would you want 90 per cent of your portfolio to be invested in Germany?

No? Why not? And in that case, why are you comfortable with 90 per cent of it being invested in the UK? This logic applies to Indians, Americans and all other nationalities.

Indians, in fact, are about the worst in the world in terms of home country bias, with something like 97–98 per cent of our investments being in India. This has partly to do with historical reasons, as Indian residents could not invest abroad in the past due to capital controls.

Even though the limits are now generous under the Liberalised Remittance Scheme (LRS) of the RBI, the earlier mindset of investing only in India still remains.

Just because you happen to be born in a country does not mean that your portfolio must be skewed towards that country. There is no logic in this. Yet most of us have a disproportionate amount of our investments in our home country, causing what I call SCCARs—single country single currency single asset risk—which can hit your portfolio hard, especially when there is a crisis.

In theory you should be underweight on your home country in the equities market, simply because in all other areas of your life—career, real estate, etc.—you are already overexposed to the country. But even if you don't go there, you should build up a global exposure of at least 30–40 per cent of your portfolio.

Remember, the world has seen many economic upheavals, from the Asian crisis of the late 1990s to the problems in various countries of the European Union (EU) after the 2008-09 global meltdown to the problems in Russia, Turkey and Sri Lanka more recently.

Bottom line: for the safety of your investments, it is always better to diversify across asset classes and across geographies.

Ideally, you want an asset manager who can dynamically and tactically change asset allocations as market conditions change. Even if this is not always possible and you continue with a fixed allocation, it is better to be diversified across asset classes and countries.

The simple route to success

The key to successful investing, over the long term, is to have every major asset class in your consideration set: across countries and currencies and across investable assets such as equity, fixed income, real estate, precious metals and other commodities.

The mantra: There is always a bull market somewhere in the world, even as there is a bear market elsewhere at the same time!

Examples of bull markets: Technology in 1998; Emerging markets in 2004–07; Commodities in 2003–08 and 2022; US tech equities in 2010–2021; Global fixed income from 2009 to 2021.

If you had invested in the right asset classes at the right time, the specific securities you bought would not have mattered a great deal.

Throughout 2010–20, fixed income gave far better risk-adjusted returns than equities in India. Even more recently, 2018 and 2019 were extremely difficult periods for the Indian stock markets. Barring a handful of stocks, most were in the negative territory.

But in this very difficult period for India, overall global markets and the global portfolios managed by us saw great returns.

Of course, post 2020, India came out of its long-term underperformance and began to outperform the world markets.

That's the beauty of asset allocation.

To optimize your portfolio, it is important to have all asset classes in your consideration set and to carry out dynamic and tactical asset allocation.

It is time to change your lens to asset allocation. That is where you should concentrate in your investment decision-making.

The answers to these big questions will determine most of your returns. And all require thought and deliberation. You will have to consider your age, financial goals, when you will need the money, and so on:

- How much should I invest in equity? This should ideally be money you don't need for over a decade.
- Within equity, look at allocation along two dimensions: countries and sectors/industries. Ensure adequate diversification and don't chase something just because it has done well in the recent past. Remember that leadership changes.
- How much should I have in debt or fixed income? Within this too there is a risk spectrum, from low-risk fixed deposits in large banks or government bonds to credit mutual funds.
- How much should I invest in real estate? If you already own the home you are living in, do you really want to tie up more of your available funds in a plot of land or a flat elsewhere? If you do, besides return considerations also consider the fact that real estate investments are illiquid and you may get stuck for months or years when you want to sell.
- How much should I keep in gold?
- If you hold unconventional, high-risk assets like crypto assets, what percentage of your total assets do they make?

The asset allocation game

- Asset allocation determines 85–90 per cent of your investment returns.
- Spend your time getting that right rather than chasing single-stock stories.
- Diversify your investments across asset classes and countries. And also across industries.
- Do not chase the asset class that has done well in the recent past. That is usually a losing strategy.

Scan the QR code to learn more

What Asset Allocation Is Not

This is something I have seen since First Global came into being. We talk about something and it is picked up by the market. Or rather, the terms, phrases and trappings are picked up—often without the deep dive to get to the meaning or essence.

Since the time First Global started talking about asset allocation, the term has really caught on. For the last few years, this term has been bandied around rather casually, including in mutual fund and PMS scheme offerings. It is therefore important to understand what asset allocation is not.

We see the words 'asset allocation' used quite widely, and we should say somewhat lightly, these days, with many wealth managers, financial advisers and fund managers claiming to adopt asset allocation strategies.

Only when one goes somewhat deeper into this does one realize that the asset allocation being talked about is in the nature of large-cap versus small-cap Indian stocks or moving from value strategies to growth strategies in terms of stock choice within the Indian stock market.

This, combined with some debt allocation, appears to be philosophy underlying the so-called asset allocation strategies.

In fact, some of the investment documents we have seen even cite the same studies that I have mentioned in another chapter which prove that 85 per cent to 92 per cent of the returns in a portfolio come from asset allocation, with specific stock selection contributing only 8 per cent to 15 per cent of returns.[6]

The problem? The studies cited take into account a portfolio consideration set that lies across countries and across asset classes—not just couple of asset classes in a single country!

For the asset allocation strategy to really work in your favour, your consideration set must include all assets: Developed market equities, emerging market equities, developed market fixed income, gold and precious metals, other commodities, real estate or real estate-based instruments across countries, and so on.

Just changing the investment allocation across different categories in the Indian equity market, or even the Indian equity and debt markets, is simply not good enough! That is like playing football on 20 per cent of the football field—which is better than not playing at all, but can it be really called football?

Even within the Indian markets, it is important to look at asset classes beyond just debt and equity.

For instance, in two of the last ten years, gold was the best-performing asset class in India (partly due to currency movements) and in another year it was the second best-performing asset class. In other years, real estate did extremely well. And now, through real estate investment trusts (REITs) and some other instruments, it is possible to get systematic exposure to real estate too.

When I talk of asset allocation, it means that *your consideration set has practically all the investible asset classes in the world.*

The other key is to have a **dynamic and tactical asset allocation model**—i.e., assets are to be reallocated based on the tactical view of various asset classes at any point in time.

Crude measures like 'At age X, you should have 60 per cent exposure to equity and 40 per cent to debt' simply don't work if you are looking to protect and multiply your wealth and to meet your specific goals. For example, a forty-year-old with two school-going kids will have different life-time requirements from someone who is not married or does not have kids. Ditto for someone running a start-up or working as a TV actor versus someone in a corporate job. Spouse, parents, one's bucket list . . . all have to be factored in to decide how one's money should be allocated to different assets. Of course, some broad principles remain. For example, the money that you invest in equity should not be required for your needs for at least five to ten years, if not longer. Thus, overall, a younger person may be advised a higher equity exposure. But there are lots of nuances to this.

An in-depth understanding of the underlying asset classes is also important. Among other things, this is to ensure that the asset classes are really largely uncorrelated. This understanding comes from studying data and from long experience.

For example, if one has a positive view on commodities and a positive view on the Brazil and Russian equity markets, increasing exposure to both may not be uncorrelated at all as commodity prices drive many of the large companies' earnings in these two markets.

Is your financial adviser or money manager well versed across asset classes, across countries, across currencies?

If not, you need to be very careful, because you may be getting trapped by the narrow expertise of your money manager, which is fine for her or him, but can be disastrous for your portfolio. That is why many financial professionals will advise you that if you want to diversify globally, you can do that by buying say ten US stocks (usually Apple, Amazon, Tesla and a few others). The reason is very simple: those are the only stocks your adviser knows anything about. Is this good advice? No. it isn't!

Currency alone, or single-country exposure, can also change your portfolio return profile dramatically. But more on that elsewhere.

The key takeaway for the time being is that you cannot afford to ignore global assets when deciding on your asset allocation.

Bottom-up stock picking is exciting. The results are brilliant when it works. Terrible when it doesn't. It is, never steady or predictable. That approach comes with high volatility or high standard deviation. And one day the loss can be high enough to toss you out of the market.

To conclude this chapter, the investment strategy you want should aim for steady returns. At times it may seem a decidedly 'unsexy' approach—this careful risk management through diversification across asset classes, countries and industries. But, as I have said in another chapter, if your aim in investing is entertainment, you will be in trouble sooner rather than later.

Which approach should you opt for?

The answer is obvious, isn't it?

True asset allocation

- Asset allocation cannot just consider two or three types of assets in a single country, the way many Indian mutual fund and PMS schemes are set up.
- The consideration set must feature all asset classes AND all geographies/countries.
- Ideally, there should be dynamic and tactical reallocation. Meaning, the region and asset mix should be changed from time to time.
- Investments should not be done for entertainment.
- Asset allocation is right for your portfolio, even when it is boring and unsexy.

The Baby Steps on Your Investment Journey

Think of how you get to some place you want to go.

You go into Google Maps or whichever your favourite maps application is, and you enter your destination, of course. But there is another very important data point you have to enter, which is the starting point. It's pretty much the same in investing.

In the first few chapters, we spoke of the investment framework. In this chapter I describe the simple steps to put it into practice.

Most of you might have investment goals. Some of you may be in the habit of making resolutions; New Year, birthday, and so on, about where you want your investment portfolio to be at some point in the future.

But my question to you is: Do you know your starting point?

This seems like a trivial question, but you would be surprised to know that many people have no idea about this—and not just retail investors. I have found large family offices to be under the impression that they are predominantly exposed to global fixed income. However, once the numbers are tabulated, you find their biggest exposure is to Indian real estate!

Therefore, as step one, I would say, get to know your starting point.

What does that mean?

First of all, *look at all your investments, where your money is, and look at how it is split.*

The following are the broad categories into which your investment pie is divided—and yes, investments include both financial and non-financial assets:

Fixed Income, which means fixed deposits, fixed income mutual funds, bonds, public provident fund, savings schemes, and so on.

Equity, which includes direct equity as well as equity mutual funds or portfolio management schemes (PMS)/alternative investment funds (AIF), investing in stocks.

Within equities you have to know how your investments are split, geographically and sector-wise.

Real estate or property. This includes land, house, apartments, etc.

Gold, silver, crypto, art and other alternative assets, held in different forms.

This will give you an idea of what your investment pie looks like. And of course, on the other side you have liabilities that you're supposed to repay, whether it is a housing, car or student loan—or debt of any other variety, including what you should never have, i.e., credit card debt!

The bottom line is: First know all of this.

Then, and only then, can you decide your goal and the path to that goal.

Only once you know all of this can you decide how you want to split your investments.

Do this as an exercise. Take a piece of paper or a spreadsheet and do this.

This gives you your present asset allocation.

Now ask yourself, are you where you want to be? Or is there some distance to go?

In either case, you have to know your starting point.

Whatever asset class you have invested in, look at it. Look at whether it is as you want it to be. Or are there some changes to be made—to take it to where you want it to be? And why is this important?

Because, as I repeat very often, 85 per cent to 90 per cent of your investment returns come from this asset allocation and not from the specific stocks or securities you buy.

The second important thing: Look at your risk-control measures. It is very important that *when you invest you must have risk-control measures in place so that you do not take a very big hit or a very crippling blow to your investment or to your entire savings or funds.*

What's required to be done for that? It is simple—at least in theory.

Have a system.

Implement that system.

And, most important, follow that system.

This is not something that can be done on the fly. You cannot think that you will decide what to do about risk control depending on the market conditions.

The system has to be put in place well in advance. It should include things like adequate diversification across assets, countries and industries.

Plus, every time you buy something, decide on a stop loss. The stop loss has to be a trailing stop loss.

What does a trailing stop loss mean? It means that the stop loss will not be

You might think that if the market goes down you will take appropriate action, depending on the situation at the time. However, in practice that almost never works.

from your purchase price. Say you buy a stock at Rs 100 and you have a 25 per cent stop loss. That does not mean you will not sell unless the stock falls to Rs 75. It means that if the stock rises to Rs 300 and then falls to Rs 225 (25 per cent fall), you will sell.

> Stocks will fall, sometimes for reasons you can identify (like margin pressure or market-share loss) but often for reasons you can't immediately identify.

Putting a system in place is relatively easy. The difficult part: It has to be followed!

Suppose you have a stop-loss level for a particular stock, and that level does get hit. Don't then try to override it and justify it to yourself saying things like, 'This time it's different,' or 'This was a high conviction idea.' Or, 'This stock will come back.' Or a thousand other excuses your mind will too easily come up with.

Get out! If that's what your system had set out as a rule beforehand, get out.

Because, the fact is that whatever investments you make, a certain percentage of them will not turn out well. They will turn out to be mistakes, i.e., they will not turn out the way you expected them to.

When that happens, your risk control system will save you from a crippling blow. That is what it is designed for. That is what it is supposed to do.

So, two simple tips:

- Draw up your asset allocation, the present allocation and the desired one.
- Plus design your risk control.

The trick is in actually implementing them.

Getting started

- Know your present asset allocation.
- Decide on the target asset allocation, depending on your objectives and goals.
- Risk control is critical. Two simple steps, at least, are required:
  - Diversify across assets, countries and sectors.
  - Have strict stop losses, because a significant portion of your decisions WILL be wrong.
- Most important, putting systems in place is easy. Implementing them is harder.
- Whatever systems you put in place, whether for picking up stocks or stop losses, DO NOT override your own systems.

Scan the QR code to learn more

Why You Need Global Diversification When You Are in the Fastest-Growing Economy

One question I get asked often is: why should Indians look at investing overseas when India itself is the one of the fastest-growing economies in the world?

Let's look at a few aspects of this.

Why be overexposed to a single market or country?

First off, *India accounted for about 4.5 per cent of the world market capitalization in equity markets,* at the time of writing this book.[7]

So what would be the reason to put 100 per cent or 90 per cent of your assets in this geography? Especially as you likely already have plenty of other kinds of exposure to this particular economy through your job, home, etc.?

In every country, investors have a home country bias—meaning, they invest disproportionately in their home markets.

For example, Canadian investors have 60 per cent of their assets in Canadian equities. Canada is not 60 per cent of the world equity markets—it is around one-tenth of this number.

Even so, in India, this phenomenon is very pronounced. And part of the reason is that historically we did not have capital account convertibility. Well after I started working, right into the 1990s, Indians could take only US $500 when travelling overseas—that too only once in three years!

Back in the day, the only way for an Indian to get some level of currency hedge was through holding gold. This partly explains why the country's obsession with the yellow metal has been perfectly logical.

Currently, the Liberalized Remittance Scheme (LRS) allows you to take out a generous US $250,000 per head per annum, which for a family of four means up to 1 million dollars every year—the equivalent of nearly Rs 8.5 crore as I write.

Nevertheless, given the long period of time when foreign exchange was never written about without being preceded by the term 'precious', many Indians have still not really gotten around to thinking about global investing.

And if they do, *they think buying a Nasdaq or maybe an S&P ETF is enough. But that is not global investing. True global investing means looking at all geographies, all asset classes.*

Why is that so?

There are risks even in fast-growing economies

I will go back to my personal history and to what turned my opinion. It was *the Asian crisis, approximately twenty-five years ago, when in just a single year 1997–98, in dollar terms, the stock markets fell between 50 per cent, in the case of Taiwan, to 90 per cent, in the case of Indonesia; with Thailand, South Korea, Philippines and other countries in between.*[8]

And these were not basket-case economies. *These were the Asian Tigers—the fastest-growing economies of the time. Yup, they were the growth leaders of the nineties. India, as I have mentioned earlier too, wanted to be an Asian Tiger.* And yet, if you were an Indonesian investor, you would have seen your net worth wiped out by 90 per cent in a single year.

For me personally, that was a wake-up call on the risks of being exposed to a single market. Hence, in 1999, First Global became the first Asian firm to become a member of the London Stock Exchange; and the next year it became a member of the NASD in the US. But that's an entirely separate story.

The rupee depreciates . . . and it adds up

A crisis is one thing, but even without a crisis, the Indian rupee has depreciated. When I started working in the 1980s, the dollar was worth Rs 12. Now, in 2023, it's worth Rs 83–84. That's an *85 per cent depreciation in the course of less than my career.*

And this implies that *over a period of time, at least 30 per cent if not more of your assets should be global.*

Therefore, when we talk of long-term planning, long-term financial goals and long-term asset allocation, we have to look at global investing. If you don't, this could well be the level of erosion in your net worth over the decades.

Coming back to financial planning, in terms of goals, many Indians want their children to study overseas. Or, if you are young, you yourself may want to study or work abroad after a few years. Several people have kids living abroad and, post-retirement, want to spend some time with them.

What all this means is that some, or even the bulk, of your expenses may at least partly be in hard currency. Those are all considerations for not having all your savings in rupees.

Therefore, even when your or your adviser's call is that India will outperform, this diversification makes sense as it is not being recommended with a one- or two-year perspective.

> It is the old adage of not putting all your eggs in one basket. It is as simple as that. Or what we call exposing your portfolio to SCCARs (Single Country Single Currency Single Asset Risks).

The US market is not the globe

The second step: if you buy only a single other market, even if it's the largest market, which is the US, that is improving things slightly. But that is still not truly global, because leadership changes.

In 2021, when there were all these Nasdaq ETFs and funds being launched, I said publicly that this was Recency bias. Nasdaq had been a great performer for three years. Did anyone think it would last forever? Nothing lasts forever. No theme lasts forever. Of course, in 2022 came the crash that brought Nasdaq close to being the worst-performing index in the world.

Going back in history, hardly anyone remembers that the Nasdaq did not cross its 2000 high until 2015!

From 2003 to 2007, we heard all these stories that the US was over as a world leader and it was the decade of the emerging markets. That was when the BRICS (Brazil, Russia, India, China, South Africa) acronym was also coined.

Why? Because emerging markets were doing extremely well. *This was a period when the emerging market index went up 3.5 times! Indian stock market indexes went up nearly seven times.* But thereafter, this huge outperformance by the emerging markets was over. The giant wheel had turned and something else had started going up.

In 2010–20, when the US was performing, those stories were forgotten.

> Always remember: whether it is a geography, an asset class or a sector within a country, no theme lasts forever.

And 85 per cent to 90 per cent of your returns, as the first page of any investing book will tell you, come from your asset allocation, not from security selection.

So get your asset allocation right—and that includes global diversification. True global diversification, not just buying a US index.

Why YOU need a globally diversified portfolio

- India is a minuscule part of the global markets. There is no need to have all your eggs in this small basket.
- Even fast-growing economies can falter, as the Asian Tigers did around 1998, when their markets crashed 50–90 per cent in dollar terms in a single year.
- The Indian rupee has itself depreciated 85 per cent over the course of my career.
- Nowadays, many people have hard-currency expenses and hence need to think global.
- Just adding US indexes or stocks is not good enough, as there are long periods when other markets outperform the US. Leadership keeps changing.

Scan the QR code to learn more

Should You Be a DIY Investor?

Now that we have a framework for asset allocation and risk management, the next question becomes: Is managing your portfolio yourself the best way to invest in equities? After all, why use financial advisers and fund managers?

If you are reading this book, it is very likely that this is something you want to do.

I'm all for DIY (do it yourself) investing. In fact, investing yourself is the best way—actually the only way—to understand how the game works.

However, do think of this another way too: based on data, are you the very best fund manager you know?

Look at all data for your own investing performance and be objective about this—not just looking at your winners but at every single stock you have bought from the beginning of your investing journey. Now that we are in the digital world with an electronic trail of everything, dig out your DP account details.

How has your portfolio done over time? What kind of returns and volatility have you seen? What was the maximum loss you made? No cheating!

Collect similar data for the mutual fund schemes or the PMS schemes that you may be thinking of investing in. In short, look at yourself as just another fund manager.

Now compare the two: Are you the best there is in terms of returns—not just over a few months but over the longer term? How did you perform in times of volatility and drawdowns (that is, when the markets or your portfolio went down)?

Objectively speaking, are you the very best fund manager there is?

If not, how much should you allocate to the fund manager called 'I/Me', and what proportion to each of the other professional fund managers you are considering?

Of course, 'I/Me' as a fund manager may not have a great past track record but now has outstanding potential and may deserve to get a somewhat higher share than one strictly based on performance.

Maybe this fund manager has now shown a much better understanding of the markets, given all the ups and downs they have seen, and is confident of doing well in the future.

Even so, how much of your money should you allocate to this particular fund manager? Should it be 100 per cent? Or even 50 per cent? Or should it be a smaller percentage? Or maybe 'I/Me' should get only a small percentage of the total corpus as play money, so that 'I/me' can be happy to have something to talk about with friends and at parties.

Also account for the fact that 'I/Me' is probably not doing it full time. 'I/Me' has limited time and other resources to devote to this activity. 'I/Me' is unlike other fund managers, who are doing this full time and who have a large team supporting them, providing them data, analysis, alerts, etc.

It's a fun mental exercise to do and will probably lead to better decision-making. You may find that you are better off investing via mutual funds, PMSes or guided investments in smart baskets, etc., at least for the bulk of your investments.

Happy investing!

Equity investing: Do it yourself or outsource it?

- Evaluate your own past results, as you would for a mutual fund or PMS scheme.
- How much would you allocate to a fund manager who showed the same results as you did?
- You may want to do DIY investing but let that be for only a limited portion of your portfolio, especially as you may not be doing it full time.

Should You Only Invest Within Your Circle of Competence?

In regular books on investing, this is the point at which you are given homilies as to how you should only invest in what you know. Usually, the advice goes something like this: if you like and understand the product or service of a company, buy the stock of that company. Buy the Apple stock instead of the latest iPhone—sounds familiar?

The examples given are from books like Peter Lynch's *One up on Wall Street*, where he has thrilling tales, such as the one about how he bought the stock of Hanes because his wife loved their pantyhose. Or from Warren Buffett's speeches about how he buys established consumer brands with predictable cash flows.

So, should you, your fund manager or financial adviser invest only in their circle of competence?

It appears a no-brainer, doesn't it? Enough investment literature repeats the mantra of investing only in your circle of competence, virtually making it the holy grail of investing.

Plenty of people, paraphrasing everyone from Peter Lynch to Warren Buffett, say this is the first step of successful investing.

But what does this magical circle of competence really mean?

In plain language, it is that part of the market which the fund manager understands and is comfortable in.

In other words, this is the fund manager's comfort zone. Therefore, I should now ask you: Should your fund manager invest only in their comfort zone?

The answer no longer appears as obvious, does it?

And this issue is real. For example, look at Berkshire Hathaway, managed by the legendary Warren Buffett. His portfolio volatility is higher than that of the S&P 500, whether you look at a horizon of ten years, fifteen years or twenty years.

This is despite the fact that Berkshire is supposed to be investing in more stable businesses. But the sheer concentration in assets and lack of diversification results in a higher standard deviation of returns for the portfolio—in other words, higher risk.

> If your fund managers are investing only within their circle of competence, they are investing in their comfort zone. Which means that they are investing in only the one, two, three sectors that they understand and are comfortable with. In turn, this implies that there is lack of diversification and lack of risk control in the portfolios they handle.

And what is worse, Berkshire Hathway has not outperformed the S&P 500 for a good twenty years now!

That, my friends, is the end result of sticking to your so-called circle of competence.

That is when you will start to underperform or lose money.

For example, let us say your fund manager is comfortable with consumer brands and banks, and invests only in those companies. Such a manager will not perform well when there is a phase when, for example, automobiles or industrial machinery or commodities are doing well.

> A fund or portfolio that invests in a limited number of sectors will do well during a phase when those kinds of stocks are doing well, but once that phase comes to an end so will the superior returns. And end it invariably will, because no sector, no theme, performs forever.

In fact, there could well be a reverse impact when commodity prices are going up. Commodities are inputs for many fast-moving consumer goods (FMCG) companies. When prices of commodities are rising, the users of these commodities see pressure on their margins and profits.

It is also important to remember that *no matter how stable a business appears to you, the stock of that company can never be an evergreen stock*.

To give just a few examples: Hindustan Unilever underperformed the market and gave practically no returns for a whole decade, from 2001 to 2010; Bata gave zero returns over a fifteen-year period, from 1994 to 2009; Nestle India compounded at less than 2.5 per cent for years on end; ITC was a huge underperformer from 2013 to 2021.

They are all companies with strong brands and have been around for decades.

None of this means that these companies are no good or anything of the kind. It is simply that no story, no theme, runs forever, as far as the stock market is concerned.

But that does not mean that it is a theme that will run forever and in every market and at any point in time.

The biggest proponent of this circle of competence—the theme of buying stable businesses, etc.—has been Warren Buffett, and his most memorable call was on Coke, which was and is one of the biggest brands in the world, with reasonably predictable cash flows. But what has been its performance over the last three decades?

From 1993 to 2022 it is up only thirteen times, versus eighteen times for the S&P 500 and fifteen times for its direct competitor, Pepsi. Obviously, it has dragged down Berkshire's absolute and relative performance.

The examples given, of buying well-known branded companies and making a lot of money from them, are all from a particular market, which is the US, and during a particular period, primarily the 1980s, when that theme did very well.

As is clear, if you invest going by your fund manager's comfort zone or understanding, which is limited, you will be confined to a few sectors, which might go through prolonged phases when they are underperforming or not doing well.

The parallel is: because I understand this, this is the part that is lit up for me and this is where I will invest, whereas the key to riches may lie elsewhere altogether.

Investing in your circle of competence is like the story that all of us have heard—of looking for the keys where the light is, rather than where you have dropped them. It isn't a very effective strategy for finding them, is it?

The bottom line: Investing in your circle of competence isn't a good secular strategy for your portfolio, although it may work for certain periods of time—purely depending on where you are in the cycle for those particular set of sectors.

The reason why this myth of consumer-stocks-being-evergreen bets persists is because the 1980s to 1990s was a particularly great period for the US market, and it was also, coincidentally, the sweet spot for consumer brands. Most of the 'famous' investors you've heard of made their fortunes during this time.

The S&P 500 compounded 4.7 per cent in the 1960s, 4 per cent in the 1970s, and then accelerated to 9.3 per cent in the 1980s and almost to 15 per cent in the 1990s.[9]

More starkly: ***Money invested in S&P 500 in 1960 would have risen 2.3 times in the twenty years to 1980, and ten times in the next twenty years to the year 2000. The myths around where to invest use data selectively, and mostly from this 1980-to-2000 period.***

And as explained above, steady businesses do not always translate into steady stocks.

Therefore, please always keep this in mind—that your fund manager must be able to invest wherever there is alpha to be made, i.e., wherever there are excess over market returns to be made, rather than be confined to a few things that they understands.

The trick is to find a fund manager or system that can actually understand and analyse a wide variety of sectors to come up with the right portfolio for you. But without that there cannot be any *sustainable* outperformance.

Circle of competence, or comfort zone

- Most of the advice you get, which is to invest in companies you know or the brands you like, is problematic, as stocks of such companies don't do well forever.
- Even steady businesses go through long periods of underperformance.
- If a fund has invested in only two or three sectors, it may outperform for a limited period but not forever, as leadership in the markets always changes.
- The examples usually given, of Peter Lynch, Warren Buffett, etc., are from a particular phase in the US markets when consumer companies did very well.
- But even Buffett has underperformed since then.

Scan the QR code to learn more

Do You Listen to the Stories the Numbers Tell You?

This chapter encapsulates the crux of what to me, constitutes training in securities research and analysis.

Elsewhere in the book, I've talked about numbers and stories multiple times, and how you must not let narratives carry you away. ***And the most fascinating part?***

Ask most people why they invested in a certain company's stock, and whether they are amateurs or professional fund managers, in addition to things like growth, margins, etc., as reasons for investments, what are the other common reasons they will give? They will say something along the lines of: they invested because the company has good management or great brands or dominance over a market, or that it has the potential to keep growing for decades—all of which are subjective and dependent on human judgement.

So, how do you make a decision based on these parameters?

Let me tell you a secret about what is one of my favourite topics: That numbers tell a story. The secret is

The numbers themselves tell you a story, or actually *The Story*, but only if you are willing to listen.

that the story the numbers tell us is the only story that matters.

The stories that numbers tell may hide in unusual places

Industry data, company financials, macroeconomic data . . . all tell stories, but only if you are willing to dig deep, listen objectively to what they tell you and piece together what you find. I consider this the best part of my job of analysing companies and industries.

In investment analysis, that is the only sort of story you should be paying attention to. And not to the recommendations that everyone, from media experts to your friends, give you, based on 'factors' that may or may not hold true once you dig deep enough.

For example, if someone tells you that a particular company has great brands, here are the questions you should ask:

- Where exactly does this brand strength show up?
- Is the company able to get more market share?
- Do its volumes not decline when every other industry player's volumes do?
- Is it able to charge higher prices than the competition for similar products, i.e., does it have greater pricing power than them?
- Does it have higher margins than them?
- A combination of the above?

Because, if the company does have great brands, this strength should show up in one or more of these areas.

At times, once you do an analysis the results can be a little unexpected, even when the basic statement or hypothesis you are testing is true.

The numbers may still tell a story that is different from the one you expected.

Many years ago, we did an analysis comparing FMCG companies in India with their global parent companies. So it was Hindustan Unilever versus Unilever; Procter and Gamble India versus Procter and Gamble in the US; Nestle India versus its parent company, and so on ... and the results were fascinating.

One, we found that for the global companies, their brand strength showed up in higher pricing power and higher margins. On the other hand, these companies were selling to organized retailers like Walmart and supermarket chains. Hence, they had to give the retailers credit in order to get their goods on the latters' shelves.

It turned out that their working capital ratios were not that great because they had significant receivables.

In India it was the reverse, where in spite of their well-known brands the market leaders were not able to charge higher prices because the consuming population didn't have the capacity to pay higher prices. Therefore, their margins at the EBITDA level (earnings before interest, taxes, depreciation and amortization) were far lower than those of their parent companies.

But their brand power showed up in an unexpected place. At the time, the distribution and retailing of consumer goods in India was entirely in the hands of players in the unorganized sector. There the branding power of these large consumer companies translated into bargaining power.

How did this manifest in the financials?

The distributors were paying these companies in advance in order to get the goods they wanted in the required quantities. As a result the big FMCG companies actually had negative working capital. This was because they had the distributors giving them cash in advance instead of their giving the distributors credit in order to get them to pick up their goods (as is usual in most businesses). This was because there was enough of a demand pull from end consumers where the brands were strong.[10]

This was a fascinating research result for me, and I could see it clearly as I did not go in with any preconceived notions and just looked at the data. Otherwise, until then, in theory and in the textbooks, one had heard of the brand power of consumer goods only impacting volumes, market share, prices and, consequently, margins.

Here the story lay in the relative bargaining power of these companies with the entire distribution chain, where their strong brands gave them an edge.

Their brand strength showed in their power over the distributor and the retailer rather than over pricing to the consumer. Of course, the brand was coveted by the distribution chain because of the consumer pull it had, but what happened was an unexpected second-order effect.

The Indian FMCG companies now have higher margins than earlier, but the signs of pressure are beginning to show on their working capital. And this will only intensify as a higher proportion of their buyers, which is the retailers (think Reliance Jio, D-mart, online retailers/platforms, etc.) become more organized.

This was over twenty years back, and of course the picture has changed again!

Once again, the numbers are beginning to tell you a story that is unfolding in real time.

Go beyond the income statement

One thing evident, even from the example above, is to also go beyond the profit and loss account or income statement of companies. This is where, invariably, a majority of the analyses stop. Most analysts or

The real nuggets are often hiding in the balance sheet and cash flow analysis—sometimes because the management is deliberately trying to hide them there!

investors look at whether sales are going up or down and what is happening to margins and earnings growth.

For example, if there is a slowdown in demand, company managements will first try to sell their products on credit so that revenues and earnings don't get impacted. This is because they know that a large number of investors, and even investment professionals, do not go beyond the revenues, margins and profits in their analysis. But if you do go into the balance sheet you will see the receivables going up.

It has happened before . . . if you look hard enough

The second point: go as far back in history as possible.

That means not just looking at growth over the preceding quarter, or year, or even balance-sheet changes over a year, but to really dig into history. You will find that this is the only way to make even subjective judgements, such as whether the management quality is good or not.

For example, let us look at cyclical industries, where there are ups and downs.

Think of cement or capital goods, or metals like steel and aluminium, where there are large profit variations from year to year as demand and supply, and hence the prices for these goods, go through ups and downs.

When it comes to companies in such sectors, it is wise for the analyst to look at their history, going as far back as possible. Fortunately, this is often possible because many of these companies have long histories.

In particular, look at the last time there was a downturn, which may have been four or five years ago.

Of course you will see what happened then to product prices! And to the margins! And to the earnings or profits!

But that is only part of the picture: now also look at what happened to receivables; what happened to inventories or even payables, i.e. creditors.

Was the company showing sales by selling more on credit and the sales were actually all sitting in receivables? Was the company not paying its own suppliers because it had not planned its production properly and was now facing a cash crunch?

And all these things, put together, will also give you a feel of the quality of management at the company.

As I have mentioned before, ultimately everything gets captured in the numbers, especially if you go back as far as possible. This holds true not just for companies but also for sectors. Too often we get stuck looking at only one- or two-year changes, which do not capture the whole picture of that industry.

> The quality of management is a nebulous concept, which people can talk about but not pinpoint anything concrete to justify their 'impression'.

For example, if you look at the two-wheeler numbers for financial year 2022 (FY22), the volumes were where they were ten years ago. So, even though the one-year growth numbers looked fine, in ten years there had been no growth in volumes. That captured real distress—and not just in that sector but also in parts of the economy. It indicated that people were not migrating from the poor to the middle class and that below the creamy layer the economy was hurting.

Thus, the numbers tell the story—not just of companies or stocks, but also of industries and economies.

The core principle in making estimates

Until this point we have been talking about past numbers, but ultimately investing is about the future, and for that we have to estimate what is going to happen in the future.

And let me tell you what the core principle of making estimates is, which even professional analysts often forget.

They might have elaborate models on Excel spreadsheets, but usually many of them just do a back-of-the-envelope, i.e. short-hand, calculation in their heads.

For example, if a company has an EBITDA margin, that is earnings before interest, taxes, depreciation and amortization margin of, let's say, 12 per cent, this is how they will go about their estimation—okay, it can go up to 14 per cent, or it can go down to 11 per cent, and draw up a few scenarios on that basis.

From experience, I can tell you that very few will go into the nitty-gritties beyond this.

> The reality is that you really need to go into the real details to do a good estimate . . . an estimate that has a reasonable chance of being accurate.

Therefore, if you are estimating sales, you can project volumes and prices for every single product of the company to an extent. And, depending on how much information is available. You'll have a better estimate if the information is more detailed.

Next come expenses. Many models just assume expenses as a percentage of sales, but in real life not all expenses vary with revenues.

Of course, there are some expenses that vary along with sales—raw material volumes, for instance, although even here you have to estimate what the raw material price will be.

To give only one example, during periods when the prices of crude oil and its downstream petrochemical go up, raw material costs as a percentage of sales go up for a whole host of industries, from textiles and chemicals to FMCG, paints, etc. The cycle plays out in reverse when the crude oil prices begin to come down.

But raw materials are only one part of the expense picture.

There are other items, like wages and salaries which, within a range, have practically nothing to do with revenues. These may continue to grow at a regular pace even if sales don't grow.

On the other hand, there will be certain expenses, like those on repairs and maintenance, which may be related to assets of the company rather than its revenues.

The point is that making reasonable estimates even on the income statement side is a very detailed exercise.

Plus, once you start to do this exercise, it also tells you what you don't know about the company, so that's a very good discipline. And **when you get your hands dirty making the estimates you realize some things that appear very counter-intuitive.** For example, if in a cyclical industry there's going to be an upturn, very often you will find that the worst company in the industry gives you the biggest bang for the buck rather than the already well-run company.

More on this phenomenon elsewhere.

Until now we have only talked of how to estimate or forecast the income statement of a company.

To get a reasonable handle on a company, you also need to project its balance sheet and cash flows, so this would include answering questions like: How do you think the receivables and payables will move? What is the capital expenditure that would be required to reach the revenues estimated? If there is a capacity increase, how will this impact other variables like employee costs?

Ostensibly, all these things are done by the research analysts preparing estimates, but I can tell you that much of this work that happens is still only at the surface level and does not dig deep

Nearly every analyst estimate for 95 per cent, if not more, of companies, assumes that profits grow every year—a feat that has been achieved by only seventeen out of the roughly 4000 listed companies in India over even ten years.

enough, or has been done without enough thought being given to alternative scenarios.

Numbers are seductive, and if you put your ear to them there is a symphony, or rather a story, that you can hear.

The only worthwhile stories in investing

- Stories about companies may be harmful when it comes to investing, but the stories that do work are the stories the numbers tell.
- The key to studying the numbers:
  - The subjective factors, brand, management quality, etc., are also captured in the numbers, and one needs to look beyond the income statement for this.
  - Look at balance sheets, cash flows, financial ratios, to really know what is going on.
- Go as far back in history as data allows to see the industry's or company's ups and downs and how its management has conducted itself in the past.
- In making future estimates, the golden rule is to go into as much detail as possible and to think through alternative scenarios.

Scan the QR codes to learn more

Understanding the Much-Abused P/E Multiple

Almost the first valuation ratios even a new investor hears of in the markets is the price–earnings (P/E) ratio. It is intuitively easy to understand. The company makes a certain profit, and you pay a multiple of that to buy its stock.

This brings me to one of my favourite interview questions to potential recruits: Why do you think the P/E multiple of stocks, especially those within the same industry, vary so widely? Why is it that one stock in the industry may trade at twenty times earnings and another at thirty-five times? Why is the market willing to pay significantly more or significantly less for the same rupee or dollar of earnings?

Before we go answer these questions, let us first define what P/E, or PE, is.

It is the ratio of the market price of the stock to earnings per share (EPS).

This is the same thing as the market capitalization of the stock divided by the net income or profit after tax. The market capitalization of a stock is the market price of the share multiplied by the number of equity shares issued by the company.

Coming back to the questions I started with, most candidates begin to answer them saying that growth is one of the determinants of PE. Therefore, if you expect higher growth

in earnings for a company going forward, you should be willing
to pay for the stock a higher multiple of current earnings. For
example, if a company has an earnings per share of Rs 10,
which is expected to grow to Rs 11 in the next year, the market
may price its stock at Rs 200—which is a PE of twenty times.
However, if that company's earnings per share was going to rise
to Rs 14 in the next year, the market may be willing to pay a
higher price, say Rs 300, for the stock. And the PE would now
be thirty times.

This much is clear—if a company's earnings are growing
faster, you will need to pay a higher price for its stock. At this
stage, if I ask the candidate to define *other* factors that would cause
the PE to change, in nine cases out of ten the answers become
a little vague—subjective factors like brand name, management
quality, etc., are sometimes talked about.

Understanding the determinants of the P/E multiple is
really crucial, since many investors and analysts may not have
been very wrong on earnings forecasts or estimates but have
often been completely off on P/E-multiple forecasts.

Warning: while I have tried to make the book simple, this
is one chapter that may be a little hard for those without a
background in finance or accounting. It can be safely skipped if
it gets too hard.

Why exert yourself with esoteric techniques when P/Es are easily available and accessible?

This is a question, whether articulated or not, that is often on
the mind when we talk of valuing companies on the basis of
discounted cash flows. The logic is that P/E ratios are easy to
understand and deal with.

However, if we stop to think, we are really evaluating companies by making conclusions like, 'A 65x prospective looks OK for, say, HUL but too high for Marico.' In analysing companies this way, we are still making a whole bunch of assumptions, except that we do not explicitly understand or articulate them.

Growth is only a partial determinant of the P/E multiple

Often, growth in earnings is cited as an important determinant of the P/E. And of course it is. If two companies had the same Rs 10 EPS in the last year but Company A is going to earn Rs 12 the next year and Company B Rs 14, you should, logically, be willing to pay a higher price for Company B, provided all other parameters are broadly in line.

But this also gives only part of the picture, because it leaves out *an important factor, which is the investment required to achieve this growth*. For example, if two companies in the same industry have similar earnings and growth prospects but one has an annual capital expenditure (capex) requirement that is significantly higher than the other, the two would, and should, be valued differently.

Here is a simplified example of two companies in the same industry:

Rs crore	Year	1	2	3	4	5
Company 1						
Net income		100	110	121	133	146
Less : Net investment		30	33	36	40	44
Cash to/(from shareholders)		**77**	**77**	**85**	**93**	**102**

Company 2					
Net Income	100	110	121	133	146
Less : Net investment	50	55	60.5	66.5	73.2
Cash to/(from) shareholders	**50**	**55**	**60.5**	**66.5**	**73.2**

It is intuitively obvious that Company 1 should be valued higher than Company 2, even though both have exactly the same income stream or net profit.

In fact, higher growth may result in depletion of investor/ shareholder wealth if the earnings from the incremental investment do not cover the marginal cost of capital.

The technical way of saying this is that *if a company that does not earn enough return on capital—that is, its incremental return on equity is lower than its cost of equity—it will only destroy value the faster it grows.* It may sound strange, but growth in profits may *reduce* the value of a company.

Your friend from a business community would intuitively understand this: *Vyaj to chhootna chahiye,* she or he will say—i.e. your business investment should earn at least as much as what you would earn as investment if you had invested it in an interest bearing instrument.

This phenomenon of not earning the cost of capital was true of many infrastructure companies in India around 2010. These companies were greatly in favour at that time in the market, and the story was: 'If India has to progress it has to invest in infrastructure. Infrastructure companies are a no-brainer.'

However, when I looked at the cold numbers, I realized that the return on equity for most of these companies had declined substantially—by between 26 per cent to 86 per cent—over the course of five years even as their PEs and price-to-book value ratios had expanded.[11]

The fact is, no matter how loved a stock or sector is, ultimately the numbers matter. They act as the force of gravity.

To me it was clear that a substantial multiple contraction was on the books, even though not many were willing to believe that.

As it happened, the crack came soon enough, and lasted for well over a decade.

A primer on return on equity and cost of equity

Think of it this way: If you set up a business investing Rs 1 crore, and then earn a net profit of Rs 15 lakh in a year, the RoE for that business in that year is 15/100, i.e., 15 per cent.

Suppose that business earns only Rs 7 lakh, the RoE will be 7 per cent. The business will not look attractive if you can get 8 per cent from bank fixed deposits, which don't even carry significant risk.

This level of profit may be acceptable at the initial stages of a business or during a bad phase in the business cycle. But if this is going to be its steady-state earnings, then that business is not worth doing.

When you invest in a business, since that carries some risk, you need to beat not just the fixed deposit or risk-free interest rates, but also be compensated for the risk. Therefore, the business is not worth doing unless you beat the cost of equity, which is the risk-free rate plus a risk premium.

If the risk-free rate is 7 per cent or 8 per cent, the cost of equity will be at least 5–6 percentage points higher to compensate for the risk. Hence the return one would expect from equity will be at least 11–15 per cent. The business will be worthwhile only if you earn at least that much on the money you have invested.

> *By investing in stocks, what you are effectively doing is buying a part of the business. The principle remains the same as for a business—the return on equity should be higher than the cost of equity.*

Cost of equity is an important driver of the P/E multiple

The other factor which would influence the valuation of a stock is the cost of equity capital for the company, implicit in which is a return expectation. This, in turn, is influenced by the perception of risk in the company's earnings (this takes into account a whole gamut of factors, from industry cyclicality to management quality to leverage).

The textbook way to factor in all these variables into your valuation model is to actually project cash flows for the company and discount them to the present. But for those looking for short-cuts, there is a quick (though simplified) back-of-the-envelope calculation:

$$P/E = \frac{1 - g/r}{k - g}$$

Where g   =   the long-term growth rate in earnings and cash flow
         r   =   the rate of return earned on the new investment (incremental net worth)
         k   =   discount rate (cost of equity capital)

The simplifying assumption here, of course, is that g and r are known and remain constant for the rest of the life of the company. The mathematically inclined can derive this formula from the terminal value calculation in discounted cash flow (DCF) analysis.

Now, assume that our discount rate or the cost of capital is 15 per cent.

For Company 1

$$g = 10\%$$
$$r = 20\%$$
$$P/E = \frac{(1 - 10\% / 20\%)}{(15\% - 10\%)} = 10x$$

Value of the company = 30 × 10x = Rs 300 crore

Rs crore Year	1	2	3	4	5
Company 1					
Net income	10	11	12.1	13.3	14.6
Less: Net investment	3	3.3	3.6	4	4.4
Cash to/(from) shareholders	**7.7**	**7.7**	**8.5**	**9.3**	**10.2**
Company 2					
Net income	10	11	12.1	13.3	14.6
Less: Net investment	5	5.5	6.05	6.65	7.32
Cash to/(from) shareholders	**5**	**5.5**	**6.05**	**6.65**	**7.32**

Let us say Company 1 can increase its earnings growth rate from 10 per cent to 11.5 per cent, but with a decline in r, or return on incremental equity, to 17 per cent. From the conventional viewpoint, the extra growth would be very welcome, but let us see what happens to the P/E:

$$P/E = \frac{(1 - 11.5\%/17\%)}{(15\% - 11.5\%)} = 9.2x$$

With additional growth, the value of the company actually declines, from Rs 300 crore to Rs 276 crore!

A company's return on capital may be lower than its cost of capital or its return on equity may be lower than its cost of equity. If this ratio were to remain unchanged indefinitely, the stock would have a negative value as incremental growth would deplete shareholder value. In fact, you would not want to buy the stock at any price unless you could foresee an improvement in returns!

Mathematically speaking, these three factors determine the P/E

- The *higher* the expected earnings growth rate, the *higher* the P/E
- The *higher* the return on incremental capital or net worth, the *higher* the P/E
- The *higher* the cost of equity (risk-free interest rate + equity risk premium), the *lower* the P/E

If you earn only your cost of capital, growth is irrelevant

In the trivial case when the return on equity capital equals its cost, the growth rate becomes irrelevant for valuation as the P/E reduces to $1/r$. This is because the company is not adding any economic value by growing.

Upper limit of P/E

Interestingly, this P/E formula also yields an upper limit of possible values, given a growth rate. Theoretically, r, or return on capital employed, can at most be infinity, which implies that growth in earnings is possible without any incremental investments. Even with this assumption, the P/E estimate is $1/(k - g)$. This, then, is the theoretical maximum for the P/E.

What about interest rates?

The cost of equity in the equation above is determined by the interest rates prevailing in the economy which determine the risk-free rate as well as the risk premium. There is a separate chapter on how interest rates influence equity prices.

Is this whole exercise only a theoretical one?

Of course, it is. But it still serves a purpose.

You may think that what we've discussed is a purely theoretical formula—after all, who can estimate what the return on net worth or growth in earnings for a company will be ten years hence. The point is that, like it or not, you are in any case implicitly making all these assumptions every time you put a multiple on current earnings, because you are valuing the company as a going concern.

Basically, the beauty of the formula discussed here is that it forces you to deliberately think about and question your assumptions. It is not magic. It is not even exact, but it does give you a range of possible multiples, given various scenarios. It is, therefore, infinitely better than theorizing about what P/E multiple a stock should get, without really knowing why.

And also for explaining why 'buy at any price' does not work.

What drives the P/E ratio

- The price-earnings ratio, or P/E, is the metric used most often to value a stock.
- P/E = stock price/earnings per share (EPS) = market capitalization of the stock/net profits.
- Most people are not really clear why different P/Es should be paid for the same rupee or dollar of earnings, and only give subjective reasons for the differences.
- Three factors determine the P/E

- The higher the expected earnings growth rate, the higher the P/E
- The higher the return on incremental capital or net worth, the higher the P/E
- The higher the cost of equity (risk-free interest rate + equity risk premium), the lower the P/E

- The real use of calculating the P/E this way is not to do an exact exercise but to see what assumptions are embedded into the price and whether they appear justified.

Scan the QR code to learn more

The Nuances in Valuation Ratios

In the previous chapter we talked about the P/E ratio and its drivers. There are also those who talk about some modifications to this to better capture what is happening in a company. Let us look at those.

Growth-adjusted P/E (P/E/CAGR of EPS)

The most popular variation of the P/E ratio is the growth-adjusted P/E, also at times called the Lynch ratio, after Peter Lynch, who popularized it. It is calculated as the P/E divided by the earnings growth rate.

However, conceptually it appears to be flawed. The intention behind the concept is to find a stock that has a low P/E relative to its growth rate. Let's think about this—what kind of company would exhibit this characteristic?

The logical answer is—a company that increases earnings growth, which in turn is usually through increases in capital employed. Unless the company management is able to keep the operating profit margin (OPM) leverage and asset turnover up (when capital employed increases sharply, there is every chance that asset turnover, at least, will decline), and return on capital employed declines in tandem with these figures declining. And, as we saw in the previous chapters, the return ratios need to be high for the market to value the stock highly.

History is replete with examples of companies of this kind, from HDFC in the 1990s to infrastructure companies around 2009–10 to companies that raised a lot of capital during the IPO (initial public offer)/QIP (qualified institutional placement) boom window.

> Very often, earnings growth comes at shrinking multiples because the market penalizes stocks for dilution of return ratios.

In the last case, since the money is raised at a premium, EPS growth remains robust but return ratios get diluted. And the Lynch ratio leads you precisely to such companies—companies that grow earnings usually at the cost of returns, and therefore (deserve to) trade at lower multiples.

These are the very companies you want to avoid!

So, do you focus on return ratios or RoE?

This is one theory in circulation—'The company that keeps beating its cost of equity by a wide margin (or adds economic value) on a consistent basis earns healthy stock returns on a consistent basis.'

How true is this?

The Indian stock market is much more efficient than it is made out to be. Companies with high RoEs often have it all

> The important point here is to relate fundamentals to price, and once the price has it all, super-normal profits can become a pipedream.

in their price, resulting in high price-to-book ratios. Often, instead of giving the investor a free lunch, it ends up pricing such stocks even higher than what they deserve. Therefore, it does not necessarily follow that high-RoE companies will give high stock returns. This often happens with steady performers like consumer companies, where peak P/Es usually value the admittedly good financial ratios too highly and the stock returns remain elusive.

That is why valuation becomes a crucial factor in such cases.

The issue with EPS growth (in a nutshell)

The drawbacks of using EPS growth is the same as the drawbacks of using the Lynch ratio. A company can have healthy EPS growth even if the fundamentals indicate otherwise.

Surprised? This is how: the company can increase its debt, called financial leverage. This can improve earnings growth, simultaneously increasing the risk inherent in earnings growth, which would not be captured in the ratio. Also, a company can show high earnings growth by issuing shares at steep premiums (despite a fall in RoE), which is obviously not reflected in the ratio.

The better way to calculate growth-adjusted EPS

If you want to calculate growth-adjusted P/E at all, you will need the growth-adjusted EPS. *The better way to do it is to take a weighted average of the estimated EPS numbers for the each of the five years, where the weights are the discount factors for the respective years.*

A similar method can be used for getting the growth-adjusted CEPS (cash earnings per share) and growth-adjusted EBITDA (earnings before interest, tax, depreciation and amortization).

The discount rates to be used are the WACC (weighted average cost of capital) for growth-adjusted EBITDA, and cost of equity for EPS and CEPS. Thus, the growth-adjusted EPS is calculated using the formula:

$$\frac{\text{Year 1 EPS} + \text{Year 2 EPS}/(1 + r) + \dots + \text{Year 5 EPS}/(1 + r)^4}{1 + 1/(1 + r) + \dots + 1/(1 + r)^4}$$

Where r is the cost of equity for the company. The market price of the stock is then divided by this growth-adjusted EPS to give the growth-adjusted P/E.

This is a ratio devised by me to better capture growth in earnings and its impact on what you should be willing to pay for the stock of a company. The point of this exercise is to give higher weights to near-term earnings where visibility is better.

This tool is also very useful for analysing commodity companies. If one has to value commodities on straight P/Es, then one can get caught at the wrong end of the cycle. Hence, growth-adjusted EPS, which captures the weighted average EPS for the entire cycle, becomes a very useful tool when looked at relative to price.

Similar calculations can be done for growth-adjusted P/CEPS and EV/EBITDA.

Parsing out the P/E further

- Many try to relate P/E ratios to earnings growth by simply dividing the P/E ratio by earnings growth and calling the result as growth-adjusted P/E.

- However, this suffers from the serious issue of earnings growth could possibly have been achieved by deploying additional capital, either via debt or by raising equity at a premium, which dilutes return ratios even as P/E grows.

- On the other hand, a high-RoE company may also be overpriced and hence not give good returns.

- There is a weighted average variation to the growth-adjusted P/E, which gives a higher weight to near-term earnings and also enables one to consider a complete cycle for commodity and other cyclical industries.

Valuing Stocks Using the Discounted Cash Flow System: The Uses, Abuses and Modifications

Ultimately, when we buy a stock in the market, the bet we are making is that the real value of the stock is somewhat higher than the price that we are buying it at, which brings us to the trillion-dollar question: How do we determine the correct value of a stock?

Traditionally, the discounted cash flow (DCF) method has been used to value stocks. This is based on the fact that what you are buying in the form of stock today is the discounted value of all the cash flows that you will receive from the stock in the future.

This is usually the source of the price targets that you see quoted in research reports. Meticulous calculations show that a stock which is trading at Rs 242 today and has a DCF value of Rs 267 will have a target price of—drum roll—Rs 267.

Do I use DCF a lot today to arrive at the value of a company?

Not really. *But just as in painting or other art forms, in order to break the rules you have to know the rules. It is therefore a sensible exercise to really understand what discounted cash flows are and how to use them.*

The methodology set out here is based on a book *Valuation: Measuring and Managing the Value of Companies* by Tom Copeland and derives a bit from Professor A. Damodaran's work too, with some quirks and modifications built over the years by the First Global research team.

Here is the methodology and glossary of terms for the free cash flow analysis.

Net operating profits less adjusted taxes (NOPLAT)

It is derived as EBIT less adjusted taxes, adjusted taxes being defined as actual tax paid less tax on other income plus tax shelter on interest, as the attempt is to get to the cash flows from the business after eliminating the impact of the financing (i.e., debt-equity mix) decisions.

Operating cash flow (OPCF)

This is the cash flow after deducting the increase in working capital from NOPLAT.

Free cash flow (FCF)

This is the cash flow left after deducting the amount spent on capex (net of depreciation for the year) from operating cash flow. It represents the cash available to debt and equity holders.

Fair value for the firm

The DCF method basically consists of discounting this projected free cash value for the entire life of the company.

This is how it is done for each year:

EBIT

   Less: Adjusted taxes

NOPLAT

   Less: Increase in working capital

OPCF

   Less: Capex minus depreciation

FCF for the year

In theory, this FCF is projected for the entire future of the company and then discounted back gives you the discounted cash flow value, or 'fair value' for the entire company or firm.

The discounting is done at the weighted average cost of capital (WACC).

$$WACC = \left(\frac{E}{V} \times Re\right) + \left(\frac{D}{V} \times Rd \times (1 - Tc)\right)$$

In this formula,

- *E* is the market value of the company's equity
- *D* is the market value of the company's debt
- *V* is the sum of the market value of the company's debt and equity (E + D = V)
- *Re* is the cost of equity.
- *Rd* is the cost of debt.
- *Tc* is the corporate tax rate.

Terminal value

A critical part of DCF calculation is the terminal value calculation.

In practice, the cash flows are projected for a few years—typically four to six years—and thereafter the earnings are supposed to grow at a certain compounded growth rate and with a certain return on incremental capital. This is called the terminal period, i.e., the period beyond the period where specific projections are made.

The per-share DCF value

The fair value for the firm is adjusted for liquid assets currently available in the balance sheet to give the firm value.

The debt is then subtracted from this firm value. In other words, the fair value of the firm is adjusted for debt to give the value of future cash flows available to equity holders.

This can then be converted into a per-share 'fair value' by dividing the result by the number of shares outstanding.

The steps in DCF analysis:

1. Project the FCFs
2. Calculate a discount rate, based on the estimated cost of equity.
3. Calculate the terminal value
4. Calculate the enterprise value (EV) by discounting the projected FCFs and terminal value to net present value.
5. Calculate the equity value by subtracting net debt from EV.

Now come the pitfalls

The DCF method is open to more abuse than almost any other methodology in finance you can think of.

First of all, almost any discounted cash flow calculation you see will assume that the company grows its earnings every year. And of course the growth in the terminal period is also positive in such a calculation.

Unless the company is currently making a loss, you will rarely see a target price or value calculation that does not assume profit growth every year.

Now for the reality.

In 2022, we did an exercise to find out how many of the nearly 4000 companies listed in India showed some earnings growth (a barrier as low as growth greater than zero) every year for just ten years.

Guess the number?

It was only seventeen, which constitutes less than half a per cent of the listed companies.

How many companies showed earnings growth every year for twenty years? It was a grand total of two: HDFC Bank and Supreme Industries. And even the latter had a profit decline in 2023, leaving HDFC Bank as the sole company to occupy this position.

In other words, precisely ONE out of 4000 companies managed to show earnings growth every year for twenty years.

We have done this exercise several times in the last few decades and the results have been the same every time. Every time, only fifteen to twenty-five companies manage to show earnings growth every year for even a ten-to-fifteen-year period.

Contrast that with what you see in over 90 per cent of the research reports, where it is assumed that every company will continue to grow earnings every single year.

Then there is the terminal value. Since this bit typically delivers about 50–90 per cent of the total value of a company, you can find assumptions of growth and returns in the terminal period becoming more aggressive than the average driver on the roads of Delhi!

Alternately, the value drivers will be hidden behind an opaque terminal P/E or EV/EBITDA multiple. And this will severely inflate the value. Inflate because most of those writing these reports recommend 'buy, buy, buy' more often than the other way around.

You can as well say that *assumptions can be tweaked to show almost any value or target price that you want to for a* stock. *This is the real issue with DCF analysis.* Consciously or subconsciously, the analyst often has a number in mind and will change the assumptions to come up with the desired result.

The real way to use DCF analysis is to draw up a sensitivity table with various growth rates and return assumptions, and then see where today's price is on that table. In other words, see what growth rate and return ratios are being assumed by today's market and then think about whether those growth assumptions are realistic or not.

Bringing the near term into focus

Given that uncertainties in any estimate rise the farther we go into the future, it is perfectly rational to make an attempt at bringing the near term into focus. But that's the tricky bit.

Many years ago, I toyed with a whole lot of approaches, testing several near-term valuation techniques. In the end, I devised a ratio that is intuitively simple:

The inherent logic of the market is that it attaches greater value to companies that generate free cash, because cash is what ultimately helps pay the bills!

So, how does one get the medium-term cash flows into focus? This is the method.

Net operating profit less adjusted taxes (NOPLAT)
Less: Working capital changes
Operating cash flow (OPCF)

Leading on from this, I reckoned a four-to-five-year cash flow forecast should be a reasonable way to go. So I designed the process thus:

This OPCF is calculated for each of the four or five years and discounted back to the present day at the weighted average cost of capital (WACC) and liquid assets added to give the discounted operating cash stream (DOCS). This value is then compared with the firm value calculated on a DCF basis. This ratio indicates what operating cash flows in, say, the next four years available to equity holders contribute to the total equity 'fair value'. This ratio can then be converted into the proportion of market price that accrues to equity holders as operating cash flows during the next four years. An example makes this clearer.

Rs crore Yr.	1	2	3	4
OPCF	100	120	140	175
WACC	15%			
4-year DOCS	425.3 + Non-operating assets (Rs 4.7 cr) = 430			
Total firm value on DCF Basis	700			
Split as: Debt	200			
Equity fair value	500			
Market capitalization of equity	650			
4-year DOCS attributed to equity holders $= \dfrac{430 \times 500}{700} = 307$				
4-year DOCS to market cap $= \dfrac{307}{650} = 47.2\%$				

We stop at the operating cash stage (and not go on to deduct capital expenditure and add depreciation) because of the reasonable assumption that over the medium-to-long term, depreciation will equal normal capex, so the net effect of the two will be zero.

Further, even though a company has strong operating cash flows, the same at the net level may be negligible or even negative for some years if the company is in the midst of a substantial expansion.

However, the market may not penalize a company (this hypothesis was borne out by back tests we did as the discounted value of free cash flows in four-five years had a far lower correlation with returns than the four-year DOCS), as long as it believes that the capex is reasonable and justified and the company will earn at least its cost of capital on the incremental capital employed.

This calculation adds clarity to DCF analysis as it allows the investor to combine both the short or medium term and the long term and makes for a clearer decision-making process. Look at the table below:

	Company A	Company B
DCF fair value (per share)	Rs 100	Rs 100
Market cap	Rs 66.6 crore	Rs 200 crore
Market price (per share)	Rs 50	Rs 34
% Undervalued (FV–MP/FV)	50%	66%
4-year DOCS available to equity holders	Rs 30 crore	Rs 40 crore
As % of market cap	45%	20%

One can see that even though company A is less undervalued than company B on a long-term basis, a larger part of its value comes from the next five years (part of the explicit period). This makes the company's value more visible than that of company B. And if you are looking for risk minimization, then company A is the one you should pick, even though it is not as cheap as company B on a DCF basis.

Short-term factors do influence the DCF analysis, and therefore the fair value

This is because the DCF analysis is a dynamic analysis, based on your (or the market's) best guess for the future. Any short-term factor whose impact is confined to a limited period has very little impact on the 'fair value'.

For example, a minor fire in a plant which disrupts production for three months does not impact the 'fair value' much, unless it is seen as an indicator of possible persistent problems in a company or industry. *Where short-term changes become significant is when they are an indication of a change in the underlying business dynamics of the company.*

So, is the DCF analysis useful or not?

It is useful to the extent that it forces you to think about all the assumptions and also to think about what kind of growth rates in earnings and cash flows would be required to justify the current market price. However, it is no magic wand, and the kind of target revisions I sometimes see in research reports, where a target may be revised from say Rs 251 to Rs 248, supposedly based on the change in the DCF value, make me laugh.

Always remember the motto: 'It is better to be approximately right than be precisely wrong.' Beware of false precision.

Understanding the
Business Drivers

Elsewhere in the book I have written about going deeper into company financials, in terms of looking beyond the income statement or the profit and loss account, delving deep into every line and every schedule in order to make estimates. But there is *one quick framework that can tell you a lot about a company's business and quality of management.*

This is generally known as the DuPont analysis, named after the company for which this was first applied. *It examines what the company's return on assets/capital employed, or return on equity, is. And, even more important, how it achieves this final number.*

Let us start from the basics.

Suppose you are a 100 per cent owner of a business and you have put Rs 1000 into that business, which now earns an annual profit of Rs 200. The return on equity or return on net worth would be 200 divided by 1000, i.e., 20 per cent.

> If you understand this step by step, it will give you an overview of many business decisions, choices and trade-offs made, as well as their execution.

In other words, return on equity/net worth (ROE) is calculated as net profit by net worth or shareholders' funds. Of course, there are some other adjustments to be made. For example, since the actual shareholders' funds available through the year are neither the number at the beginning of the year or the year end, it is usual to take an approximation by averaging the two.

Now let us see how we come to this final return on net worth. What are its drivers? How can we further break it up? The DuPont analysis is one way to compute, and hence analyse, these drivers.

For a company, the ROE, which is net profit divided by average net worth, can be broken up into a product of:

1. Net profit divided by sales or revenue, which we know as the net profit margin.
2. Sales or revenues divided by assets, which captures how much revenues the company is generating on its. That is what is called the asset turnover.
3. Assets divided by shareholder funds. As assets in a balance-sheet sense are the same as the capital employed by a business, in this ratio you have debt + equity (net worth) in the numerator, and you have only equity in the denominator. Suppose you put in that Rs 1000 invested in the business as equity, based on which you borrowed Rs 2000 and put it all into the assets of the business. So now, with this last factor, the calculation will be 3000 divided by 1000, i.e., three times, which represents a debt-to-equity ratio of 2:1.

The equation for this would be:

$$\text{Return on Equity} = \frac{\text{net profit}}{\text{net worth}}$$

$$= \underbrace{\frac{\text{net profit}}{\text{revenue}}}_{\substack{\text{net profit} \\ \text{margin}}} \times \underbrace{\frac{\text{revenue}}{\text{total assets}}}_{\substack{\text{asset} \\ \text{turnover}}} \times \underbrace{\frac{\text{total assets}}{\text{net worth}}}_{\substack{\text{financial} \\ \text{leverage}}}$$

This is the basic construct of return on equity. It is the net margin multiplied by the asset turnover multiplied by the financial leverage. Now, what are the trade-offs involved?

And is it a good idea to increase one or the other of these ratios?

The possible trade-offs between margins and asset turnover or Can you invest more and have higher margins and profits?

Let's look at the first two factors in the formula. Now, there are business decisions where there are trade-offs involved between these two factors.

For example, if you are the management of Tesla and you decide to make a majority of the components of your car in-house, what does that mean? You have to set up extra facilities in terms of a new factory or add more machines—basically, you have to invest more in assets, which brings down the second factor, which is the asset turnover.

But if you are doing more activities and value-addition in-house, your margins should go up as you are capturing within the company the margin that would have otherwise been made by an independent components manufacturer. In short, Tesla is investing more in land, plant and machinery to make the components so that it can make higher margins on an ongoing basis.

Therefore, all other things being equal, Tesla's profit margin should go up even as its asset turnover goes down.

If I go back several decades, when Gujarat Ambuja Cement set up its first cement plant, it did many things that were a first for the Indian cement industry. The company management decided that they'd have their power plant in-house, they'd have a railway siding in-house, and also port facilities in order to use the ship route to transport cement to markets like Mumbai.

Now, all of that meant a larger investment in fixed assets, but they were capturing more value, so that meant that their margins went up and their asset turnover went down.

Can margins of different players within an industry converge, even theoretically speaking?

Now, when we compare two companies in the same industry, we often just look at the margins and then apply logic of this sort: Company A has a high operating margin or a high net profit margin, and therefore the other rival, Company B, in the same industry can hope to reach there if it is managed better or more efficiently.

However, we have to look at the full picture to know what is actually possible for Company B.

For example, if a rival of Tesla's decides to outsource many of the components that Tesla is making in-house for itself, what will happen is that the rival has opted for a higher asset turnover—basically, it has decided not to invest much in assets.

The corollary to that is, they will also not capture as much value in the profit and loss account as they otherwise could, so logically their margins will be lower.

In essence, they have opted for higher asset turnover but lower margins, whereas a company like Tesla which is making all this in-house has opted for higher margins and lower asset turnover.

The company which is outsourcing components cannot get to that higher operating margin unless it also integrates its operations vertically, which would involve higher investments in assets and hence a lower asset turnover.

There can be a direct trade-off involved in management decisions taken. This can define the range of the operating margin and the asset turnover combinations possible. The range of possibilities for margins depends for instance on the level of vertical integration, i.e., the extent to which components are made in-house or whether any input material is purchased or made by the company itself. Decisions can also involve upfront investment in fixed assets for other facilities, like a railway siding or port facilities, as in the case of Gujarat Ambuja Cement, which can reduce the company's transportation costs.

> In short, the balance-sheet decisions of companies have to be taken into account in order to project their margins and profits.

And then comes financial leverage

The analysis so far has involved the first two drivers of return on equity—the operating profit margin and asset turnover.

The third factor or driver of ROE, which is assets divided by shareholders' equity, captures the financial leverage of a company. This is calculated as assets divided by shareholder equity and can also be described as capital employed by shareholder equity—that is, debt + equity divided by equity.

If the total capital employed is Rs 3000 crore and the shareholder equity is Rs 1000 crore, that means this factor is three and the debt-equity ratio for the company 2:1.

Hence, even if two companies have the same return on equity of, say, 20 per cent, they can have different returns on capital employed depending on their financial leverage.

Even if the ROE of two companies in the same industry is similar but there is a significant difference in this last factor, which is leverage, you, as an investor, should not be neutral between the two. That means one company's ROE has been enhanced as it has taken higher leverage—meaning, the company has taken proportionately higher debt. And higher debt usually means taking on higher risk, which is something all of us understand.

If one company has a leverage (debt–equity ratio) of 2:1, this last factor will be 3. If the other company has a leverage of only 1:1, this last factor will be 2.

In a sense, taking on higher debt or financial leverage is not an ideal way to improve ROE.

This is not to say that all companies should have zero debt.

But debt does increase the riskiness of a business, and therefore a company should only take on debt that it can service comfortably, even during a downturn in the business.

All else being equal, if the final return on equity is the same for two companies, a rational investor will prefer a company that has got there with lower leverage or debt rather than one that has got there with higher leverage.

Of course, we are talking about companies within the same industry, because leverage can vary widely between industries.

To summarize this chapter . . . it is important to look at the ROE of a company rather than only margins or profitability, *as it is possible for a company to improve margins by investing more in fixed assets. Therefore, higher margins do not necessarily mean better management or greater efficiency.*

Plus while taking on debt or increasing financial leverage does boost ROE, it also increases the riskiness of a business and hence, all analysis has to take both aspects into account.

The trade-offs involved in driving return on equity (RoE)

- An understanding of the drivers of RoE helps you become aware of the business drivers and the trade-offs made by the management.
- RoE is the multiplicative product of the profit margin, the asset turnover and the financial leverage.
- Decisions on matters such as how many components to make in-house can involve trade-offs between the first two factors. Hence it does not make sense to only compare companies on their margins and profit and loss accounts.
- Increasing the debt, i.e., the financial leverage, can also improve RoE, but this is the least desirable way for a company to do so.

Scan the QR codes to learn more

SECTION II

Myths and Mantras

The investment field, especially the stock market, is a place of stories and myths. Surprised?

Isn't everyone looking for the keys to the magic kingdom, or the '*khul ja sim-sim*' that will open the door to the treasure room? Some easy-to-implement mantra? But this is a place not just with dragons and pitfalls but also many shimmering illusions that attract you, only to take your portfolio down a ruinous route.

Here are some of the common mantras that are touted:

'*Buy and forget.*'

'*You can't go wrong buying this type of stock.*'

'*Just follow what the FIIs are doing.*'

'*THIS is a sure-shot way to get multibaggers.*'

'*My friend has made a fortune in the markets. Let's follow him.*'

In this section we look at what works and what doesn't.

Should you buy the dominant brands in the business?

Should you track what the institutions and big investors are doing?

What IS the magic way to get the multibaggers?

And much more.

Plus, I will share my own hard-won lessons and mantras in the market, which you will do well to remember when navigating your way through it.

Value or Growth Investing? The Winning Theme

A question I often get . . . as does almost every fund manager and investor, is '*Are you a value or a growth investor? Why?*'

The answer is not quite as simple as the question makes it seem.

What exactly IS value?

One, value and growth are artificial distinctions, especially the way most people define the terms, which is at a very rudimentary level.

Most people define value as buying stocks with a low price to earnings (PE) or low price to book (PB) ratio.

Many foreign institutions calling themselves value investors entered the Indian market in the nineties and bought stocks trading at single-digit PE multiples without understanding why those particular stocks were trading at such low multiples.

They burnt their fingers buying stocks of many promoter groups like the Mafatlals, Scindias, Videocon, etc., either because the businesses were in their sunset phase or because their management was not quite clean. Either way, most of these stocks have since faded into oblivion.

The Indian market, which is generally a smart one, was pricing them low for a reason.

> Indian stock markets rarely give anyone a free lunch, which is why companies with good, steady cash flows, even without very high growth, are normally valued very high.

Companies with good, steady cash flows, even without very high growth, are normally valued very high, for example, the FMCG bunch. For the same reason, it is almost impossible to construct a portfolio of high-dividend-yield quality stocks in India, because a company with steady, predictable dividends will trade at a high multiple to the book value of the share. The dividend yield on the market price of the stock will be consequently low.

Two, *low PE or PB ratios might not be the right definition of value at all*.

When Benjamin Graham, the patron saint of those who swear by value, was alive, he himself changed this 'low multiple as value' definition, and in the last editions of his book, *The Intelligent Investor*, had written that intangible assets were becoming more important and had to be incorporated into the value equation. He meant that the traditional way of looking at the stock price as a multiple of its book value no longer held. This is what he wrote:

> It may be pointed out that under modern conditions the so-called 'intangibles, e.g. good-will or even a highly efficient organization, are every bit as real from a dollars-and-cents standpoint as are buildings and machinery'.
>
> Earnings based on these intangibles may be even less vulnerable to competition than those which require only a cash investment in productive facilities. Furthermore, when conditions are favorable the enterprise with the relatively

small capital investment is likely to show a more rapid rate of growth . . .

We do not think, therefore, that any rules may reasonably be laid down on the subject of book value in relation to market price, except the strong recommendation already made that the purchaser know what he is doing on this score and be satisfied in his own mind that he is acting sensibly.[12]

Think about how much truer this statement must be now, nearly five decades later, when we have moved on even more to intellectual capital than physical capital.

The twist in the tale? ***Ben Graham himself made the bulk of his fortune in Geico, an insurance company—not at all the sort of value stock he wrote about all his life!***

As I always say, pay attention to what investors and fund managers actually do and not just to what they say. But that topic is covered elsewhere in the book.

How stocks are classified also keeps changing. Facebook, or Meta, was classified as a growth stock till 2021. When its stock price crashed, it began to be talked about as a value stock! Therefore, don't spend too much time on labels.

The golden rule: No theme runs forever

Three, whichever way you define value or growth, no theme runs forever. Therefore, you cannot be locked into a single investing philosophy.

The key rule in investing is to be flexible.

The market does not care about any fancy stories you spin, or for that matter, for any philosophy or -ism!

> Certain geographies, sectors, asset classes and also types of investing themes work for a period of time, and then they stop working.

To give only one example, the 'steady' FMCG stocks in India performed well in 2019 and 2020, and thereafter became laggards . . . just as they have several times in the last few decades. After all, even the venerable Hindustan Unilever had given almost no returns from 1999 to 2010.

A corollary to this is that investors and fund managers who say they invest in their circle of competence are essentially saying that they invest in their comfort zone.

The types of stocks, sectors, themes or investing strategies they like won't be the right places to be in all the time.

These go in and out of favour.

Plus, a portfolio that contains only one type of stocks, whether from particular sectors or 'value' vs. 'growth' types, has higher volatility and drawdowns for precisely these reasons.

We talked about three things:
* *How you define value*
* *Whether something you buy as value will really deliver or is it just going down the tubes*
* *No theme runs forever*

Let us delve a bit more into the last one. At the beginning of year 2023, many started to say that it would globally be the year of value investing as rising interest rates had made growth stocks less attractive.

The reasoning was that growth stocks depend on future earnings rather than current earnings. Hence as interest rates go up, future cash flows get discounted at a higher rate and their current value goes down. Meaning that logically the stock should be worth less today than it was when interest rates were higher.

For example, when the interest rate is zero, $100 received five years hence will be valued the same as $100 received today.

But if the interest rate becomes 5 per cent, the cash flow received five years later is worth less than $80 today.

Unfortunately for them, the market rarely works on a very simple thumb rule.

Thus, Nasdaq was one of the best-performing markets in the world in 2023. And Nasdaq is considered the epitome of growth investing!

> It is not just important to understand the direction of the economy and the interest rates but also to what extent the markets have already discounted those—or in other words, how much all of it is already priced in.

Not only that, 90 per cent of the movement of the S&P 500 was also accounted for by just seven tech stocks—i.e. the growth stocks—from January to October 2023.

Why? Partly because Nasdaq had a disastrous 2022, where it was among the worst-performing markets in the whole world.

The markets don't make it that easy for you to remain one step ahead . . . but that is the whole fun thing about them.

No theme runs forever . . . the biggest rule for building wealth in the market

- How you define value itself keeps evolving. Just buying low PE or PB stocks is not good enough.
- You have to check whether something you buy as value will really deliver or is just going down the tubes.
- No theme runs forever. Hence, value stocks will perform for some time, and then some other theme will take over. It is the same for 'growth'.
- It is not just important to understand the direction of the economy and the interest rates but also to what extent the markets have already discounted these, or in other words, how much all of it is already priced in.

Scan the QR code to learn more

Should You Invest in Monopoly or Dominant Businesses?

We are all familiar with those do-it-yourself investing principles that are supposed to make investing simple and profitable, so simple that the woman or man on the street can follow them easily and effortlessly to make super-normal returns.

One of the favourites in this genre is, *'Buy monopoly businesses. Buy the largest company in the sector, with the strongest brand. You can't go wrong with the 800-pound gorilla in the business.'*

But what does history show?

You might say that this is the nature of the technology businesses.

But it is not as simple as that.

In any case, when Kodak was running its film-based business, nobody thought it was a fast-moving high-tech area. The issue is far more fundamental.

Remember Nokia, Kodak, BlackBerry (Research in Motion)—all dominant businesses, with magazine covers featuring them, asking whether anyone could ever catch up with them? Where are they now?

Does having a dominant market share make a company more vulnerable?

> When a company is the dominant player in the business, even if it does nothing wrong at all, any new player in the business will end up taking share and sales away from it.

When you have a 60 per cent or 70 per cent market share in an industry, as Bajaj Auto did in scooters or Maruti in cars in India before new, foreign players came in, it is an obvious fact that the new players will take away some sales from the incumbent.

The same is the case with, say, an Asian Paints.

For the largest player in the market, it is nearly impossible to grow faster than the market, whereas for a new or smaller player, taking away 1 per cent, 2 per cent or 5 per cent share from a large player is not such a big deal.

This is the reason why growth projections for smaller players have very little to do with what is happening in the economy at the macro level, or even with what is happening in their particular industries.

When a small regional player launches a biscuit brand or inexpensive washing powder, it is not banking on overall market growth but on only nibbling away at the share of the 'Big Daddy' in the business.

When Tata Motors took over Jaguar Land Rover (JLR) in 2008 and introduced some great new models in Jaguar, it was able to grow sales far faster than its competitors. This was something we at First Global had bet on as we realized that it had only a 4–5 per cent global market share in luxury cars at that time. For this reason, it was not very dependent on the overall growth in the luxury car market. It could grow by taking away share from the bigger players.

A new player can nibble away at the niches

Another threat from a new player for the market leader is that it can target niches. For example, in a paints or dyes business, a new entrant can target a particular type of dye or paint—let us say, a type of exterior paint—rather than compete with the dominant player across segments.

In other businesses like detergent, hair oil, tea or confectionery, small players can target certain states or regions and can even tailor their product to suit the preferences of that particular region.

That is how many players have made dents in the market share of larger players in their businesses, from hair oil to detergent. Often, this story ends with bigger players like Hindustan Unilever, Dabur or Marico having to then pay a premium price to acquire these brands and their market share, as otherwise their own market share keeps getting chipped away.

Tactics and countermoves

What also happens is that the new player often cuts prices, gives discounts or freebies, like free service on vehicles or appliances. This becomes an issue for the number one company in the business, which has to decide whether to follow the new entrant or not.

I remember a case discussion back during my MBA days in a marketing class which made this very clear. It was about a new entrant in a business cutting prices.

The professor asked one of us what the dominant player in the business would or should do. The student said it should match the discounts. The professor then asked us to calculate how much of a hit the bigger player would have to take on its large revenue base if it went on to match the pricing of the smaller player, and it became clear that the impact would be huge.

It becomes a big decision for the incumbent, as to whether to follow the smaller player and take a hit on its margins and lose a hefty amount of profits on its high revenue base, or cede market share to the new entrant.

It also happens that smaller and later entrants often have lower cost structures and overheads compared with the old, established companies, which tend to accumulate legacy costs over a period of time. Their pay structures are higher, they may be using more expensive equipment and have better facilities and offices, in keeping with their reputation and history.

How do you gauge whether brand value exists

It is, in any case, a good exercise to see how the so-called brand value of a company gets captured in the financials. For example, twenty years ago, the FMCG companies in India, like Hindustan Unilever, Nestle, P&G, etc., did not have very high operating margins, but their brand value was captured in their leverage over the distribution chain where they got money in advance from distributors and as a result had a negative working capital cycle.

Often, the biggest player in a market has a choice in terms of pricing, and companies can opt for different options that determine their profit and margin trajectory.

Now their margins are higher, but as retail gets more organized in India, the bargaining power of these manufacturers with the trade is reducing. This has been discussed in detail in an earlier chapter.

As a simple example, certain strategies can result in lower revenue growth but with margins being maintained, or they may opt to chase market share at the cost of margins.

Should you make your business unattractive?

Amazon, for instance, deliberately keeps pricing and margins extremely low, especially in new businesses it enters. For example, when it entered cloud computing, it did so at prices that did not appear to make economic sense. The reason? It did not want to make the business too attractive for other entrants . . . and the strategy worked!

A business that is growing well or has high margins is a double-edged sword as it attracts new players too. Amazon could use this tactic as it had a large-enough business to cushion it before starting these new ones.

Take Nykaa as an example. As I write this in 2023, it is the dominant player in the beauty D2C (direct to consumer) business, but now that it has created the business it has, it is far easier for other players to enter. The exception to this rule would be the platform business where, when a large community of buyers and sellers on a single platform itself becomes an entry barrier. Facebook, Instagram, WhatsApp, YouTube, etc.,

> Whichever way you look at it, it is really impossible for the dominant player in a market to grow faster than the market itself, whereas this is not a constraint for its small competitors.

are examples of these—where new users sign up because everyone they know is there or there is a ready library of content that a new player cannot replicate easily.

Why do disruptions come from smaller players?

It is also mostly true that the big disruptions in a business come from new entrants or smaller players. It is extremely difficult for a giant to do this, especially when it involves destruction of its current cash-generating business.

A famous example of this: Kodak had the digital camera technology but could never scale it up as it would have destroyed its existing business. It was making most of its money from selling and processing films rather than selling cameras, and this business would have taken a crippling hit had it scaled up in digital technology.

Microsoft, for instance, with its existing cash-generating businesses, missed out opportunity after opportunity in Internet browser, search, cloud computing and more— all because these appeared too small relative to its existing businesses. It has caught up only recently in some of these areas under Satya Nadella's leadership.

Of course, we know how that story played out, with Kodak's business getting disrupted anyway and the company eventually going out of business.

There is also some inertia when you have a substantial profitable business and the new business is too small to get top management focus. When your main business is generating billions, how do you get adequate focus on something which is only a couple of millions at the moment? Whereas, some smart group of youngsters with their start-up maybe giving their all to their small, nascent business.

Even if it is a great business, is it a great stock?

Until now, we have only been talking of business issues that can derail the story for a dominant company in an industry. An additional complexity as an investor arises when you buy a big, dominant company at the wrong price.

Even if there are no big disruptions in its business, it may still be an underperformer, even over a long period of time.

A good example of this is Coke, whose stock price over a period as long as thirty years (1993–2023) went up only twelve times, when the S&P 500 went up 16.5 times over the same period and its competitor Pepsi 19.5 times.

In India too, large companies with big brands have underperformed for lengthy periods—a good example being Hindustan Unilever, which underperformed massively from 1999 to 2010, a period during which its business also showed very low growth.

Another example is Colgate India, which saw a stock price decline of 75 per cent over the nine years from 1993 to 2002!

Or Bata, which gave zero returns over a fifteen-year period from 1994 to 2009.

Moral of the story: Buying companies with large market share and established brands will not lead you to investment nirvana. A whole lot of additional analysis is needed.

And remember, a large market share can actually be a vulnerability rather than a strength.

Is investing in dominant players a no-brainer?

- A large market share can be a vulnerability as a new player can nibble away at it. The dominant company cannot grow faster than the market.
- Smaller players can also target niches.

- Innovations usually come from smaller players as the top company wants to protect its existing segments and profits.
- A large player may neglect a nascent business area as it appears too insignificant for it, whereas a smaller player may focus on it and manage to grow it to a substantial size.
- Even if the business is doing well, if you buy the stock at the wrong price you will not get returns.

On Mathematics and FII Flows

In class 7, I had a mathematics teacher, Mrs Rangan. She was what used to be called a 'strict marker'.

So in a maths answer, if you missed any of the steps, you would obviously lose marks, but even if you wrote all the steps but did not write '*this implies that*' to connect one step to the next, you would still lose some marks.

The training I got with her has held me in good stead, not just in my academic career but throughout my life.

I got this compliment often during my college and IIM days from my teachers—they'd tell me they did not know where they could cut even one mark in my paper; and I always sent a silent thanks to Mrs Rangan.

Check for unsupported leaps in logic

But this training went a lot beyond maxing a maths paper. The really important part was the drilling into one's head to *think through every step and to debate internally whether the previous step did indeed imply the next or whether you are just making an illogical, or at least non-data-driven, leap.*

I find gaps in the reasoning I see all around, in the media, in research reports and so on; assertions and claims are made, but if you go through them step by step, you realize that there are gaps or leaps in their logic. Conclusions are claimed without checking the facts or data as to whether what is being said really holds at all.

Has anyone checked if FII flows change market direction?

Let me explain with an example something that you hear talked about in the press and on TV every day.

In fact, this is a question almost every interviewer asks me: What will FII (foreign institutional investors) flows into the Indian market be? Sometimes, this would be related to something happening in the global markets or economies.

It has always amazed me that no one wants to look at the data to see whether there is a correlation at all between FII flows and Indian market movements!

Erudite commentators in the newspapers write long analyses along the lines of: 'For XYZ reasons, FII flows will go down (or up) and this will have a negative (or positive) impact on Indian stock market'—or the bond markets, if they are talking about inflows and outflows in the Indian debt market.

The last statement is made almost as a throwaway line—as if it is very obvious that nothing further needs to be proven. If FII flows change, it will OBVIOUSLY impact market direction.

But think about where this conclusion has come from. Who has tested it and proven it to be correct?

Whether FII flows cause the market to go up and down, meaning whether one causes the other, is a second step that will need to be tested if we do find a correlation.

As someone who has done this exercise, I can tell you there is no correlation itself to be found.

FIIs first came to India three decades ago, at a time when there was no domestic fund management industry to speak of, let alone large-scale retail participation. Therefore, logically, the impact of the money they brought in should have been even more than what would be the case today, when other players have become more sizeable too.

According to the logic followed currently in the media, FII flows have a very sizeable impact on the Indian market.

Remember, this was fresh, new flows of money, literally tens of billions of dollars pouring into the Indian markets for the first time. But what happened?

1994 is the year when the FII inflows started in earnest.

And 1994 to 2003 is the only nine-year period in Indian market history where the Sensex return was a net zero!

This new slew of money came in and did absolutely nothing at all for the markets.

Even on a month-to-month basis, there was no correlation between FII flows and stock market movements, as we used to track it closely during the nineties. Strangely enough, the very first month when the FII flows turned negative, meaning the FIIs were net sellers, the market was up.

That was further proof to me that *market movements could not be predicted by forecasting FII flows. It was an exercise in futility.*

The media has to fill up the hours . . . you don't

To repeat something I say often: Do not spend your time on what the media is trying to fill its pages and time with. They have to keep saying something twenty-four hours of the day.

You, on the other hand, have to utilize your time sensibly and, in this case, on something that actually improves your portfolio returns.

Thus, the media will try to explain every move in the market—never mind that daily moves are mostly purely random and devoid of any logic. The same macro data or news can be used to justify both an up move or down move!

Look at where the data leads. Remember Mrs Rangan and check if you are making any unsupported jumps in the intermediate steps in your reasoning.

There is only one God, and that is data.

Do not fall for fallacies or generally accepted narratives. Just because people on TV say something every day doesn't make it true.

Besides everything else, it will save you a lot of time, which would otherwise be spent in chasing, collecting and analysing data that's, frankly, irrelevant.

Logic and data in the markets

- A maths lesson I have not forgotten: in any train of reasoning, stop and see if every step follows logically from the previous one—that you are not making any unsupported leaps in thinking.
- Do not fall for fallacies or generally accepted narratives. Just because people on TV say something every day doesn't make it true. Always check against data.

- For example, there is a lot of talk about how much foreign institutions will or will not invest in India and how that will impact market direction. But no one checks to see if there is actually any correlation between them.

Scan the QR code to learn more

Interest Rates and Why They Matter Even for Equity Markets

Often, on TV channels and the like, you hear talk about changes in the interest rates and how they are likely to impact equity markets. Especially in the 2022–24 period, this chatter has been everywhere.

And sometimes it is not clear why this should be so.

After all, interest rates define the return you get on fixed deposits, bonds and other fixed income instruments. As interest rates go up, the returns on these instruments also increase. On the other hand, equities are not apparently linked to interest rates. So, why all the talk linking equity markets and interest rates?

Interest rate changes are inversely related to bond prices

Suppose, for example, a government bond pays 4 per cent per annum. That means it pays an annual coupon of Rs 4 on a face value of Rs 100. For ease of calculation, we are assuming that this is a perpetual bond that will just keep paying interest.

Now, if the investor expects interest rates to go up from 4 per cent to 6 per cent, the bond price will need to come down by one third from Rs 100 to Rs 66.7 in order to now give an yield of 6 per cent. Let me explain this. Since the bond pays Rs 4 per year, for this Rs 4 to be 6 per cent, the price would need to be Rs 66.6 because 4/66.6 = 6 per cent.

> Of course the price of a bond yielding a fixed coupon will go down as the interest rates in that economy or currency go up. Similarly, the price of the bond will go up as the interest rates go down. This much appears straightforward.

This much is intuitively clear to anyone with a school-level knowledge of arithmetic.

What is not so intuitively clear is why should this impact shares or equity markets.

Interest rate changes impact expected return from equity

Let me try to simplify it a bit. I have explained in another chapter what the determinants of the P/E ratio are, but at the simplest level it is calculated as the earnings per share divided by the stock price, which is also the same as net income divided by market capitalization.

Let's look at what it really means and let's play around with it.

What if we invert the P/E, where the numerator becomes the denominator and the denominator becomes the numerator?

What does P/E inverted become? It becomes E/P, which is known as earnings yield.

E means earnings or profits, divided by price.

This ratio tries to capture what you are earning in terms of profits—or the rate of return in a crude sense, when you invest in a business—which is what you do when you buy a stock.

Think of it this way: if you are running a small business where you invest Rs 5 lakh and earn a profit of Rs 75,000 in a year, your E/P, or earnings yield, is 75,000 divided by Rs 5 lakh, which is 15 per cent.

But you could have invested the same amount in some debt instrument too and earned maybe 10 per cent. The higher risk you are taking by starting a business is being compensated for by the higher yield, which is 15 per cent instead of the 10 per cent on debt.

Therefore, the acceptable, or expected, return from an equity investment in a business is some percentage over and above the return you can make from lower-risk debt, so interest rates are implicit in the calculation of what is an acceptable or desirable P/E.

> As interest rates go up, you want to earn more from equity as well. Plus, you want to earn more than what you would get from a fixed deposit if you come to the equity markets.

So, if the interest rate on bonds or fixed deposits goes up to 15 per cent, you will want to earn more from equity, otherwise you would not want to take the higher risk of investing in equity.

That is why, when interest rates go up, the acceptable or expected returns from equity also go up.

In the equity markets, this means that the E/P that you want goes up, which in turn means the P/E goes down. Effectively, the market now wants to pay less for the same rupee of earnings.

Why the interest rate impact varies for each company

> As interest rates go up, the market P/E goes down.

But this effect is not the same for every company.

The reason is that earnings or accounting profits are only an approximation. Ultimately, the value of the company is the discounted value of all future cash flows of the company.

For example, around 2020, interest rates in most of the Western nations were around zero—and in some even negative.

When interest rates are low, the future cash flows don't lose much value in being discounted back to today.

When interest rates are zero, then you don't care whether you earn $100 today or $100 five years later, because the 100 dollars being received five years later also has the same value.

However, if interest rates go up, then five years later, that $100 of cash or profit is no longer as valuable as it is now. Say, if the interest rate goes up to 4 per cent, the value of the $100 of cash received five years later will be:

$100/((1.04)^5)$, which is 82.2. That cash is now 18 per cent less valuable than when the interest rates were zero, making stocks less valuable.

In short, when interest rates go up, what happens is that the present value of later-year profits and cash flows goes down.

And where is this impact seen more?

Think of so-called new-age companies like Uber, Doordash or Peleton in the US, or companies like Zomato, Paytm and PolicyBazaar in India, which were not profitable when they came out with their IPOs but were supposed to become profitable in the future—maybe five or ten years later.

The effect of changes in interest rates or cost of capital is more on the so-called growth companies— companies that have relatively low profits or cash flows today but have a lot of promise that they will make much higher profits or have much higher cash flows in the future.

In these cases, all that you are buying is the promise of future cash flows as little or no cash flows existed at the time of their public issues.

Now, if in the interim, interest rates go up, those future profits and cash flows will be valued less and less.

It is said that value does better than growth when interest rates go up. Because value is supposed to capture companies which have more profits, book value and cash flows today as compared with those which have only the promise of these in the future.

And therefore, as interest rates go up, the value of these companies falls much more than the value of companies which have profits and cash flows today.

That, my friends, is the story in short, of interest rates and equity markets and why the two are linked.

Of course, the equity cash flows are not discounted at a risk-free rate in the economy, but at the cost of equity capital, which is a risk-free rate plus an equity risk premium. However, when interest rates go up, so does the cost of capital.

Why interest rates impact equity values

- Interest rates have a direct impact on bonds and other fixed income investments. As rates go up, their value falls. But why should they impact equity?
- As rates go up, equity values also fall because now you need higher returns from equity too.
- The discount rate used for future cash flows goes up, which means their present value goes down.
- The impact is the most for 'growth companies', where the cash flows are more in the future than in the present.

Scan the QR code to learn more

It's Not Just Financial Markets That Forget History

Every now and then one hears of a bubble building or bursting in some asset class or market somewhere in the world.

There is a pattern to them—in every bubble people forget what has happened in the past and once again get mesmerized by rosy projections of what are ultimately the same old things. Or, in some cases, people are aware of the excesses happening in the market but still believe they can get out ahead of the mob, till one fine day everything blows up.

You can learn more about this phenomenon in several books that have been written on financial or market bubbles, including John Kenneth Galbraith's concise and brilliant *A Short History of Financial Euphoria*.

Here is one of my favourite quotes from the book:

'*There can be few fields of human endeavour in which history counts for so little as in the world of finance.*'[13]

Whether it is IPOs in 2024, the crypto/NFT frenzy of 2021 or the Silicon Valley Bank collapse in 2023, all market bubbles follow a pattern, set out beautifully in this book.

The classic bubble

The sequence of a classic bubble in the financial market

- In the euphoric phase, every member of the mob believes they are smart and all the money being made by them is well deserved.
- While the euphoric phase is on, those sceptical about the bubble are hated. They are called stupid for not making money, accused of having ulterior motives, and so on.
- Even those who see the problems jump in, thinking they can get out ahead of the crowd.

The bubble-burst

THEN comes the burst—which always comes with a bang . . . it's never a slow grind. Thus, all those who planned to exit too can't.

And following on its heels comes the blame game:

- Some heads have to be sacrificed, whether of corporations/ other entities or people.
- What remains sacred or sacrosanct are the markets and the 'common' speculator. They are never blamed . . . but maybe they should be.

Whether it is SME IPOs or the crypto/NFT frenzy or the Tulip Mania or any of the past madnesses in markets across the world, all were/are as much about 'common' people thinking they had found a way to quickly multiply their money as about their being misled.

It was a willing suspension of disbelief on their part.

This is different from real mis-selling, which too unfortunately happens in the financial markets—for example, the selling of ULIPS and other insurance products as investments to totally unsuitable customers, or getting retirees to invest their money in products that make maximum commissions for their 'personal' bankers.

These are the areas where a crackdown is required.

One of my pet peeves is the selling of thematic funds at the peak of a theme. Remember the slew of Nasdaq funds in 2021, or the sectoral funds that come unfailingly around the peak for that sector, or the defence-theme funds being launched in India in 2024.

But the thing is this:

Forgetting history and its excesses are not just a feature of the financial or capital markets.

You see this play out in multiple industries!

Sometimes it is the entrepreneurs and business people who are misled repeatedly about the prospects of an industry . . . they forget the many past busts.

> In many cases there is little justification for people to invest a large chunk of their savings in the 'flavour of the time' . . . except sheer greed.

Booms and busts are a feature of many industries

Let us look at the airlines industry, for instance.

Damania, Moduluft, East West and NEPC Airlines were among the first lot of private airlines in India in the 1990s and early 2000s. All of them eventually shut down, but this fact was merrily forgotten when Kingfisher, Deccan and Jet Air started off a few years later.

When their story was about to get over, in came Spice Jet, Go Air, etc., in next lot . . . that's how it goes on.

Bank licences are considered a gold mine, in view of examples like HDFC Bank and Kotak Mahindra.

Centurion Bank, Times Bank, Global Trust, Yes Bank and many, many more banks started by experienced professionals, (besides the many PSU and cooperative banks), which had to be shut down or restructured, are forgotten!

These examples are about business people forgetting the track record of their industry and setting up companies not very different from the failed ones, thinking they will succeed where others haven't in the past.

> After a spectacular bust in an industry, it takes only a few years for all the lessons from it to be forgotten . . . there is no institutional memory of it.

We see the same tendency among investors, whether they are retail investors or sophisticated institutions.

For example, in financial services, the same phenomenon of giving people loans to buy things is packaged differently, and there is excitement among investors to get in every time. Of course, it usually ends in chasing of marginal borrowers by the lenders till there is a small or big crisis.

Of late, the flavour of the season is something called BNPL, or 'Buy now pay later'. This is supposed to be an exciting new innovation. The reality? It's nothing but the literally centuries-old buying on instalments . . . but BNPL sounds fancier and, most importantly, 'new' and 'innovative'.

People laud growth in lending businesses. But think about this: how difficult it must be to give out more and more money faster and faster . . . this simple fact is forgotten when people chase lending businesses without a thought in the world. The real

difficulty for a lending business is in getting the money back, but that shows up only years later.

How many remember the first round of EdTech scam companies, topped by Educomp, headed by the IIM-pedigreed? There were many others too at the time, like Treehouse, Everonn, Zee Learn, Jetking, etc.

We at First Global did a report on why none of the financials of Educomp made sense in 2007, when it was a much-owned stock.

These were the red flags for Educomp:

- Revenues sitting in sky-high receivables
- No cash flows
- No cogent explanation from the management for this

Eventually, most of these education tech companies went bust. The Educomp stock made a peak of Rs 1100 plus in January 2008 and over the next few years drifted down till it became a penny stock. The last quote was at Rs 2 (no zeroes missing there!). But the interesting part lay in what happened thereafter.

After a decorous mourning period of a few years, once again EdTech, or education technology companies, became the darling of the investors, this time more in the unlisted space, where the likes of Byju's raised over US$5 billion(!) in spite of very well-documented holes in its business model as well as corporate governance.

Yet the funding rounds continued, probably fuelled by the greater fool theory that investors would get an exit by palming off their stake to someone . . . maybe in an IPO.

Except that the story began to unravel and the sequel to the earlier EdTech story is in the theatres now, as I write this in 2024.

As the cliché goes: those who forget history are condemned to repeat it.

Can we all beat the odds?

Why does this sort of behaviour happen?

None of us is inclined to think about data when we start a new business, or for that matter any new activity.

Besides greed, there is also another reason: We always think we will beat the odds in any game or don't think about the odds at all!

That is how so many get taken in by fancy courses promising that you can make a living by trading, specially trading exotica like options and other derivatives.

A visit to the SEBI website shows that not even 10 per cent of the traders in options make money, and even among those, most of them make only a paltry amount. But human beings don't like data.

As Rolf Dobelli writes in *The Art of Thinking Clearly*, 'We respond to the expected magnitude of events (the size of the jackpot) but not to its likelihood. In other words, we lack an intuitive grasp of probability.'[14]

In simple terms, when we think of a big pay-off later, we set our sights on someone who has made a fortune in trading. We cannot process the fact that only 1 per cent or 0.1 per cent of the traders have made that kind of money. We just see the amount of money they have made and chase it . . . only to come to grief.

Daniel Kahneman has written extensively about this phenomenon, calling it 'base rate blindness', giving examples from his own life where he either did not think about the data at all or was comfortable in the belief that he was way better than average and hence would beat the odds.

For example, he talks about his confidence about finishing his book in a few months without asking this question of his publisher, 'How long does it typically take for two authors to write a non-fiction book together?'

When he was part of a committee redesigning part of the curriculum for Israeli schools, they did find out how long such an exercise typically took to implement. It was a few years, and in many cases the work never got completed. Nevertheless, the committee was convinced that this particular team was smarter and better than the previous committees and they would get it done in a matter of months. The reality? In their case the change dragged on for years and was never implemented.

It turns out that even the great Daniel Kahneman who knows all about such pitfalls still did not beat the odds in either of the examples above!

Therefore, force yourself to look at the data. Of people/companies doing a particular activity . . . how many have succeeded in the past? What has been the history of this particular industry you are looking at? Ask these questions, whether you are starting a business or investing in one.

All of us are not, and cannot be, hugely above average. This is not a glamorous or maybe even happy thought, but your bank balance will thank you for having thought this through.

Why history and probability matter

- Human beings have a tendency to forget history, and that is why patterns repeat.
- Similar bubbles form in various assets again and again.
- Even in industries, same mistakes are repeated. In airlines, there have been at least three rounds of investments by private companies in India over the last twenty-five years, but the lessons were never learnt. It is the same for education technology companies.
- We remember the successes, for example in banking, but forget the failures.

- Humans also either never find out about averages and probability while embarking on any of their ventures or ignore them thinking they will always do better. This is a trap.

Scan the QR code to learn more

What Do Past Stock Market Returns Tell Us About the Future?[15]

If I ask you whether equity is volatile as an asset class, you will say every school kid knows that it is. But the key question is, what do you understand by a volatile asset class?

Most of us think volatility means that equity returns will vary from year to year, may even be negative in certain years, but that it all evens out over the long term.

That is our thought process. But what **do you think constitutes the long term? Do you think annualized returns would be more or less equal over five years, ten years, or at least over twenty years?** Let us see what the real numbers are.

Let's start with the question: What returns do you expect from the equity markets?

And the figure most have in mind is a compounding of 15–16 per cent per annum, at least in India.

That has been roughly the rate at which the Sensex has annually compounded returns in the little over four decades it has been in existence.

We all know this. But what most investors, even seasoned ones, do not realize is that these returns vary hugely, not just from year to year but over very long periods of time too.

Returns vary widely not just every year . . . but every decade

The returns, i.e., the compounded annual growth rate (CAGR) of the Indian market each DECADE for the last four decades has been the following: 21.6 per cent in the 1980s, 14.2 per cent in the 1990s, 17.8 per cent in 2001–10, and a mere 8.8 per cent in 2011–20!

A LOOK AT PAST RETURNS

Period	SENSEX Index	NIFTY Index	NSE500 Index
1981-1990	21.60%	–	–
1991-2000	14.20%	14.30%	–
2001-2010	17.80%	17.10%	18.40%
2011-2020	8.80%	8.60%	8.80%
2021-2023*	12.40%	13.00%	15.80%
CAGR Since Beginning	15.20%	12.20%	11.30%

*As on August 31, 2023
Source: First Global Research, Bloomberg data

And even these numbers do not really capture the magnitude of the variation we are talking about.

Thus, Rs 100 invested in 1981 would have become more than Rs 700 by 1990—i.e., up seven times.

In contrast, money invested in Indian equity indexes in 2011 would have gone up only around 2.3 times over the whole decade.

Once you account for inflation having averaged over 5 per cent in that decade and bank fixed deposit rates having been at

7–8 per cent for a number of years in this period, the investor in the Indian equity market did not get compensated at all for taking the additional risk of investing in equities.

Rs. 100 INVESTED IN THE INDEX BECOMES

Period	SENSEX Index	NIFTY Index	NSE500 Index
1981-1990	707	–	–
1991-2000	379	382	
2001-2010	516	485	541
2011-2020	233	228	233
2021-2023*	136	138	147

*As on August 31, 2023
Source: First Global Research, Bloomberg data

And this is without picking and choosing the entry and exit points.

Not only do returns vary, capital can also get eroded in the interim

If one looks at highs and lows, the differences can be even starker.

For example, *the top five losing streaks of the Sensex brought it down by a range of 40 per cent to a whopping 60 per cent-plus.*

. . . in case you needed any reminders that equity returns can be volatile!

Subconsciously, many investors think of volatile returns as meaning that equity markets returns can vary widely within a range, that returns from it can go up and down. But the real killer is that your very capital can be eroded substantially in the interim.

As this table shows, there have been at least five times the Indian market has fallen by 40 per cent to 60 per cent, and it has often taken years to come back to its earlier high—the longest it has taken being almost four years.

SENSEX (INR)
Top 5 Drawdowns

Sr No.	Peak	Trough	Back to Peak	Max Drawdown	Days
1	09-Jan-08	09-Mar-09	04-Nov-10	-60.90%	1,030
2	14-Feb-00	21-Sep-01	02-Jan-04	-56.10%	1,418
3	28-Apr-92	26-Apr-93	12-Aug-94	-47.70%	836
4	28-Feb-86	28-Mar-88	03-Oct-88	-40.60%	948
5	13-Sep-94	04-Dec-96	14-Jul-99	-40.30%	1,765

*As on August 31, 2023
Source: First Global Research, Bloomberg data

And this is not a peculiarity of the Indian market.

There is a reason why most of the famous American market gurus made their fortunes in the 1980s and 1990s!

If one looks at the well-known US indexes, we see this same pattern of very stark differences in compounding, not only in individual years but over decades too. Thus, *the S&P 500 compounded at 4.7 per cent in the 1960s, 4 per cent in the 1970s, and then accelerated to 9.3 per cent in the 1980s and to nearly 15 per cent in the 1990s.*

Of course, in the first decade of this century, the US indexes gave no returns whatsoever!

GLOBAL INDICES
CAGR PERFORMANCE FOR DECADE

Period	Dow Jones Industrial	S&P 500 Index	NASDAQ 100 Index	MSCI ACWI Index	MSCI Emerging Market Index
1951-1960	11.60%	12.90%	-	-	-
1961-1970	3.10%	4.70%	-	-	-
1971-1980	1.40%	4.00%	-	-	-
1981-1990	10.60%	9.30%	-	-	-
1991-2000	15.10%	14.90%	27.90%	9.80%	6.10%
2001-2010	0.70%	-0.50%	-0.50%	1.30%	13.20%
2011-2020	10.20%	11.60%	19.20%	6.90%	1.20%
2021-2023*	4.90%	7.20%	7.30%	2.30%	-10.00%
CAGR Since Beginning	4.30%	10.90%	13.50%	5.50%	6.60%

*As on August 31, 2023
Source: First Global Research, Bloomberg data

During that time, emerging markets did brilliantly. And then it turned again.

Now you know why all the big-name US investors and fund managers you have heard of, from Peter Lynch to George Soros to Warren Buffett, usually made their billions in the 1980s and 1990s.

Even if one looks at a twenty-year period, money invested at the beginning of the 1960s in the S&P 500 would have risen to only 2.3 times over the twenty years to 1980.

But equity investments rose nearly ten times in the next twenty years of the 1980s and 1990s!

US $100 INVESTED IN THE INDEX BECOMES...

Period	Dow Jones Industrial	S&P 500 Index	NASDAQ 100 Index	MSCI ACWI Index	MSCI Emerging Market Index
1951-1960	299	336	-	-	-
1961-1970	136	159	-	-	-
1971-1980	115	147	-	-	-
1981-1990	273	243	-	-	-
1991-2000	410	400	1,168	255	180
2001-2010	107	95	95	114	345
2011-2020	264	299	581	195	112
2021-2023*	113	120	120	106	76

*As on August 31, 2023
Source: First Global Research, Bloomberg data

You might think that understanding history is all very well, but is this information of any use in the real world?

The short answer: it is.

Watch out for the changes in trends

Just because a market (or a sector/stock) has underperformed for two years, three years, five years or even ten years does not mean that it will outperform in the next period. However, if a decisive change in trend does happen, it is likely to be sustained.

> When the Indian market came out of the 2011–20 decade of low returns, it was clear that the outperformance would continue—which was a call I made in 2021.

The years 2011–20 was a period when the Indian market came out of its trend of underperformance, both relative to its own history as well as relative to the global markets. And it did outperform global markets significantly in 2021 and 2022.

Therefore, when making a projection about the markets, consider long-term charts that go back as far as possible and see, first of all, whether the market is far above its trend line or below it.

Always step back, look at data, analyse the big picture, and you will get insights that you never will when you are caught up in trying to 'understand' day-to-day stock price movements, which (surprise surprise!) are actually mostly random noise with no underlying causes.

Here the analysis has taken into account the mainstream indexes like the Sensex and the Nifty, which are mostly large-cap indexes consisting of securities that have high market capitalization.

But the small and micro-caps space marches to a somewhat different tune.

The history of small caps

What does the history show here?

As John Kenneth Galbraith explains in his excellent book *A Short History of Financial Euphoria*, financial market participants are programmed to forget history.

This truth becomes even starker when the number of new participants in the market keeps rising, as has been the case in India.

Looking back: How brutal have the bear markets in small caps been?

While stock markets in general are volatile places, this is only exaggerated in the case of smaller companies. Let alone individual small caps and mid-caps, even the indexes for these stocks have shown extreme moves.

The NSE Smallcap index fell 78 per cent from its January 2008 peak over the subsequent fourteen months.

It crossed its high only in July 2016, after more than eight years!

And even the small-cap bull run of 2016–17 didn't last long. There was another 65 per cent fall from the January 2018 high over fourteen months. This high was crossed again only three and a half years later.

SMALL-CAP INDEX BIGGEST DRAWDOWNS

NSE SmallCap 100	
Max Drawdown	-77.50%
Longest DD Days	3124
Volatility (ann.)	24.10% (till March 2020)

Sr No.	Start	Valley	End	Days	Max Drawdown (%)
1	08-Jan-08	09-Mar-09	28-Jul-16	3124	-77.5
2	16-Jan-18	24-Mar-20	07-Jun-21	1238	-65.1
3	11-May-06	14-Jun-06	10-Nov-06	183	-34.7
4	18-Jan-22	20-Jun-22	21-Aug-23	580	-33.4
5	05-Jan-04	17-May-04	21-Sep-04	260	-29.3

Source: Bloomberg, First Global Research

Yes, but my stocks will do much better

The response to this data from a number of investors/intermediaries is along the lines of: 'Yes, the index may have fallen, but I am choosing my stocks very carefully, and no matter what happens to the index, my stocks will do well.'

Let's examine this too.

Let's see how many small caps did not go down in the 2008–09 crash? A grand total of 1 per cent!

What are the odds that you would not only have held these stocks but that these would have comprised the majority of your portfolio?

> It is plain foolish to ignore base rates and averages and assume that you will be the exception to the rule and do brilliantly well even as everything collapses around you!

In fact, 90 per cent of small caps were down more than 50 per cent during this period.

And what about the 2018–20 small-cap collapse?

78 per cent of the stocks were down more than 50 per cent.

Only 8 per cent of the small caps were up in that period.

SMALL CAP FALL COMPOSITION

Start	End	Small cap Index Drawdown (%)	% of Stocks down more than 70%	% of Stocks down more than 50%	% of Stocks down more than 40%	% of Stocks up for the period
08-01-2008	09-03-2009	-78%	72%	90%	93%	1%
10-11-2010	06-08-2013	-44%	38%	58%	67%	15%
16-01-2018	24-03-2020	-65%	55%	78%	82%	8%

Universe considered for above analysis is 1500 stocks between market cap rank of 250-1750 at the beginning of fall.

Source: Bloomberg, First Global Research

Did small caps ever recover at all?

And what I have said so far is still not the worst part of the small-caps collapse.

We said that the Nifty Smallcap index took more than eight years to come back to its 2008 levels in 2016.

The real sting?

It is that 18–20 per cent of the constituents of the small-cap index change every year in most years. Yup, the churn is as high as that. In about five to six years, the index changes almost completely. It is, to all intents and purposes, an altogether new index.

Therefore, even after eight years the small-cap stocks that made the highs in 2008 never recovered; many just vanished from the face of the earth or became penny stocks.

Even if you had been 'patient' enough to hold them for eight years, you would not have recovered your money.

A sobering thought, isn't it?

The liquidity question

We have so far been talking about price movements in small-cap stocks. However, the truth is that these are stocks where there is ample liquidity when they are on their way up, but when they start to crack, not only does their price go down but you often have no exit at all. Liquidity dries up and many hit the downward price circuit for days in a row, leaving you trapped.

How to play this segment?

FOMO (fear of missing out) isn't the right reason to get on a train which has already left the station long ago.

This is always a risky end of the market and must be played extremely carefully.

Plus, much of the data that is talked about to prove that small caps give outsized returns is also not accurate, because it is not survivorship-bias free—meaning, you are only looking at the success stories.

In the US, where mutual funds have a much longer history, some studies had shown that small-cap funds outperform the general mutual fund universe.

However, once the data was adjusted for mutual fund schemes that had closed or had to be merged because of non-performance, it was found that small-cap schemes had actually not outperformed at all, even on a returns basis, let alone on risk-adjusted returns basis.

Investing is a Loser's game, as I explained later. You must ensure that you do not have big losses on your capital in order to have any hope of winning the investment game.

As a general rule, never have more than about 20 per cent of your portfolio in companies whose market cap is below Rs 5000 crore. That is the discipline we at First Global maintain, both in our PMS schemes and our Smallcase, FG-HUM. The latter is an offering on the Smallcase platform which recommends a basket of stocks that you can buy.

Even more caution is advised when small caps have already run up.

How volatile are equity returns?

- The Sensex went up seven times in the 1980s and only 2.3 times in 2011–20. That is the kind of variation possible in equity returns.
- Money invested at the beginning of the 1960s in the S&P 500 rose to only 2.3 times over the twenty years to 1980. But the same index rose nearly ten times in the next twenty years of the 1980s and 1990s.

- Success in markets is often hinged on which time period the person is investing in.
- Small and micro-caps have seen much bigger losses than big caps, and many stocks in this space disappear forever. Be very cautious in these spaces.

Apparent Mispricing May Be a Result of Perfect Hindsight

What is the one truth about investing that most experts never speak about?

All those talking heads on television hold forth with full confidence about what will happen to the markets or to particular stocks. The research analysts come up with a particular value and target price for a stock. At times they revise the target price even from, say, Rs 267 to Rs 262, as if this was a game of precise measurements and forecasts!

The truth? Investing is about making peace with ambiguity. Ambiguity is at the core of investing!

For the last thirty years, this has been among my first lessons for aspiring analysts and investors.

The nature of this business is such that you have to make decisions working with ambiguities and partial information.

As I almost always hired freshers, mostly straight out of engineering college and business school, this was a difficult concept for them to grasp.

It was a tremendous leap for those trained in science, mathematics and engineering, where equations and questions have only one answer—I should know, being a mathematics graduate myself.

Investing . . . and life, are about ambiguity and probability

In life and investing you may not know what all the independent variables at play are—that is, you will not even know what factors can affect the outcome in terms of the business, financial performance or stock price movements of companies and markets.

The fundamental truth is that life in general, and investing in particular, are about probabilities, not certainties.

Who in the beginning of 2020 could have said that the hotel and airline businesses would go to zero for most of that year? And if I had told you that this would be the case, would you have predicted that most stock markets in the world would see a tremendous bull run?

Even in 2022, when *The Economist* was drawing up a list of major global risks in January, the Russia-Ukraine conflict was not even part of that list of ten. And yet Russia invaded Ukraine less than a month and half later.

Even leaving aside outlier events, the business of companies is full of uncertainties. No management knows for sure what their profit will be even two or three years hence—heck, even what it will be in the next quarter!

Let alone the stock price, even the financial performance of the company depends on very many factors, including the economic environment, inflation, input price changes, competitors' moves and changing customer preferences. *The management has no control over most of these factors. But while the company management may be uncertain, research analysts make projections that make it appear as if they can see the future.*

The core of investing lies in getting comfortable with two related concepts:

- *Making decisions with incomplete information and uncertainty. When everything is known, the time to invest is often already past.*
- *The flipside: all decisions have been made on the basis of unknowns and hence can be wrong.*

If you passed up an opportunity to invest in Apple or Tesla, did you make a mistake?

This is the reason why something that may look like a no-brainer opportunity in hindsight may not have appeared so in real time.

For example, sitting here in 2024, you may think that anyone who gave up the chance to invest in Apple made a mistake. There are even some articles deriding the classification of Apple's IPO as a high-risk offering at the time of its launch.

In hindsight, we know the path these companies and their stocks took, but the point is that when making the decision this path would not have been certain and may well have been a low-probability one.

But what is the truth? For not one or two but a full twenty years after its IPO, Apple was a huge underperformer, compounding only 3.2 per cent and coming close to bankruptcy several times. And this includes a seven-year period after the return of Steve Jobs, who is now considered a magician.

Similarly, Tesla compounded only 4.9 per cent from 2013 to 2019, and it is only the 90 per cent-plus compounding thereafter that makes its overall CAGR look so good. Plus, it came close to bankruptcy not just once but several times.

In hindsight, all those stories of Tesla, Amazon and several others being rescued at the last minute with an investment or bank loan appear very thrilling, but before the event, as a sensible investor managing risk tightly, you may well have been right in not investing in those stocks. After all, many other companies of that vintage did not get a last-minute rescue and went under. *There was no way of knowing who the survivors would be, beforehand.*

And this is not just a characteristic of the recent past or of only highly volatile technology stocks.

I will quote from First Global's report of 1997 on brick-and-mortar stocks like Indian Hotels and TVS Suzuki, which had been huge outperformers at the time. But the logic remained the same, *that before their big take-off, their actual trajectory may not have been predictable or may have been a low-probability outcome, or an outcome that was predicated on changes which took place thereafter, from changes in the tax rate to the exchange rate.*

At any given point there will be future macro and micro factors which may change the trajectory of a company or stock.

During the period that this report talks about, the 1991 liberalization brought about a number of changes, both positive and negative, for the then existing Indian companies. Here is the extract from our report:

Going back to Dec '91, we find that a good 80% of the stocks were trading at prices such that the fair value fell beyond the + 20% range of prices. From this statistic, it appears that the market was mispricing a significant proportion of the stocks. However, this impression could be way off the mark due to a simple reason—we are using historical financials for the period FY92-96 as forecast numbers to calculate the fair value.

However, were you actually sitting down to do the DCF (Discounted Cashflow) analysis in Dec.'91, you would not have had the benefit of 20-20 hindsight and therefore, the assumptions could well have been different. There have been some (or rather a lot of) changes in the interim which logically could not have been anticipated in 1991.

To give only one example, the corporate tax rate has come down from 51% to a soon to be 35% which naturally would not have been foreseen. The liberalization process has changed the growth trajectory of several industries both for the positive (e.g. the hotel industry) and the negative (e.g. commodities, where import tariffs have declined).

Sitting in 1991, would you have projected a $/Re exchange rate of Rs. 35 and therefore found East India or Indian Hotels to be undervalued? In fact, even if you'd projected the exchange rate correctly, you may well have combined it with a much more pessimistic view on inbound foreign travel—not very illogical considering the magnitude of the macro-economic crisis that India was facing in 1991.

Then there are unforeseen regulatory changes—the easing of restrictions on foreign currency allowances for outbound travelers meant Thomas Cook's growth zoomed. A similar effect was noticed for Castrol when controls on volume sales were effectively dismantled with freeing of lube oil imports and rationalization of base oil tariffs.

There is another category of stocks that appears hugely undervalued in 1991 with the benefit of hindsight—the turnarounds like TVS Suzuki and Carrier or new companies like Infosys. This is simply because turnarounds are awfully hard to predict correctly, as when the company is down-and-out, there may be several possible outcomes of the future of the company. For instance, if you were studying TVS Suzuki

in 1991, you would actually be sitting at an uncertainty node
of a decision tree with, let us say, three possible outcomes:

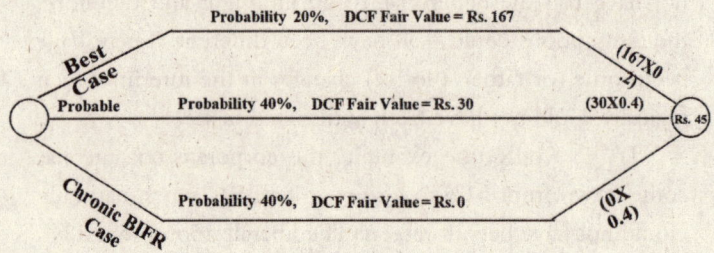

Note: BIFR (Board for Industrial and Financial
Reconstruction) dealt with sick companies back then.

The expected value of the 'fair value' is about Rs. 45
(167 X 20% + 30 X 40% + 0 X 40%), which would be the
expected Monetary Value of your investment. But as a risk
averse investor, you may have wanted a greater margin of
safety in a stock like this where there was a 40% chance of
having to write off your investment, so you may not have
been willing to cough up the EMV. Or put another way,
you'd have used a higher discount rate and therefore arrived
at lower fair values under each outcome. Of course, since
TVS Suzuki operates in the auto sector which was generally
undervalued in 1991–92, it may still have been undervalued
but not by as much as it appears by comparing the Rs. 167
'fair value' with the market price of Rs. 28.[16]

This was written over twenty-seven years ago, but the principles
of uncertainty in investing don't really change.

Ambiguity and probability: The core of investing

- Investing is about ambiguity, and hence is a game of probability.
- The future is unknown, hence every investment has an element of uncertainty. Even a carefully selected investment can go wrong.
- When we look at investments that have given great returns, we often forget that the actual path taken by the company may have been a low-probability event and passing up on the opportunity may have been the right decision. This holds for companies like Tesla and Apple.

Scan the QR code to learn more

Smart Money or Dumb Money?

Everyone in the Indian markets wants to emulate Rakesh Jhunjhunwala—or at least his investment results. RJ probably made the largest-ever fortune made by anyone in the Indian markets from investing alone.

There are many theories about his investment methods and philosophies, and why he succeeded and managed to make a fortune investing exclusively in Indian equities.

A recent book written about his life and investments, *The Big Bull of Dalal Street: How Rakesh Jhunjhunwala Made His Fortune*, by Neil Borate, Aprajita Sharma and Aditya Kondawar, makes all sorts of assertions about his methods and abilities. But the line that stood out for me was a quote from Jhunjhunwala himself: '*Not every year I make money. I make money in spurts, like 1989–92, 2003–07, 2009–11. In 1994–99 I would not have made any trading income.*'

If you want to internalize one RJ superpower, this is it: To understand and act on the fact that stock market returns are lumpy, not even.

Not only do they vary from year to year, there can also be long periods when there are no returns at all. On the other hand, you can make mega returns in just two or three good years.

If you remain disciplined through downturns or frustrating sideways moves, which can go on for what seems like an interminably long time while you are living through them, you'll be way ahead of the rest of the pack.

Between 2003 and 2007, the market indexes themselves went up about six times. But that was after nine years of zero returns.

Struck by FOMO

Instead, the way most investors behave is to get struck by FOMO (Fear of Missing Out) and jump on to a theme when it has already run up and is in all probability peaking.

A few examples:

All the Nasdaq ETFs and funds in 2021 that were heavily subscribed. I kept warning against those at the time because the Nasdaq had been on the tear for two or three years.

Almost all the thematic funds, whether for sectors like IT or pharma, or some other theme like Greater China or small cap, are launched near the peak of the cycle for that particular theme. The fund houses well understand that this is the easiest way to gather assets . . . even if it brutally drags down portfolio returns for investors.

And this FOMO issue is, predictably, compounded by panic selling on the other side . . .

So suddenly the same Nasdaq that looked so attractive in 2021 appeared very risky once it was down 40 per cent in 2022!

Thus, many compounded their problem of buying at the wrong price by also selling at the wrong price.

Nasdaq, which was at the bottom of the global league tables in 2022 then, rather predictably, rose again in 2023.

Data shows that the majority of mutual fund investors in the Indian markets do not remain invested for even two years in a single scheme, let alone longer. All talk of long-

> The flip side of this mindset of chasing wherever the run-up has been of late is that investors get jittery with the lack of performance in a particular market, asset class or strategy too soon and jump ship.

term compounding in the equity markets comes to nought when most investors are not invested at all for those long decades, or even for five years.

At various points we hear comments like this one: 'When your India PMS is doing so well, why should we invest anything in your global funds?'

Then the logic of global diversification over the long term starts to dim.

Another time it is: 'Why invest in equity when I made more in fixed income last year?'

Or, 'Gold has given great returns in the last six months. I lost out by being invested in equity.'

Thus, asset allocation decisions for the long term are made based on how some asset has performed in the last three months or six months . . . a complete recipe for disaster!

It is the same thing with investment strategies. The small caps may fall by 80 per cent, after which they show a dramatic five-fold increase. Investors conveniently forget that all of this would have

> It can be proven that chasing the strategy, sector or geography that has done well of late will *systematically* reduce your investment returns.

brought them back to zero returns (in actual fact far lower, because the small cap stocks that fall often just disappear and it is a different lot that gives the five-fold increase). They will crowd into small-cap fund schemes and strategies again, forgetting the risky nature of the

product. Anyone who tries to explain risk mitigation at that stage would be considered a 'fuddy duddy'.

This discipline of investing is where most retail investors falter. They end up chasing the asset class or strategy that has recently done well, forgetting about the long-term patterns.

Watch the sentiment . . . as a contra-indicator

Remember that sentiment is always a contra-indicator.

When you are feeling buoyant and confident about some part of the market, that is exactly when you should be wary, as the returns in the next period are likely to be below average.

On the other hand, if the general feeling is one of anxiety and frustration, the returns in the next period are likely to be above normal.

All this has been confirmed by a host of academic research studies across the world.

Unfortunately, if you get out of the market during the scary times, you'll never be able to catch up when the up move comes.

In theory, we all know that equity might give higher returns over the long term and that it has a lot more volatility than a host of other asset classes. But in reality, we get rattled when the returns are volatile/not there/ even negative for a period of time.

If you missed out on just the ten best days of the Indian stock market in a full forty years, you would have lost out on two thirds of the total market returns over this period.

Miss out on the thirty best days over forty long years and you have missed 90 per cent of the returns you could have made. The pattern is the same for the S&P 500, where missing out on the 100 best days in 100 years would bring your returns to negative territory!

As it happens, these sharp up moves normally come when there is fear, anxiety and uncertainty in the markets. Markets rarely go up that rapidly in a bull phase.

For example, if you did not get back into the markets by end March 2020 after the horrifying COVID crash at the beginning of the month, you'd have missed the 30 per cent move of the next five weeks, both in India and globally. It is a gap that would have then been impossible to bridge, no matter how smart an investor you are.

In an ideal world, you would get out before a big crash and get back in time—something we at First Global did manage to do, both with our India PMS and global funds during the COVID crash of 2020. We called out the turning points in public in real time.

At other times we used hedges to cushion a possible crash when things looked uncertain.

But overall, in the scheme of things, it is bigger damage to your portfolio returns if you are out of the market at the wrong time than if you remain invested and face a decline in your portfolio.

The takeaways

Please think carefully about your India-versus-global allocation.

Within India, think about your fixed income, gold, equity, real estate, etc., allocation.

Then don't keep tampering with your portfolio on an everyday basis.

These are the returns on Indian equities (and the First Global equity PMS, India Super 50) over the last four years.

Facing Volatility

	Returns		Return/Volatility (Equivalent of Sharpe Ratio)	
	FG-IS50	BSE 500	FG-IS50	BSE 500
FY21*	57.9%	36.0%	2.8	1.1
FY22	31.1%	22.3%	2.2	1.4
FY23	–3.0%	–0.9%	–0.2	–0.1
FY24	50.6%	53.4%	4.7	5.2
Total Returns#	177.7%	131.0%	1.9	1.2

For a 13-month period, i.e., from our first full month of operations since inception, i.e., from 1 March 2020 to 31 March 2021.

 # From our first full month of operations since inception, i.e., from 1 March 2020 to 31 March 2024.

 # These returns are after fees and expenses, as reported to SEBI.

FG-IS50 (First Global India Super 50)

Let there be two months of gold prices going up or fixed deposit rates increasing and investors start to diss equities.

But let the stock market go up 25–30 per cent and the same people will then come running back, compounding their problems.

If you have to learn one thing from Rakesh Jhunjhunwala's investing career, it is this.

> Equanimity, discipline and an ability to stick to your long-term plans—basically control over your mind—are the keys to successful investing.

Want to be the next Rakesh Jhunjhunwala?

- If you want to internalize one RJ superpower, this is it: To understand and act on the fact that stock market returns are lumpy, not even.
- Not only do they vary from year to year, but there can also be long periods when there are no returns at all. On the other hand, you can make mega returns in just two or three good years.
- But missing out on just a handful of days can take away almost all your returns. That is the danger of NOT being invested.
- Remember that sentiment is always a contra-indicator. When you are feeling buoyant and confident about some part of the market, that is exactly when you should be wary, as the returns in the next period from that part of the market are likely to be below average. On the other hand, if the general feeling is one of anxiety and frustration, the returns in the next period will probably be good.

The Secret to Having a Portfolio of Multibaggers

If I had even Rs 10 for each time I get asked a version of this question, I could have a few lakhs on this account alone!

And the question is: can you name one stock I can buy for my infant daughter or son so that they have a huge corpus when they grow up?

First the back story. First Global had a strong buy on Amazon at a price of $15 (split-adjusted $0.75) back in 2001, post the tech crash.

> What's the next HDFC Bank or Amazon that we can buy and forget about for twenty-five years?

This was at a time when there was no other buy, let alone a strong buy on the stock, from any firm on Wall Street. Jeff Bezos even sent us an email thanking us for our support.

At the very same time, *Business Week* and other major business magazines were predicting bankruptcy for Amazon. Even the Wall Street firms, which had been big supporters and promoters of Amazon, were all now 'throwing in the towel' on the stock, as they put it.

Amazon's ride since then is there for everyone to see!

Similarly, we had a buy on HDFC Bank at a price of Rs 38 (split-adjusted Rs 3.8) in 1996, just a year after its IPO.

On the cover of our research report was a picture of a baby, saying this was where the company was now, and then a picture of Mr Universe, Arnold Schwarzenegger, with a blurb saying this was where it was headed. We also saw that transformation play out over time.

Both these calls were based on analysis of business prospects, financials, and so on. For example, Amazon had made a free cash flow of over $200 million in the preceding quarter after having been free cash flow negative forever. It was clear that it was in no danger of going bankrupt, which was what the rest of the Street was pricing in. So we were confident enough in the company not just to have a buy, but a strong buy on the stock.

In the case of HDFC Bank, it was a bet on the market for banking growing post-liberalization as well as a bet on the prospect of an efficient, branded, private-sector player taking away share from nationalized banks, which were the only players of size at the time.

There was also the secret ingredient of knowing the management of the bank and hence being more confident about its risk management, which is a critical component in the success of any lending business.

But here is the thing: *When you are writing a report like this, the visibility is not for twenty or twenty-five years, or even a decade.*

At best, at that stage, you can only say that Amazon at $15 will go up to $50 or a Rs 38 HDFC Bank to Rs 100, or maybe Rs 150.

Even Aditya Puri and Jeff Bezos, who headed these companies, could not have foreseen the full extent of the business or stock price trajectory. Yes, they may have been confident of their businesses doing well, but not that their company's stock would give thousands of per cent in returns.

Jeff Bezos may have wanted to become the richest man in the world.

But could he have said twenty years ago that he would get there even for a day? No way.

Rakesh Jhunjhunwala could not have predicted upfront that Titan, CRISIL, Lupin Labs and a few other stocks in his portfolio would wipe out the sins of many more losers in it that went nowhere.

Warren Buffett himself has said that net of his top few calls, the rest of his portfolio has been below average.

The truth is that no one can know beforehand which stocks in a portfolio will become multibaggers. Anyone who tells you otherwise is only fooling you and maybe, themselves.

He puts the number of winning stocks at about a dozen. His recently deceased partner, Charlie Munger, put it lower at about four or five.

Don't get fooled by stories of great long-term foresight. Life is about probabilities, and at every stage there are multiple outcomes possible for a company/ stock.

No one can build a portfolio of only multibaggers. Or even one consisting of 80 per cent or 60 per cent of multibaggers. In the history of the world, there has not been a single person who has been able to do this.

The formula for winning in this game is to have a well-chosen portfolio of at least twenty-five to thirty stocks across sectors, built with some thought and analysis, and using a system.

Still, be prepared for some of them to turn out to be duds. As a rule of thumb, you may find that possibly five are absolute write-offs, another five do nothing very much either way, ten to twelve give you reasonable returns and then, and only if

Any story of multibaggers conveniently forgets all the other stocks that looked equally promising at the same point in time but did not give anywhere close to the same returns over the long term. It is the classic survivorship bias, which I have written about elsewhere.

you have chosen your stocks well, there is the likelihood that two to five of them will turn out to be multibaggers.

The bottom line: to get the elusive multibaggers, you have to cast the net wide rather than convince yourself that you have found the one or two stocks that will perform to all eternity.

Want a portfolio of multi-baggers?

- Want the next HDFC Bank or Amazon? But no one knows the multibaggers in advance. Not even the managements of the companies.
- No investor or fund manager has ever had a portfolio consisting of even 80 or 60 per cent multibaggers, let alone 100 per cent.
- The only way to do this is to buy at least twenty-five to thirty stocks, chosen carefully, and you may end up with some multibaggers.

Scan the QR code to learn more

Diwali for Your Portfolio[17]

Diwali has a close relationship with Goddess Lakshmi, and hence with our wealth and prosperity.

What if we look at our portfolios through the prism of Diwali?

First comes the clean-up

Step one in celebrating Diwali is the clean-up, which is such an integral part of the festival.

This time, ensure that it goes beyond just your home and cupboards.

Truly celebrate the essence of Diwali:

Declutter and remove the cobwebs of your mind.

Re-examine everything.

Throw out beliefs, opinions, theories and ideologies that no longer make sense.

Be flexible and open to change and to data—even inconvenient data.

And as far as your portfolio is concerned:

First take stock (pun intended) of it.

> Get rid of all the junk . . . it may not even be junk, but simply make room for your money to go where there are better opportunities in the market.

You have to do this consciously and ruthlessly, even if you are kicking and screaming inside—and let me tell you, your insides will resist every bit of it.

The reason is very simple: we hold on to our losers as evolution has hardwired us to avoid booking losses.

Remember, transaction costs are minuscule now, so that can't be the reason to hold on to something that is sub-optimal.

Also, waiting for the stock 'to come back to my purchase price' is irrational . . . The market has zero interest in YOUR purchase price!

> Most people hang on to bad and losing positions and, in the process, miss out on investment options that really do well out in the future.

It is much better to invest in something that will give you higher returns.

Know that you don't have to make it back in the same stock. Your bank balance doesn't care where the money has come from.

As a general rule, one of the pillars of successful investing is to get rid of bad investments, irrespective of the price at which you have to do this and choose good investment options.

Do this and I can tell you greatness awaits!

What is your relationship with your dhan?

On Dhanteras day, think deeply about your relationship with your dhan.

Don't invest haphazardly and without a system.

This is the time of the year when *all of us worship Goddess Lakshmi but think about whether we really show her the respect that is due to her.*

Think about the time you bought your mobile phone. You researched online, read articles, compared phones feature by feature, asked a dozen friends and then made a decision. Even to buy a saree or a shirt, we check around a bit as to which shop or website is reliable.

Now think about the way you made your last portfolio decision or bought a stock.

Don't you spend more time and effort researching a Rs 25,000 or even a Rs 10,000 purchase than you do a Rs 1 lakh or maybe Rs 5 lakh stock investment?

Very often, the latter is done based on some tip from a friend or even someone anonymous on a chat group, maybe a half-heard 'expert' opinion on a TV channel or some buzz about a new IPO, or something of the kind.

There is little thought that goes into the typical investment decision: What parameters is your stock buy based on? Where does it fit into your portfolio? What does your portfolio look like in the first place? How is it split between various sectors or asset classes? Most questions of this kind are not addressed at all.

As a result, you may not even be aware that this is the fourth bank you are buying, and now your portfolio consists of stocks where 80 per cent of them are in just two industries. It is all done on an ad hoc basis.

Even less thought goes into monitoring that portfolio or making changes when required.

Once you think about all this, you will realize that no matter how many lamps you are lighting before Goddess Lakshmi you are not really showing her enough respect.

This Diwali, take a pledge to really start respecting her— which means respecting your own hard-earned money and investment corpus—Your *khoon-passeene ki kamai.*

Whether you are doing it yourself or have an investment adviser of some sort, decide today that you are going to use a proper system for investing and for monitoring your portfolio. Don't invest haphazardly and without a system.

The Smallcase platform is a good one to help you choose an equity portfolio basket that fits in with your goals and world view and will help you formulate the best portfolio management plan for yourself, if you're not of the PMS size.

Our own offering, FG-HUM (Human + Machine), for instance, uses a very sophisticated artificial intelligence model, combined with decades of human expertise, to come up with a curated, diversified, multi-cap, multi-sector list of twenty-five to thirty stocks that solve your investment dilemmas in one shot. And the investment process is also super simple, which helps in better portfolio management.

Why twenty-five to thirty stocks? Because, regardless of what anyone tells you, no one knows in advance which stocks are going to be multibaggers.

No investor or fund manager in the world has had a portfolio consisting solely or even mainly of multibaggers. More on that phenomenon elsewhere in the book.

You have to buy based on a system, but even then you will have some duds in your portfolio and will be lucky to find 10–15 per cent of your stocks going up several times.

It may not be Diwali, but you can still resolve to respect Lakshmi Maa and not just worship her.

How to have permanent Diwali with your portfolio

- First the clean-up! Get rid of the junk in your portfolio, no matter how much your heart resists it.
- Get rid of bad investments, irrespective of the price you get, and choose good investment options.
- We worship Goddess Lakshmi, but do we really show her the respect that is due to her?

- Don't you spend more time and effort researching a Rs 25,000 or even a Rs 10,000 purchase than you do a Rs 1 lakh or maybe Rs 5 lakh stock investment?
- Decide today that you are going to use a proper system for investing and for monitoring your portfolio. Don't invest haphazardly and without a system.

When to Sell a Stock

Almost any book on investing will have chapters, explanations, equations and analysis—pages of them—explaining how you should pick stocks for investing. In other words, it is all about what you should buy for your portfolio. It is the same with videos or courses on investing, or for that matter, with most of the airtime on business channels.

Very little is written or understood about when to sell a stock

> Look for when to sell something and the space and time spent on it will be minuscule.

Even when something is written about selling a stock, it is usually asking you to look for turns in the business cycle or in the company financials or valuations. Many of these involve bets about the future, which may be completely incorrect as you do not know how the company's future may pan out.

Selling, it is implied, is even more of an art than buying. Of course, there will be some experts recommending a blind 'buy and hold' or 'buy and forget' strategy, usually with cherry-picked examples. Meaning they will only pick the success stories which demonstrate that holding something for ten years or twenty years has worked very well.

They will not discuss what happened to all the other companies or stocks that an investor would have bought at the same time as these successful stocks, but which went nowhere. They will not point out that many successful stocks of the present went through long periods of no returns at all. Apple, for example, was a very poor performer for a good twenty years following its listing. This is something I have discussed in another chapter.

The best thing you can do for your portfolio returns

Coming back to the question we started with: when should you sell a stock that you hold?

As I have written in the chapter on following the famous investors, Warren Buffett sells nearly 80 per cent of his positions within two years. This means he recognizes that 80 per cent of his bets are wrong. Many talk about his buy-and-hold philosophy, but the data is completely to the contrary.

> The very first thing to remember is that some of your buy decisions will go wrong, and this is meant to happen. And this does not imply that you are necessarily an unskilled investor.

The best thing you can do when investing in a security is to tell yourself that you may be making a mistake, as a certain proportion of your decisions will certainly not have the outcomes you had expected or desired.

This may happen even when the decision process has been correct, but the very fact that you are making a decision about the future, and that the future is unknown, means a certain number of times things will not go as you expected them to.

Why you shouldn't have a price target . . .

So, when do you sell?

Let's start with what not to do. Which is, ***don't decide at the time you buy a stock that you are going to sell it if it goes up to X.***

If you're buying a stock at Rs 60, don't decide that you will sell it when it quotes at Rs 100 or Rs 150 or Rs 200, because that way you will miss out on the multibaggers.

When you are buying a portfolio of twenty, twenty-five or thirty stocks, you don't know which of them are going to be multibaggers—which are those that will go up several times. You do hope and expect that maybe one, maybe two, maybe three of them might be multibaggers.

But you do not know in advance which of the stocks are going to be in that category. So let your profits run.

As an aside, what most investors do is the opposite of this strategy—meaning, they let their losses run, at times waiting for their cost price to come back, whereas they book profits on their winners.

This is the exact opposite of what you should be doing, as I have said. The reason we don't do that is because very painful for human beings to book losses. It is called loss-aversion bias and is the cause of losses and underperformance in many portfolios.

. . . But always have a stop loss

What you must have when you buy stocks is a stop-loss level. Decide what the stop-loss will be—say, 25 per cent or 30 per cent.

For our First Global portfolios, we use a complex algorithm to decide on the stop-loss levels, depending on factors like the volatility of each stock, or how much it goes up and down normally.

But even a simple stop-loss level will work. The important thing is to decide on it upfront and stick to it.

The stop loss has to be a trailing stop loss. That means it is not from your purchase price. If you buy something at Rs 60 and have a stop loss of 25 per cent, it does not mean that your stop loss is at 75 per cent of Rs 60, i.e. Rs 45.

What does trailing stop loss mean? First, it means that the stop-loss price keeps changing as the market price of the stock keeps changing.

If a stock goes up from Rs 60 to Rs 200 and you have a 25 per cent stop loss, then you will sell if it falls to Rs 150. You won't wait till it falls to Rs 45, which is 25 per cent down from your buying price.

So if your stock falls from Rs 200 to Rs 150, you sell.

Does this mean that if you sell at Rs 150, the stock will not go up again?

Of course not! There may be cases when the stock keeps falling and there may be cases when the stock goes up again. But overall, on the average, this strategy will save you serious money.

Averaging down?

Some 'experts' will advise that you average down in stocks that you have high conviction in when their prices fall.

This is an extremely dangerous strategy as your mind will always trick you into saying that your conviction was right and the market is currently wrong.

That is almost never the truth.

At times, you might, at a later stage,

> If you are not a professional investor, it is best that you just follow this simple rule: Decide on a trailing stop loss and get out if the stock falls from its high by that per cent.

even go back into that stock at a lower price, or even at a higher price, but that's a separate decision altogether. And you should look at it as a fresh investment, without letting your history with the stock be a hangover on that decision.

Put in place a system . . . and don't override it

The important part lies in following the discipline of keeping to this rule. For example, in our portfolio management we say the decision is by human plus machine on the purchase side, but strictly by machine on the risk management side, including implementation of stop loss. Simply because human beings do not want to admit their mistakes. Machines, on the other hand, have no problem in admitting mistakes.

When a stock you hold hits a stop loss, your instinct will be to say, *'This time it is different', 'It doesn't apply to this stock', 'Let's wait a while', 'I have high conviction on this'*. All these are justifications, or rather excuses, the human mind is sure to make up. This approach will result in poor performance or underperformance for your portfolio over a period of time.

The other side of this is that you should let profits run—meaning, do not sell a stock that is going up.

The exception to the rule

The exception to this rule is when a stock becomes an outsized part of your portfolio.

If a single stock becomes 40–50–70 per cent of your portfolio because it has gone up multiple times, then you might want to trim it and book some profits just so that you don't have such an outsized exposure to a single stock.

The other exception would be in the case of small-cap stocks, where stop losses do not work well as when some of these stocks fall, they go down so fast that you are unable to exit.

There, to err on the side of caution, you may book part profits even when the stock is going up.

These are simple rules but will help you improve your portfolio management returns tremendously if you keep to the discipline.

Selling your stocks: The neglected part of the equation

- Almost all investment books and experts talk and write about what to buy most of the time, but an equally important part of the equation is when to sell.
- If you want some simple rules, the first principle is to understand that a significant portion of your decisions will prove to be incorrect. Therefore, always be ready to admit this and rectify wrong decisions.
- When you buy a stock, do not fix a target price at which to get out, as that way you will miss out on multibaggers.
- Always have a trailing stop-loss and keep to the discipline of exiting if the stock hits the stop loss.
- Book losses when you need to but keep profits running.
- However, you may want to book some profits and trim your holdings in one or two stocks if they become an outsized portion of your portfolio, or partially book profits on your small-cap stocks that have gone up.

Scan the QR code to learn more

The Investing Mantras

All spiritual gurus give you mantras to chant to calm you down or to bring you success, good health, etc.

This chapter is not about how to choose stocks, i.e., what parameters to look at, whether growth, returns, management quality, etc., work. It is really about how to think about investments: the framework, your attitude, emotions, objectives, and so on.

Investment mantras are the same for your portfolio health—except that they are not something you chant every morning for fifteen minutes.

They are what you believe are at the foundation of your whole investment and portfolio management strategy.

So, let's go down the list of the nine mantras I have for you. Yup, as in the gurus' nine planets, or the navratnas, the nine gems, nine is the magic number.

Be the 'house', not the 'gambler'

This is a phrase borrowed from the casinos. The house here means the owner or the management of the casino.

How does the casino work?

It is actually pretty simple. The management has an edge, at least a slight edge, in all the games.

Let us look at the simplest game, roulette. There are 37 slots in all (there are some variants to this, but that isn't relevant for this purpose) from 0 to 36.

As a gambler, you can bet in various permutations and combinations on 36 of them, from 1 to 36, depending on colour, number, etc. For example, you can bet on the reds or the blacks, or on a particular number.

But if the wheel stops at 0, no one betting gets anything and the house pockets all the bets. Clearly, the house has a consistent edge of 1 out of 37, depending on the version of the game.

If it is a fair wheel, it will land on 0 roughly 1 by 37 times—so 2.7 per cent of the times—and the house gets a certain payoff.

The payoff is not certain even if the wheel is spun ten times or even a hundred times, but the house gets thousands and millions of runs, and over these many runs it is nearly certain that it will 'win' 2.7 per cent of the time.

In certain online games, the system pays out to the players 85 per cent of the money pooled in by them, and 15 per cent is kept by those running the game.

On the other hand, it is statistically certain that if you are the gambler and keep gambling, you will lose money. Again, this may not happen with every single person betting but holds true in the aggregate.

How does this translate into investment wisdom? When you take very few bets—meaning, invest in very few securities—you are essentially banking on luck,

> In short, the expected value of your payoff is negative if you are placing bets, and positive if you are running the show.

which may even help you get returns for a certain period of time. But you need to understand that this is still luck, not skill.

If you really think you have the skill to pick the right stocks, then it can be mathematically proven (see the chapter on diversification) that the only way to ensure that your results reflect your skills is to take a large number of bets—that is, have a large number of stocks in your basket.

With only twelve to fifteen stocks, the results will not reflect your skill level—whether it is good or bad.

> If you, your adviser or your fund manager has some skill in picking the right securities, the only way to ensure that your results actually reflect that skill is to have a large number of bets, i.e., a diversified portfolio.

In statistical theory this is called the law of large numbers. It is only when your sample is large enough will the real value—of your returns, in this case—be predictably close to the expected value.

Even when you are managing your portfolio yourself, have a minimum of twenty-five to thirty stocks—all, of course, chosen by a system you have set in place, but even then you will not and cannot know in advance which would be the best five or ten out of those.

Protect in down markets; participate in up markets

This is the golden mean to aspire to.

Different strategies work in different markets.

In reality, it is very difficult to outperform a runaway bull market because that is the time nearly everything gives you returns.

The trick then is to at least understand and acknowledge that it is the bull market that is giving you your returns and not your extraordinary skill in picking stocks!

This is where most rookie investors, and not a few markets stalwarts, falter. After a while you begin to look smarter and smarter in your own eyes.

It is the classic attribution bias!

If you ask anyone what proportion of their previous-period returns they attribute to luck or skill, their answer will depend on how they have done in the immediate preceding year or period.

If they have done well, it is all because of their extraordinary stock-picking skills, but if they have not, there are a thousand unforeseen risk factors to blame—from politics to market operators to central bankers to unexpected geopolitical events.

This is how the human mind operates—which is why systems and discipline work. In down markets, your risk management systems should kick in.

In fact, if you can limit your drawdowns in a down market, that is the easiest way to generate alpha or outperformance. That is also because investment is a loser's game (as discussed later), so your focus has to be first on not losing rather than on swashbuckling moves that will generate the maximum returns.

The boring mantras of diversification across sectors, creating stop losses, hedging, asset allocation, et al., are what will save you when the market crashes, and over a period of time that is what is going to help your portfolio outperform.

In a 'winner's game', you would have won by concentrating only on picking the best stocks, but with all the data in the world available to everyone and the best brains in the world working on identifying the winners, it is unlikely that you will be the outlier in identifying the winners every time.

The competition is far less on managing risks and avoiding losses—but that is from where the big outperformance points come.

For example, the day the Russia-Ukraine war broke out, the Nifty fell 5 per cent. But our PMS portfolios lost only 1.6 per cent, precisely because our portfolios were geared towards minimizing losses.

In the markets, it means not always having an aggressive stance, and that when there is uncertainty it makes sense to buy hedges. In our portfolios we do it in the form of out-of-the-money puts. Of course, this is insurance, which costs money. Hence you will never be hedged 100 per cent of the time for 100 per cent of your corpus, but whenever there is uncertainty of any kind—for example, geopolitical uncertainty—it makes sense to buy hedges.

The proof of the pudding? An ET Money study in February 2024 showed the best-performing mutual fund schemes had one thing in common—they outperformed when the markets fell. A MF scheme outperformed 93 per cent of the up moves but was still nearly the bottom fund in its category as it did not outperform the falls.

Play for singles, not for sixes or home runs

We all want to score the thrilling six that wins the game for India, but if you try to hit a six on every ball you are most likely to be out of the game before you know it.

Do asset allocation right. Get in reasonable global diversification. Within equity, do not be over-concentrated on any single stock or sector, and so on.

In most games, and on most pitches, it make sense to aim for a steady run rate.

In managing your own portfolio, this would mean aiming for the steady, sensible route even if it appears somewhat boring.

That will get you much further than trying to identify one or two multibaggers that you can boast about. *In real life, the quest for these multibaggers more often than not ends in tears because many of the stocks on a tear can go down just as easily as they have gone up.*

Ask those who bought small-cap stocks in the bull run of 2007–08, and then in 2017–18, only to see the small-cap index itself getting wiped out by 65 per cent to 80 per cent and individual stocks sometimes disappearing into thin air.

Also, remember that lack of diversification increases the element of chance or luck in the results, which means that it becomes a hit-or-miss affair. That is why we at First Global find potential clients coming to us and saying

> Boring can be good in portfolio management if your aim is to maximize your returns over a period of time rather than be the centre of attraction at parties.

they had invested in this fund or PMS scheme which did very well for two years and now has been underperforming hugely for the last three years, or vice versa.

Play everything, believe nothing

Conventional investing wisdom tells you to have high-conviction ideas and put all or most of your money in those.

I am here to tell you the exact opposite. Buy stocks based on facts and data, but don't have a love affair with them. Love your family and friends. Never forget that stocks and stock markets exist for one purpose only—to maximize your wealth.

In short, do not invest your emotions in any position.

That is the first step to being able to invest sensibly and also to exit when you need to.

> High conviction is the enemy of high performance. This sounds strange, but that is the truth.

Simply because no theme runs for ever in the markets. Soon after we started our PMS management in 2020, due to a variety of reasons, including COVID-related supply constraints, prices of certain chemicals began to zoom, and along with that a grand bull run happened in some of the companies making those chemicals.

We bought several of those stocks, and they were among our top performers in 2020 and 2021. However, we did not build up a story in our heads that these were the best businesses or best managements of all time. So we were able to quit those positions when the time came without emotion and without a sense of loss.

On the other hand, we also bought ITC, and then later capital goods and industrial machinery companies in our India PMS in 2021 when they came out of their twelve-year-long period of underperformance.

Related to this is the truth that *while a business maybe steady and predictable for at least a few years, the stock market trajectory rarely is. Even companies with the steadiest of businesses have their stocks go through long periods of underperformance in the market.*

> Within reason, no stock is a Permanent Hero or a Permanent Dud.

Not bullish, not bearish, be hare-ish

When people ask me whether I am a bull or a bear, there is only one answer I give them: I am a Hare.

Why did we choose the hare as our mascot at First Global?

Because the hare is alert, it is fast, it is agile. It can run swiftly, but it can also change direction quickly.

That is the way to be in the markets. You cannot be wedded to a point of view because ultimately life and markets are bets about the future.

By definition, the future is not known or can only be known as a range of possibilities. *Therefore, it is entirely possible that even if you have done your homework well, what you consider as the most probable outcome may not come to pass. Something else may happen and you may need to change your strategy.*

You may need to be a hare!

Of course, the hare has another characteristic, which one can only aspire to: it has 360-degree vision, and thus it can see in all directions.

Great trades are like buses, there's always one coming

Some of the biggest mistakes in the markets come out of FOMO, or fear of missing out.

Your friend got an IPO allotment during an IPO boom and flipped it out in a few days at double the price; Nasdaq had a great run for three years and you did not invest; small-cap indexes are up 50 per cent and your friends are talking about the stocks they made pots of money in; some industry has been doing very well (say, tech or pharma or infrastructure or defence) and you did not invest in those stocks and now every expert on TV is telling you 'I told you so'. What do you do?

If you are like most investors, you will pile on to the next IPO, the next small-cap NFO (New Fund Offering) or that industry-theme fund.

The result almost certainly is an underperforming portfolio.

The reason for this is simple—*when a theme has been doing well for some time is when it comes on your radar and you want to clamber on to this bus which has already left the bus station. In running after a fast-moving vehicle and trying to climb on to it you are more likely than not to just fall to the ground.*

As Richard Branson said in his book, and which is one of my favourite quotes, 'Opportunities are like buses . . . there is always another one around the corner.'

The world is not running out of opportunities. Investing in something which has been already doing well

The thing to remember is this: this is not the last bus or the last opportunity that will come your way. If you have missed this one, never mind; there will be another one just around the corner.

over a period of time will usually just result in underperformance of what you have bought. This is the data. This is the same reason why you should avoid thematic funds.

In fact, it can be systematically proven that if you invest in the best-performing sector or asset class of the recent past, you will equally systematically underperform the benchmarks.

No storification, just datafication

As I have discussed elsewhere in the book, as human beings we want stories, and especially stories about why we are invested in certain companies.

When I started in this business as a broker to large institutional fund managers, this was one of the things that struck me. The fund managers were supposed to be managing money professionally and objectively, but whenever you went to a fund manager to explain why a certain stock was a good buy, almost invariably the question was: 'What is the story?'

It came to a point where, in a ironic hat-tip to this all-pervasive question, all our research reports would start with a one-pager called 'The Story'.

But of course, then you were catering to your clientele and their needs—which, in spite of the whole front of a fund was really still a human being who needed to be convinced with the story.

When you are dealing directly with the market you know that the market has no use for stories. It does not care how well you have crafted your story about a security or a sector, how emotionally invested you are in the story, how many people you have told that story to, how heart-broken you would be if the story does not come true. . .

The market will do what it has to do, and if it spoils your story, then so be it. It frankly doesn't give a damn.

Even now, when we go to market our investment management services, investors want to know the stories behind why we hold certain stocks. Surprisingly, the larger the investor the more inclined they are to be dissatisfied without the juicy stories, probably because everyone else in the market is only too happy to paint these grand pictures and tell them some fascinating stories.

So, why don't we at least make up some stories to satisfy the finicky family-office investor or ultra HNI (high net worth investor) or a big bank?

One reason we don't is because if we tell and repeat stories, we will also begin to believe them ourselves.

> To keep to the discipline of sticking to data and objective facts means you have to let go of the temptation of telling fascinating stories. That is the price you pay for predictable outperformance over a period of time.

Rigidity kills, in arteries and in investing

We all know this for our cardiac health—that our blood vessels must remain flexible. Rigidity means higher risk of heart attacks.

The same thing holds in investing. If you believe you have the keys to the kingdom and that every single investment of yours is going to be a great one, you hold on to that conviction even when the market price for the stock is telling you something else. Basically, you remain rigid. The net result? Your portfolio, or your clients', will soon be full of gaping holes.

There are both known unknowns and unknown unknowns.

This means that *any investment*

> Rigidity simply does not work in the markets. Investing is a game where you are making a bet on the future, which is by definition unknown.

you are making, any bet you are making, is one based on probabilities. This in turn means that your bet can be wrong, even if you have made the decision carefully.

By holding on to your so-called convictions even in the face of contrary facts, you are only going to go into a downward spiral.

Fascinating artificial intelligence videos show how AI finds a way around one or more physical obstacles by trying various tactics. It may be that some of them work, but the environment may change and then the techniques stop working after a while. The trick lies in acknowledging what is still working, what has stopped working, and undertaking course correction accordingly.

> There is no merit in holding on to your convictions in the face of truth which is to the contrary.

Avoid big losses

I have explained in another chapter how investing is a loser's game, where fifty or sixty years ago you may have had an edge in terms of understanding companies or having information or data no one else had.

> The real way to get an edge in this business is to ensure that you do not suffer any crippling losses. If you can protect on the downside, the market will give you plenty of room to make gains.

However, by now, across the world everybody has the same data. Not only that, the very best minds in the world work in this business of trying to identify investment winners.

In such a situation, it is foolish to expect that you will be always ahead in identifying the winners.

At First Global, we have a fairly elaborate system of risk management—in fact, we tell our clients that more than half the money they pay us is for risk management and only the balance for returns management.

Nevertheless, even when you are investing on your own, have a disciplined risk management system that even you cannot overrule.

This includes things like not taking a concentrated position in sectors or stocks, having strict stop losses, and so on.

The biggest risk management hack?

When you are buying a stock, tell yourself you may be making a mistake, because no matter how super-smart you are, a certain percentage of your investment decisions *will* be mistakes.

One other reason to have strict risk management is that when stocks go up and down, their increase and decline percentages are not symmetrical.

If a stock or a portfolio falls by one-third, it will need a 50 per cent move to come back to zero base. If it falls by 50 per cent, it will need to double to come back to zero returns position. The only way to win this game is to ensure that drawdowns, or losses, are limited.

So, here is a quick recap of what I consider important investment mantras to live by. Although, in a sense, this whole book is dotted with many of these mantras.

The nine investment mantras

1. Be the 'house', not the 'gambler'.
2. Protect in down markets. Participate in up markets.
3. Play for singles. Not for sixes or home runs.
4. Play everything. Believe nothing.
5. Not bullish. Not bearish. Be hare-ish.
6. Great trades are like buses, there's always one coming.
7. No storification. Just datafication.
8. Rigidity kills, in arteries and in investing.
9. Avoid big losses.

Scan the QR code to learn more

Why Investing Is a Loser's Game

I often say that in investing it is more important to manage risks than to try to maximize returns. But why do I say that?

Because investing is a loser's game.

And what is a loser's game?

This goes back to a mind-opening concept in an old article written over forty years ago by Charles D. Ellis, called 'The Loser's Game', which classifies everything in the world into a winner's game or a loser's game.[18]

Can the same thing be two different types of games?

Interestingly, the same game can be two different games, so to speak.

For example, in tennis, if you look at the Grand Slam level, there you have to serve brilliantly and return every volley. You have to play superbly in order to win. That is a winner's game.

However, when you are playing at your mohalla or club level, you just have to make sure that you don't make mistakes, i.e., you must not lose. Your objective should be just to keep the ball in play and hope the other side will make enough mistakes for you to win. This is what makes it a loser's game. The outcome of the game is determined by the actions of the loser.

And games can transform—a game can change from a winner's game to a loser's game.

> And games can transform—a game can change from a winner's game to a loser's game.

A great example is aviation, which in the early years was an adventure sport. This was the time J.R.D. Tata and Charles Lindberg were flying. Here is a part account of J.R.D. Tata's famous Karachi–London flight:

> JRD had taken off from Karachi on 3 May 1930 in a Gypsy Moth G-AAGI plane. He faced significant headwinds as he flew towards Jask, a small, hot and dusty town on the coast of Iran. There he stayed overnight and then took off towards Basra in Iraq. He drifted a little and had to double back from the salt marshes north of Lingah to reach Basra. From Basra, he flew towards Baghdad, and then towards Cairo.
>
> En route, his faulty compass led him to drift out again and land on an old, disused World War 1 airstrip covered in anthills at Haifa. But he recovered quickly from this error and reached Cairo . . .[19]

This was an adventure where pilots used faulty instruments and there were lots of deviations from the original plan, risks, etc. It was the quintessential winner's game.

> Aviation transformed from a winner's game to a loser's game—as did investing.

But now there is only one way to fly an aircraft: Go by the checklist. Do not make mistakes.

How investing changed from a winner's game to a loser's game

Coming to investing, let's look at, say, your grandparents' generation. At that time there was significant information asymmetry. They may have known of companies which other people had not analysed; maybe they were able to go more deeply into their financials at a time when spreadsheets were not available and were able to invest in something that became a multibagger. Even getting annual reports of companies was a competitive advantage!

Even up to fifteen or twenty years ago, fund managers and professional analysts could go and meet companies and get differential information. The investor on the street was not invited to analyst meets or conference calls. In short, there was substantial information arbitrage, not just in India but even in the more developed countries. Even in the US, a big fund house like Fidelity could have a meeting with, say, a Walmart or an IBM and get information, which was otherwise not generally available.

But today, by law, all data and information, including conference call transcripts and presentations, are available to everyone. Plus, there is a large number of extremely smart people in the market in every country.

Therefore, for you to have a consistent edge in making the best possible investment every time is very difficult. Even professional fund managers cannot say that all their picks will do well; that they will find hidden gems no one else has found. To claim the contrary is another way of saying that they will be consistently smarter than the combined wisdom of all the many smart people in the markets—and this is always an illusion.

Fund managers having not come to terms with this reality is the reason why so many of them underperform the benchmarks.

With the change in how information is available in the markets, the required skill sets have changed—from trying to get an information edge to being able to analyse tonnes of information and data. More on that elsewhere in the book.

For example, in the COVID crash of March 2020, most retail investors and even professional fund managers just went down with the market, 30–35–40 per cent, or even more than the market.

Since you cannot be ahead of the market in identifying investment opportunities each and every time, your first priority should be to avoid taking a big hit on your capital and ensure that you do not lose substantial money.

And from that kind of loss it is very difficult to come back. For one thing, if your portfolio comes down by one-third it will need to go up 50 per cent for you to break even. If it goes down by 50 per cent you will need to double your money to come to zero returns.

Making sure that you don't take a big hit on your capital should be your priority number one rather than going all out on a high-risk bet in order to maximize returns.

Asymmetry between buys and sells

One additional point relating to investing is that the competition is high in identifying investments. In other words, ***most market participants are jostling to identify or find and buy the next hot stock.***

Focus and competition are far less when it comes to when to sell a stock. It therefore makes sense to focus on that side of the equation.

Optimization of when to sell may provide a more sustainable advantage than concentration on when to buy, because the latter is where almost all market participants concentrate.

Investing, a loser's game

- You should first manage the risk in investing rather than try to maximize the returns. Because investing is a loser's game.
- A loser's game is an activity where the final result is determined by the actions of the loser. In such cases the winning strategy is to play to ensure that you do not lose.
- In investing, this means managing your portfolio so that you avoid big drawdowns or losses on your capital. You will win if and only if you do not lose (big money).
- Investing may have been a winner's game once upon a time when information was not easily available. Now, by law, plenty of data is available, and the skill required is in crunching the data.
- As a corollary, because most market participants focus on what and when to buy, a potentially winning strategy is to have a good focus on when to sell.

Scan the QR code to learn more

The Logic of Diversification

Diversified or concentrated portfolios: Which to choose?

Till a couple of years ago, the generally accepted 'fact' was that only concentrated portfolios could get you alpha—that is, outperformance of the market.

The logic went something like this: if you are buying a number of stocks in large quantities, then you are replicating the market, and how can you do better than the market then?

Most of the players, especially in the PMS industry, would pitch themselves as providing value because they were buying only around fifteen stocks, which was different from the strategy of mutual fund schemes, which held a large number of stocks.

Of course, of late I hear more and more fund managers talking about diversification. *Many of the same people who used to say that only a concentrated portfolio could make you outsized returns, or at least give you outperformance, are now saying that diversification is better.*

Can you outperform with a diversified portfolio?

First the facts: in most years, more than 50 per cent of the stocks in the market outperform the market index. The average is more like 55 per cent.

There are roughly 750 stocks in the Indian market with market capitalization greater than Rs 1000 crore, and each year close to 400 of them outperform the market.

Even if you are holding forty or sixty stocks, if they are mainly from this outperforming bucket, your portfolio as a whole will outperform the index. You do not need to be super concentrated to ensure outperformance.

Therefore, it is clear that you can very well outperform the market with a diversified portfolio. But let us invert the question.

Does a diversified portfolio lead to outperformance?

What is the magic formula for outperformance? Is it that if you hold forty rather than fourteen stocks, your portfolio will automatically give you outperformance, or alpha?

There is a nuanced answer to this. People talking about diversification versus concentration often do not understand the logic of a diversified portfolio. They only know of the term 'diversified portfolio' and not what the underlying first principles logic is.

It is not that if you hold more stocks your performance will be better.

So, what is the logic for diversification?

Why is it that I speak about diversification and advise it?

Why is it that since First Global started its PMS four years ago, its performance has been topping the charts in the multi-cap PMS category, especially on a risk-adjusted basis—and this has been achieved with a diversified portfolio?

Is holding a large number of stocks the magic formula?

Not quite. But this is something that many professional investors and fund managers copying First Global do not understand.

It is not as if buying a higher number of stocks gets you to outperformance.

Diversification reduces the element of luck and increases the contribution of skill

What diversification does is this: It makes sure that your actual returns are closer to the expected value of the returns, or that the results are close to what you can expect given your skill levels.

Let me explain.

This might sound complicated, but it is actually quite simple.

Think of this: you know a coin is expected to have a 50 per cent probability of heads or tails when tossed.

Nevertheless, if you toss it only ten times it may happen that you might get only two heads, or you might get eight or nine heads. Basically, the predictability is not very high when it comes to a small number of tosses. However, if you toss it 100 times, it is going to be closer to that 50/50 number.

Now, investing is a game of skill and luck.

Diversification increases the component of skill and reduces the element of luck.

Suppose you are skilful enough to pick the right stocks 65 per cent of the time. Why only 65 per cent of the time? Because no fund manager or investor in the world is ever right 80–90 or

> In short, if you actually have the skill, diversification will ensure that it shows up in your results.
> But if you do not have the skill, then just increasing the number of stocks is not going to help.

100 per cent of the time—forget about that. So, even if you get your picks 60 per cent right, actually it is pretty good.

What diversification does is that if you are buying, say, fifty stocks instead of fifteen, you are more likely to get close to that 60 per cent or 65 per cent hit rate.

With only a few stocks you are playing luck mainly

Of course, with fewer stocks, what happens is that the element of chance coming into play increases. So if you are buying only twelve or fifteen stocks, there is a great element of chance that comes to play—and at times it may even favour you—so there might be one or two years when that kind of strategy does very well.

Nevertheless, diversification increases predictability and makes the results more foreseeable as they will be closer to reflecting your skill level.

In summary, diversification works only if you have the skill. Only if your system is designed such that it gives you outperformance will it ensure that in the real world too you have outperformance.

It is that simple!

Diversified or concentrated portfolios: What works better?

- It was earlier accepted that to significantly outperform the market you needed a concentrated portfolio.
- However, this is not correct because more than half the stocks in the market outperform the market. Hence it is possible to have an outperforming portfolio even with a large number of stocks.
- But neither is there any magic to having a large number of stocks in one's portfolio.
- Investing is a game of skill and luck. All that diversification ensures is that the element of skill plays a bigger role than luck in the final result.
- In short, a concentrated portfolio relies more on luck, whereas a diversified portfolio gives results which reflect the skill level of the investor/fund manager more closely.

Scan the QR code to learn more

SECTION III

Human Behaviour and Investing

If you had to choose to work on one area in order to improve your portfolio returns, it is this: Understanding your own thinking, biases and decision-making, and how to change things about yourself. It is about internal work, rather than merely reading pages and pages of techniques and equations.

This is not to say that understanding numbers, finance or accounting, even economics, is of no consequence for investing well. It is quite the reverse. As you know, I am a very numbers- and data-driven person, but the other side is equally important.

That is why I said that while you can afford to skip the numbers and equations chapters early in the book, you must read everything in the coming pages super carefully.

It is a truism that intelligence and wisdom are different attributes.

As has been said, you can have an intelligent serial killer, but never a wise one.

To be an investor in the markets, you can read a lot of books, and you should. But, as they say about mathematics, that part is a necessary but not sufficient condition for success in investing, or even trading.

What is required is something more: experience, living through the ups and downs of the markets (that's very different from merely looking at past charts where you can easily decide what you would have done in specific situations), plus understanding your own mindset, emotions and biases . . . in short, you need wisdom along with knowledge.

That's why people who are outstanding success stories, whether it is in investing or for that matter trading, usually come into their own usually at fifty-plus.

George Soros, Warren Buffett, Jim Simons and many others came into their best years at age fifty, or even past fifty-five.

On the other hand, there is no magic to that age, unless and until you've also put in the 10,000 hours of hard work that is necessary.

And no—watching business and stock market channels all day long does not count!

In fact, that's a time sink, and all the more a trap because it 'appears' useful.

What is required is for the investor to read solid books on finance, investment techniques, the history of both markets and businesses, and much more. All this knowledge has to go into your brain, and only then, along with experience and wisdom, will you be able to put what you have learnt into practice.

Only when you live through market ups and downs will you be able to understand your own emotions, your own mindset, your ability to be disciplined and to keep to your system (or not) . . . where your particular pitfalls lie and how you can guard against them.

Investing is as much about what goes on inside your own head as it is about what is going on outside. This is what the following section concentrates on.

Why Following Successful Investors May Set You Up for Failure[20]

If you want to know how to become rich or how to become a good investor, how would you go about it?

A logical way to do it appears to be look at the richest people in the world, or the most successful investors, study the techniques they have employed and use them in your own life.

It seems logical, doesn't it? To do as well in the markets as, say, Warren Buffett, Rakesh Jhunjhunwala or Ray Dalio, you need to just study their methods and replicate them. It seems simple enough.

Following successful investors, in fact, is not logical at all!

There is in it an inherent and major logical fallacy—in fact, several fallacies—that can lead you to absolutely erroneous conclusions and decisions.

Just a note, before we plunge into this topic . . . the examples here have been chosen simply based on which investors and their methods have been studied well and extensively—basically the best-known ones. They are, by no means, chosen to prove a point or to exemplify the 'worst in category'.

First, are they buying the sort of stocks you think they are?

If you ask any follower or fan of Warren Buffett's to tell you in detail what kind of stocks Buffett buys, I am sure that fan can provide you a checklist that goes something like this: steady businesses, mostly with great brands, predictable cash flows that can be forecast decades into the future, available at a reasonable price, etc.

Then the fan may add: Buffett does not buy businesses he does not understand, or which are vulnerable to changes in technology.

All these are 'principles' extracted from writings by or about him.

Coca-Cola, which has been among his big holdings, exemplifies this sort of stock (more on Coke later), but let us see what he actually holds. As I write this, at the beginning of 2024 *almost 50 per cent of Berkshire Hathaway's total investments are in a single stock: Apple.*

Does Apple really fit this bill? Sure, it is a dominant player in mobile phones and certain devices—at least at the high end. But can anyone say with any degree of certainty what that business will look like at an industry level ten or fifteen years later?

As for being dominant, there was a time when Nokia and the smaller Blackberry were considered unbeatable in the devices business, but they are now consigned to the dustbin of history.

Now, with artificial intelligence and many other new technologies moving very fast, who knows who the big winner of the next round will be. Who knows even what devices we will be using a few years hence?

It has been very rare in the last few decades of technology that a winner in one round remains the number one in the next round too.

And Apple is not the only example. Berkshire Hathway has invested very widely over the years in derivatives, in structured deals, and so on. And it has often made a large chunk of money from these activities.

These are not the value stocks everybody thinks Berkshire has bought. The sweetheart deals it got after the 2008 financial crisis with the likes of Goldman Sachs and Bank of America are examples of that. Not only did Buffett invest in them, he influenced the US government to bail out the banking sector, bolstering his own returns.

In fact, Warren Buffett's folksy, avuncular image allows him to get away with deals that would get others classified as vultures or sharks. He is always sniffing the waters when there is blood around.

Is their holding period what you think it is?

Again, ask anyone who follows Buffett how long they think he holds a stock, and the answer will be that his favourite holding period is forever, that he thinks of himself as part owner of the business and never intends to sell.

The reality? Ninety per cent of stocks that Berkshire buys are sold within two years, and 75 per cent sold within ten months. This is the data from a study carried out for the company's entire activity over the period 2006 to 2015.[21]

Panel B: Holding period and number of stocks held by Berkshire Hathaway

Holding quarters	Number of stocks	Percentage	Cumulative percentage
1	39	16.96	16.96
2	29	12.61	29.57
3	16	6.96	36.52
4	55	23.91	60.43
5–10	34	14.78	75.22
10–20	20	8.70	83.91
20–30	15	6.52	90.43
30–40	13	5.65	96.09
40–50	2	0.87	96.96
>50	7	3.04	100
Total	230	100	

Hence, Berkshire Hathaway's holding period is not forever—it is far from it. In fact, somewhere Buffett clarified that he meant the 'hold forever' mantra was only for the businesses that Berkshire is majority owner of, which is obviously a small fraction of its holdings. And which is really making a virtue out of a necessity, because unless Berkshire makes a strategic sale, it is unlikely it can get out of those businesses.

Are their results as spectacular?

Another assumption we make without actually checking the data is that certain investors like Warren Buffett–Charlie Munger and Ray Dalio are 'successful'. But what does the data actually show?

Berkshire Hathaway, which was run by the legends Warren Buffett and Charlie Munger, has not outperformed the S&P

500—not for one or two years but for fifteen and twenty years. This is in spite of the huge crash in the US markets in 2022, which should have theoretically provided them alpha, what with their supposedly conservative and risk-averse strategy.

CAGR	Bridgewater Associates, LP, Pure Alpha Fund II	Berkshire Hathaway Inc. (Class A)	S&P 500 TR
10-Year	3.0%	11.5%	12.2%
15-Year	5.7%	8.7%	10.1%
20-Year	8.3%	10.4%	10.4%

Data as of March 2023. Source: Bloomberg. RCM Alternatives

While Berkshire's results have at least been somewhat close to the market returns, Dalio's Bridgewater has had a frankly disastrous run for a good two decades. Over fifteen years, the fund has only compounded at 5.7 per cent, as against the S&P 500's 10.1 per cent.

Yet the glow of being smart and successful continues to surround these names because they can talk the talk.

In other words, $100 invested in Ray Dalio's fund fifteen years ago would have grown to only $230 instead of the $424 that an investment in the S&P would have yielded over the same period.

Do you really understand how value is defined?

Many of the well-known investors I am talking about are thought of as value investors, and most of the people in the public market think they know what value investing means, which is mostly buying stocks at low price-to-earnings or low price-to-book.

However, for one, that is too restrictive a definition of value, and as shown above Berkshire's top holding is Apple, which you anyway cannot call a low multiple or value stock.

The interesting thing is that Benjamin Graham is considered the patron saint of value investing, but in every edition of his book he kept refining the definition of value, in the later editions speaking about how intangibles were contributing more and more to the value of companies. That edition itself was written almost half a century ago, and I am sure that if he had been alive today, he would have redefined value again. More on that elsewhere in the book.

The point is that people do not go into the depth of what he wrote and just go by the key/kunji or CliffNotes version and think they understand what value is.

Even more important is the fact that Graham made almost all his money in Geico, which is an insurance company and not in the value stocks that he is associated with.

It is all about the timing!

We also spout many homilies about not timing the market, but the well-known success stories of investors are almost always a function of when they were investing.

In India, if you had invested in the Sensex in 1981, your Rs 100 would have become Rs 700. Invested in 2011, Rs 100 would have become only Rs 230 at the end of ten years in 2020.

If one looks at the well-known US indexes, we see this same pattern of very stark differences in compounding, not only in individual years but for decades altogether. The S&P 500 compounded at 4.7 per cent in the 1960s, 4 per cent in the 1970s, then accelerated to 9.3 per cent in the 1980s and to nearly 15 per cent in the 1990s.

Even if one looks at a twenty-year period, $100 invested at the beginning of the 1960s in the S&P 500 would have risen to only $230 over the twenty years to 1980.

But equity investments rose nearly ten times in the next twenty years of the eighties and nineties, making certain investors and fund managers appear brilliant.

That was the time when investors like Warren Buffett saw their biggest compounding. Not only that, the opportunities thrown up at the time made others like Peter Lynch of Fidelity look outstanding. *As an aside, my respect for Lynch is not so much for his skill in stock picking as for the fact that he recognized that the fourteen-year super-run he had at the Magellan Fund could not and would not be replicated and retired at the peak of his game when he was still in his forties.*

Many who taught this philosophy of buying businesses that you understand (example: Peter Lynch talking about buying the company whose pantyhose his wife loved), great brands, predictable cash flows, etc., are merely parroting stuff from books written in the 1980s when those were the kind of stocks that performed.

> Not only do markets compound at different rates for even decades at a time, different types of stocks do well at various points in time.

The fact is, no sector outperforms forever—not even steady consumer businesses. In India alone there have been whole decades at a time when steady FMCG companies like Hindustan Unilever or Nestle India have underperformed the market hugely.

Now we know that the investors you admire may not actually be holding the kind of stocks you think they do, their holding period may be very different from what your impression of the same is, and, even worse, their results are nowhere close to the huge market-beating returns that you think they made.

Their money, in short, may have been made very differently from the public perception of how it was made, and may have more than a little to do with which period of the market they managed to catch.

But there is something even more fundamentally wrong in the very question we started with.

Let us say these investors had been very successful even in the last ten or fifteen years, but there is still something really fundamentally wrong in the question we started with.

Should you copy the methods of the most successful investors in the first place?

There is a really fascinating story from World War II, when the US military was examining its bomber aircraft to see where to reinforce them. The aircraft returning to base were examined to see which parts had taken the maximum hits, and plans were afoot to reinforce these parts.

That was when mathematician and statistician Abraham Wald pointed out that this analysis could be totally off, because it did not take into account the aircraft that *did not* return to base.

The parts which showed no hits were probably the parts where, if the aircraft took a hit, it would not survive and be able to return to base. The bullet holes in the returning aircraft, contrary to conventional thinking, represented areas where a bomber could take damage and still fly well enough to return safely to base.

So Wald proposed that the navy reinforce the areas where the returning aircraft were unscathed, inferring that planes hit in those areas were lost. It was a brilliant piece of analysis that totally inverted the conventional way of looking at a problem.

A not-so-happy piece of trivia: Wald died in an air crash over Kerala in the 1950s while going from a talk at the Indian Statistical Institute at Calcutta to another at the Indian Institutes of Science.

You must be wondering what this story has to do with following successful investors?

Are you even asking the right question?

In the analysis given above, your starting point is investors who are/appear successful today. Then you look backwards, at the strategies they have employed in the past.

You are starting with success stories of, say, billionaire stock investors and attempting to reverse-engineer a personal pathway to similar success. The stated or unstated presumption is that if you follow their strategies, you will see similar levels of success.

Now, suppose some of these entities/investors had opted for extremely high-risk strategies, where most of those using these strategies went out of business. However, the few that were left standing became successful or rich beyond their wildest dreams!

But your analysis does not take into account the entities that followed the very same strategy but failed or even went out of business. Or, in short, your analysis suffers from survivorship bias.

You think you are answering the question as to which strategies lead to success, but your actual analysis is inverted in order.

Instead of starting with what happens to investors or fund managers who follow a particular strategy, you are instead looking at the strategies followed by the successful entities. The two are entirely different inquiries to make.

It is a core principle of probability that the probability of event A, given that event B has occurred, is not the same as the probability of event B, given event A has occurred. By inverting the pathway, you are ending up with completely wrong results.

It is the equivalent of saying that if you want to become as successful as Bill Gates, you should drop out of college.

An example will make it clearer. Suppose there is a way of investing which is extremely high risk but can give high returns. Every year, 90 per cent of the people opting for it will go bust, but the balance 10 per cent will make ten times their money.

Suppose 100,000 people start playing this game. Five years later, there will be only one person left out of these, but this person would have made $1,000 into $100 million. She will be the most successful investor in the market.

Now, when you are evaluating options and know of this person who has converted $1,000 into $100 million, you will naturally want to emulate her methods, except that because of survivorship bias, you will not realize that 99.999 per cent of the people opting for this method or system will go bust.

In general, of investors that follow the most aggressive strategies, a few of them will make extraordinarily high returns whereas the others will flame out.

The most successful outliers on Dalal Street, or for that matter Wall Street, over any given short-term period almost always took some extreme amount of risk that just happened to pay off big.

Think about this very deeply when you hear that all the richest investors in the world are optimistic, or risk takers, or whatever other defining characteristic of a rich investor is supposed to be.

Outliers often take extraordinary risks to produce those magnificent returns.

But just because a particular strategy worked one time for one person doesn't mean it's a good strategy to follow.

It's extremely unlikely that someone who has an investment strategy that generates significantly higher returns than the market has found a strategy that is safe and consistent.

It is more than likely that he or she has simply 'survived', a very dangerous approach to investing. In short, he or she got lucky.

It is like meeting a centenarian who has been drinking and smoking and eating lavishly all her life and assuming that following a similar lifestyle will get you to live to 100. It is not going to happen.

That particular person may have been extraordinarily lucky, in terms of her genes or some other factor, and is actually the exception that proves the rule.

Even when the odds are not as extreme as in the example above, there is a general rule that holds. If you look at only the picture of who has made the most returns, we would say that being extremely aggressive is good.

In reality, maybe 90 per cent or 95 per cent of those who had these aggressive positions lost all their capital. And there are maybe 5 per cent who made outsized returns.

In short, for any evaluation, start with all entities that followed that strategy and understand their trajectory rather than look at only the successful ones.

> Even for systems that are not as high risk as this one, due to the sheer chance there will be some people who will make extraordinary amounts of money. But that does not mean the system that they followed was the best system to follow or will give the best risk-return trade-off.

Following successful investors

- While the formula for success in investing appears simple—do what successful investors do—there is a whole host of fallacies in this path.
- First, the type of stocks they are said to hold may be very different from what they actually hold. Warren Buffett has NOT made most of his money in steady consumer businesses.
- Is their holding period what you think it is? Buffett, for instance, doesn't hold 80 per cent of his stocks for even one year.

- Have you even checked if these investors are 'successful'? Neither Buffett nor Ray Dalio has beaten benchmarks for over two decades!

- Success is often a product of how markets have done over a period of time. Both in India and the US, market returns have varied by three to four times even over a decade.

- When following successful investors, are you even asking the right question?

- Instead of following the path of the grand successes, you should ask what happened to all the entities who followed the same strategy.

- A high-risk strategy can have very few winners, but the ones that survive can have spectacular results. That doesn't mean it is the right strategy to follow.

Why Does the 'Hold' Rating Exist in Securities Research?

Even if you'd never heard anything about the securities market, you would still understand buy and sell ratings.

But hold? That's not quite as intuitive, is it?

The question is: Is it even rational?

The whole construct of a 'hold' rating is to hide from us the fact that we are being irrational by putting a covert premium on something precisely because we are already holding it.

Think about it—if a security is not worth buying today, why is it worth holding?

This irrationality arises out of something called the endowment effect, or endowment bias.

Anything that belongs to us automatically has higher value for us. This holds true even when it comes to mundane objects, like a coffee mug.

The seminal study on endowment effect was carried out at Cornell University by Richard Thaler, Daniel Kahneman and Jack Knetsch.[22]

It was a simple experiment. Half the students were given coffee mugs with the university logo on them and half were not. They were then asked the price of the mug, i.e., what they would be willing to buy or sell it for.

Logically, whether or not they had the mugs should not have made a difference to the estimated price or the price they were willing to trade the mugs. But the reality was very different. The students who had got the mugs were not willing to sell them for less than $5.25 on average compared to the students without mugs who were prepared to buy them for between $2.25 and $2.75 on average.

Similar experiments have been replicated many times in different settings.

When we get attached to even everyday objects like coffee mugs, securities or other investments we hold are much closer to our hearts, because first they are more closely aligned with our well-being.

Secondly, investing in a stock or other asset means that you have analysed the options and made a conscious choice. Now you don't want to change your mind because that would mean accepting that your earlier choice was incorrect.

As a result, you are likely to be even more invested mentally (pun intended) in a stock that you own than in other objects that you may own.

That's why most people will keep defending the choice of stocks they hold in their portfolio and hold on to them for too long.

In fact, endowment bias is the single reason why a 'hold' rating exists at all in the lexicon of market analysts.

Don't kid yourself!

You may even kid yourself that you are holding on to this investment because you do not want to incur unnecessary transaction costs, but the fact is often that the investment may not make sense even if you net out the transaction costs involved.

The comfort factor with something familiar could keep one holding on to stocks too, or it could be decision paralysis that leaves your portfolio unchanged for long periods because you want an irrational premium to sell something you hold.

And this isn't even confined to the stock or securities markets. Many who want to sell an apartment or household

> Usually, the transaction cost of a switch in investments is negligible compared with the potential loss of holding on to the wrong investment or the potential profit that was not realized by not switching to the right asset or security.

on to a price they have anchored themselves to. For example, you hear many people say, 'I won't sell unless I get Rs 2 crore for this flat.'

That may not be the market price. They may wait two, four or five years till they get that price, and may even feel happy about having held on, but that may have been an economically irrational 'hold' decision. If they had sold the house all those years ago and put the money even in a fixed deposit, they would have been better off.

In financial markets, the problem is that these rationalizations that keep you from taking the required action can be detrimental to your financial health.

The price at which you bought a stock is irrelevant

Listen to the questions viewers ask 'experts' on television. They typically go something like this: 'I had bought this stock X years ago at Y price. What should I do with it now?' Other than the name of the stock, all other information in this question is completely irrelevant.

The right answer to this question should explain that *the market has zero interest in the viewer's purchase price for the stock. It is completely and totally irrelevant.* But of course, such a thing is never said.

Very often people are of the mindset that they must get out of a stock or even a fund when that holding comes to the break-even point. Meaning if the stock price or the mutual fund NAV has fallen below their purchase price, they think they will sell only if the price comes back to the level at which they had bought, so that they don't have to book losses on the investment. But this completely irrational.

Understand that you do not have to make it back through the same investment. Your bank balance does not care where the money has come from.

On a related note, do not fall in love with stocks—meaning, do not invest your emotions in them. Your portfolio will thank you for it.

How to fix your attachment to stocks

Since you now know that this is a cognitive bias, you need to guard yourself against it. The only real way to make a start is with a zero-base portfolio approach.

Do not think about how you can bring yourself to sell Hindustan Unilever shares bought by your parents, or that you have made a ton of money on HDFC Bank or Apple so you should continue to hold them.

The only rational way to deal with this is to think about how you would deploy your money if you had the equivalent of all these shares in cash today. Do this at least once and twice a year. Preferably with another set of eyes too—your life partner, your financial adviser or someone who has no stake in proving that the initial decision to invest was correct.

Why what you hold is of no relevance

- Is having a hold rating rational? If a security is not worth buying today, why is it worth holding?
- The whole construct of the 'hold' rating is to hide from us the fact that we are being irrational, by putting a covert premium on something precisely because we are already holding it.
- Anything that belongs to us automatically has higher value for us than it otherwise would.
- The market does not care what we hold and at what price we bought it. Do not invest your emotions in your portfolio or wait for your purchase price to come back.
- Do a zero base rebalance of your portfolio and hold what makes the most sense today. What you hold already is not of real consequence, especially as transaction costs are very low now. Assume you have all cash today and then allocate.

Scan the QR code to learn more

Humans and the Art of Storytelling

When you switch on your laptop or mobile, sometimes a disconcerting ad pops up talking about a young girl with three siblings who cannot afford food or school fees, or maybe featuring a parent asking for money for a life-saving surgery for their child.

An ad like that is bound to generate a degree of guilt if you do not respond.

Now, flip the situation. Ever wonder why, in contrast, there is negligible emotional response to news reports saying 30 per cent of children in your district are malnourished or that lakhs of cancer patients do not have the money for treatment?

The reason is simple: **_human beings are hardwired to respond to stories. While impersonal statistics are easy to ignore, stories are not!_**

Anthropologists say that stories exist in all cultures across all time periods, regardless of their level of sophistication.
It can be said that stories, in a very real sense, are what make us human.

Human beings have always been tellers of and listeners of stories. Go back to when humans were still living in caves—they would return and tell stories about their hunts, which are what people see illustrated in cave paintings.

Stories are the best way to pass on knowledge, wisdom and information to the next generation. Children everywhere not just like stories, but they also find them the easiest way to learn things—something that was well understood by Vishnu Sharma when he wrote the Panchatantra.

Great. So, what is the point being made here?

Stories make us human . . . but the market is not human!

The issue is that it is not just stories but also many other ways of thinking that make us human, are the very aspects that derail our investment journey.

As I've talked about elsewhere in the book, what we call quirks of thinking or biases today have had a real and valuable role to play in our evolution. So, at some point in the evolutionary cycle, these were very good attributes to have—possibly when humans were hunter-gatherers or when they had to escape from wild animals.

It's not accidental that almost all ads, including the ones mentioned in the beginning of this chapter, are in the form of stories rather than a dry list of facts or statistics. Stories work when there is a human being on the other side listening to them.

For example, if a fund manager is trying to convince investors to invest with her or him and comes up with this nice little story: 'I am investing in this company because it has great brands, predictable cash flows, manages logistics very well,'; or about why this company's management 'has a magic touch'—as investors, most human beings will get convinced.

> Stories are much more powerful and memorable than any other way of conveying something, and hence satisfying to us.

But the problem is that when you're investing, there is no human being on the other side. There's only the market, which doesn't really care about how beautifully your story is crafted or how many people believe in it.

Here are the reasons why stories do not work when it comes to investing.

One: Stories don't play out the way they are sold

Most of you will be able to think of instances when the story that was told to you about the market or some stocks did not play out the way 'everyone' or the experts said it would!

Let alone the stories about individual stocks, even on an aggregate basis, almost every story of a stock or company that is talked about or a valuation that has been done assumes that the company grows its earnings out into infinity. Yet, of the 4000-plus stocks listed on the Indian bourses, only sixteen (no typo here!), have shown some profit growth every year for even as short a period as ten years.

That is a mere 0.4 per cent of the stocks!

This goes to show that the stories you are being sold are just tales, with little probability that they will come true in the future.

Two: Stories have to be deterministic and simple . . . but life is complex and probabilistic

A story, by definition, has to be reasonably simple. So there has to be a beginning, a cause-and-effect segment and an end. That's what you want.

However, life is much more complex. A company has hundreds of financial parameters and there are many decisions that can change its business outcome.

Then there are not just its own decisions, but others that are allied with them—how the market is changing, how the consumer is evolving, and what the competition is doing.

For example, if the monsoon fails, the demand for a paint company's products will go down. The same happens if consumer inflation spikes up and the consumer has very little

In the interest of a good story, one needs to discard all this complexity and uncertainty and turn it into a very simplified, and therefore inaccurate and under-analysed, narration.

money for left for discretionary consumption. To some extent these are at least known factors, but what if a cement company which was not in this segment at all decides to enter the paints segment? It would surely nibble away some market share from the older company.

But when someone is selling a story about the paints company, whether it is a fund manager, an analyst or the company management themselves, they will usually brush aside all the possible negatives in the interest of a story that leaves you starry-eyed.

Three: Life is not deterministic

Life is not deterministic. It is about probabilities. But stories have a beginning, middle and end.

No one would want to watch a movie that ends by saying there is a 60 per cent probability that the hero and heroine will get together and get married, a 30 per cent probability that each will get married to someone else, and a 10 percent probability that they don't get married at all.

You will walk out saying what the hell, that's not a good story!

In investing, there is a whole range of outcomes with different probabilities attached to them. But a fund manager or investor often gives her holdings a rosy future without risks, ignoring the discordant elements (industry cycle, favourable policy or plain luck), and that is where investing becomes dangerous and risky. The world is a lot more complex than what simple stories tell us.

Also, **remember that for a fund manager or investor to be wrong does not mean that they were talking complete nonsense all along. Nor that their stories did not have a kernel of truth—good stories always do**—to make them plausible. It is only that the story was being used to describe something that was much more complex, like an industry, a company or a country, which had many more moving parts, and what actually happened was a lot different from what was predicted.

As Morgan Housel, partner at The Collaborative Fund and a former columnist, writes: '. . . *something that's true but incomplete might be more dangerous than something that's wrong because a little truth is a fuel for a lot of overconfidence*'.[23] More on this phenomenon elsewhere in the book.

Four: The story misleads the storyteller as well

As human storytellers, we get invested in our stories because they then determine our self-worth and net worth. Ultimately, the story is perfectly capable of misleading the storyteller just as much as it misleads the listener. That is the beauty as well as the pitfall of storytelling.

As we repeat our story, we get more and more convinced about it. **We become invested in not just the stock, which is the subject of our story, but also in our story about the stock. And because of that, it becomes very difficult to change our mind.** And the best among us fall for this!

If you look at Warren Buffett, he sold—in a sense—the Coke story for a long time. That it was great brand (of course, it was the number one brand in the world for decades), had predictable cash flows, a moat around its business, etc.

Of course, like all great stories, none of these factors was incorrect or untrue, but these factors still did not capture all the changes that were happening in the company and the industry around it, including how the consumer was evolving away from sugary sodas, Pepsi was moving faster on a variety of fronts, including reducing its dependence on sodas, and so on.

Now, look at what happened to Buffett's Coke position. Mind you, it did very well for several years after he bought it, but then things changed. However, by then he was arguably so invested in his story that he could not change his mind. He held on for far too long!

Then if you look at his investment in Coke, it went up only eight times between 1993 and 2020. In that time the S&P 500 itself went up thirteen times, and Pepsi thirty times!

The story derails not only the audience but also the storyteller, because ultimately the storyteller also gets convinced by their own story.

How to challenge a story

Ask yourself what investing story you are buying into—maybe about a whole market, a sector or a stock.

Check whether it makes complete sense or are you discarding some facts and data which do not fit in with your story.

Even if the story currently makes sense, can it permanently do so?

Consciously challenge all the assumptions that have gone into that neat little story in your head.

Do all this, and you just may be able to distance yourself just a teeny-weeny bit from the storification bias!

> Think of alternative endings to the story instead of the one you've been told or are telling.

How stories mislead you in the markets

- Stories are what make us human. But markets don't care about your carefully crafted stories.
- Many stories don't play out in the real world.
- Stories have to be deterministic and simple; but life is complex, probabilistic, and hence unpredictable.
- Stories mislead not just the listener but also the storyteller, who ultimately becomes a believer as well.
- Ask yourself what investing story you are buying into—whether you are discarding some facts and data which do not fit in with your story.
- Even if the story currently makes sense, can it permanently make sense?
- Think of alternative endings to the story instead of the one you've been believing or propagating.

The Story behind Our High-Conviction Ideas[24]

Recently, one of the large banks which distributes our products asked for the 'stories' and narratives behind why we have bought certain stocks or exited them. Plus, they wanted to understand our high-conviction ideas.

The issue we faced?

Why I deliberately avoid stories about the stocks I hold

All studies and data have shown that while human beings love stories, one of the systematic biases that bring down investment returns is storification.

It is a trap that all of us are very prone to because stories are, in a real sense, what make us human.

As I explained in the last chapter, one of the things common across all human civilizations across the ages and across geographies is storytelling. Humans

> First Global's entire investment process is anti-storification and anti-high-conviction— deliberately, consciously and systematically so.

communicate by means of stories. We remember stories, we are moved by stories and we teach through stories.

In some sense, you can say that not having stories to tell is a disadvantage when you are trying to convince someone to do or buy something, whether it is a lay investor or even an investment professional (it is just not as satisfying without stories, isn't it?).

I have earlier in this book written about how at First Global we used to have a page called 'The Story' in our research reports, when our primary business was being a broker to fund houses. It was a take-off on the constant demand from the banks and fund houses for the stories behind our picks.

While humans love stories, the market doesn't care

Of course, this was only an ironic take. And, over time, I began to understand the phenomenon more and realized that with tools to deal with big data groups it was only a matter of time before the story was confined to the rubbish heap of history.

There was no doubt then that if you were trying to outperform the market, going by data instead of stories was what would give you results. Hence our entire investment process was geared to take advantage of this truth.

In theory, we all want to say that we make investment decisions based on data, but if I tell you that we bought a particular stock because the return ratios were expanding, growth across quarters was consistent, asset utilization was the best in class, it had no apparent corporate governance issues and it was in the top 10 per cent in most of the factors that we like to look at, it does not sound as exciting as stories of a superb brand, visionary management or huge orders in the future, etc.

As human beings, we do not want dry data and statistics; we want juicy stories, and that is exactly how the market entraps us. Because the market is not a human being and does not mind breaking our heart over a carefully crafted story.

Steer clear of conviction and emotion when it comes to your securities

The data-based approach has served us very well, and the results are there for all to see. At the time of writing this book, First Global has the top-performing multi-cap PMS since its launch, and the gap on the risk-adjusted return measures with our nearest competitors is even higher.

By way of a few illustrations, we went overweight in industrials and capital goods based on our systems way back in October 2021 when most fund managers began to understand and tell that story only in 2023!

> By not attaching conviction, and therefore emotion, to our ideas, we have been able to move in and out of sectors and stocks far ahead of the market.

While that sector had been an underdog for twelve years, from 2009 to 2021, the fundamentals were changing because of the order book and sales pick-up. Plus, the many lean years had resulted in cost efficiencies, so once the business came in, the margins began to expand.

For many fund managers it remained in the dog category for many more quarters and their investors missed the major move in the stocks. *Because, for human beings it is very hard to change the stories they have formed in their heads.*

At a time when everyone started to pile into the sector, we began to evaluate whether that story had run its course or not.

Similarly, when FMCG was the story being sold throughout 2020, we were among the few fund houses to say that it did not make sense to us, based on data. However, those who loved the sector, barely ever spoke about ITC or Gilette India as FMCG companies because those particular stocks were not doing well at the time.

On the other hand, almost the first FMCG stock recommended by our systems was ITC, which we bought in early 2021 and which became a huge winner for us because we had no bias against it. Ironically, a number of fund managers who were proponents of the FMCG story never bought ITC, at least in the initial period of its upward move, because they were wedded to their old stories.

A system is designed to get rid of human bias, as well as noise, which is introduced any time human beings make judgements and decisions.

As Daniel Kahneman says, '*A well-designed system will always outperform a human expert.*'

To give another example, we evaluate all our holdings on a zero base every quarter, essentially answering the question as to where we would be invested if we had cash today. This is to get rid of endowment bias, which makes us hold on to things when there are better opportunities available in the market.

The story misleads not just the listener

As I have said before, the worst thing about storification is that *in the end it misleads not just the listener but also the storyteller!*

The narrators repeat the story so many times that they also begin to believe it. And the best among us fall prey to this.

That is reason enough to steer clear of building high conviction in your holdings, which is nothing other than building stories about them in your head.

As for high conviction, what better example than that *the companies profiled in the books* In Search of Excellence *and* Good to Great *were UNDERPERFORMERS compared with the S&P 500 basket in the decade after the publication of the books. They were laggards not just in terms of stock price performance, but also sales and profit growth*.

Even when we look at the list of the top contributors to our PMS performance previous years, we find that we don't hold many of these stocks any more—for example, the chemical companies that did so well for us in 2021–22 disappeared from the portfolios thereafter.

If we had gotten married to these stocks by telling ourselves great stories about them, we wouldn't have been able to get out in time!

How many people even remember that Cisco was the highest market-cap company in the whole world and was the most coveted investment? Or the dream run of ABB? Not to mention Enron?

> Stories can always be found to justify why the performance of a stock or even a company was great at some point in time, but most of them are merely used to justify what is happening in the present.

There are plenty of such examples in the Indian market too. *The initial Sensex list had textiles, shipping, Premier Automobiles, Hindustan Motors and groups like the Mafatlals, JK, Thapars, etcetera, dominating—all of whom have been consigned to history now.*

At one point, the major indexes had zero weightage for banks and financials. As I write today, they have the highest weightage in the indexes. There were also seven or eight PSUs

> Fashions, performance, themes, narratives, all come and go.

in the Sensex at one time. And then everyone forgot about them for almost a couple of decades.

And it is also another human bias to forget what we were actually thinking and saying once the time and facts have changed. Hindsight bias makes us believe that we always knew what was going to happen.

That's the data!

The rest, you've guessed it, stories.

Should you invest in high-conviction ideas?

- It is considered the right thing for you to have high conviction in your investments. But my whole investment process is anti-storification and anti-high conviction—deliberately, consciously and systematically so.
- All studies and data have shown that while human beings love stories, storification is one of the systematic biases that bring down investment returns.
- By not attaching conviction, i.e., emotion to its investments, First Global has been able to move in and out of sectors and stocks ahead of the market.
- Even well-known companies, brands and stocks fall out of favour.
- Data-driven investing brings far better results than those dependent on stories and emotion, which is what conviction is about.

Investing in Stocks or High-Profile IPOs Because Some Big-Name Investors Have Done So?

Most investors look at the names of investors that have invested in a company as shorthand for the credibility of the company.

For instance, if large institutional investors, including mutual funds, well-known venture capital funds, foreign institutions, etc., are holding a stock, or large or foreign securities firms are recommending a stock, many investors take that as a Good Housekeeping stamp of approval. They take it as a cue that they can buy those stocks with their eyes closed.

This has been especially the case with IPOs, where the list of investors is flaunted—most recently by the so-called new-age tech and consumer tech companies.

The investor list looks very impressive, featuring large venture capital funds, private equity players, sovereign wealth funds, and so on.

The common investor thinks that all these institutions must have done their due diligence, and that by putting their money where their mouth is, they have already done the work for the smaller investors who can go along for the ride.

The problem? It doesn't quite work that way. A few pointers:

Does the entity recommending the stock have the competence to do so, or is it pushing an agenda?

For any investment, study the numbers, financials and logic yourself. Or outsource it to a reliable fund manager or adviser—a lesson I learnt early on.

The big names may lack either the competence or the integrity (or both!) to give the right advice. They may not be capable of doing a good job of analysis or may not spend enough time and effort on it. Alternately, they may be pushing some agenda.

If that were not the case, you could blindly buy those stocks in the public market which have the maximum number of buy ratings at any point.

In most cases you will find this strategy will lead to underperformance.

This is because large players have their own institutional imperatives where they are trying to keep either their internal or external consumers (meaning their bosses or clients) happy by saying what they want to hear.

Thus, securities firms will not say negative things or have sell ratings on companies from which they have hopes of getting future investment banking business. Also, they will not have sell ratings on stocks that are major holdings of the funds which are their clients.

The net result? Every study of Wall Street has shown that of all the stock ratings by research houses, only between 1 per cent and 7 per cent are sell ratings at any point. All the rest are buy or hold ratings. So, over 90 per cent of *research reports recommend that you buy or hold that stock!* This itself illustrates how skewed the game is.

The proportion will be no different in the Indian market.

This alone should tell you of the uselessness of relying on such ratings and what the results will be if you make investment decisions based on them.

It is safer to be in the consensus

Not only are the research ratings mostly buy ratings, the research analysts also tend to move in herds. After all, *it is comfortable and also safe from a job retention perspective to hold the same view as the consensus, rather than try to form an independent opinion.*

A very good example of this is in the case of Amazon in the year 2001. I have elsewhere written about how First Global was the only firm with a buy rating on Amazon when it was trading at less than $15 (75 cents adjusted for split).

The remarkable thing is this: much of Wall Street was positive on Amazon for the few years leading up to this period, and then all of them turned negative, most of them even predicting bankruptcy for the company. If they had bothered to actually focus on the financials, they would have seen that for the first time in its history Amazon was making huge cash flows and was no longer a bankruptcy risk.

However, as I have explained above, the incentives in this business are such that the research analyst is safer if she writes what everyone else is saying rather than go out on a limb and take the risk of being wrong. *In short, it is okay to be wrong if everybody else is also in the same boat, but not otherwise.*

So far, this has been about analysts either not being able to analyse fundamentals correctly or working with an eye on incentives, which makes it difficult for them to express an independent opinion. But this is only part of the story.

What if the institutions have themselves invested?

There's also another aspect to consider when you take the list of investors in a stock as a signal to invest in it yourself. It is not even as if these players are telling you to invest. You are only taking a cue from their investment. And therein lies a problem . . . or rather several.

For example, if you are being pointed towards new valuation metrics like gross merchandise value (GMV), number of transactions, market share, etc., and told not to focus on current profits (or lack thereof) or cash flows, remember this: There is only one way to value a security or a company. Ultimately the value of the stock is the discounted value of cash flows that it will be able to generate in its lifetime.

Should you consider new valuation metrics?

Every time there is euphoria in the market, these type of new valuation parameters raise their heads. In the 2000 tech boom it was eyeballs on the Internet. It did not matter whether the company was making any money or had any hope of making any money as long as it was getting the eyeballs!

> New valuation parameters are primarily ways to justify a valuation, NOT to do a valuation.

We hear similar stories of how just getting the market share of, say, food delivery or ride share or whatever businesses, is good enough to make those stocks a good bet and that the profits can be thought of later.

VCs assume that most of their investments will go down to zero

There is also a fundamental difference between a normal investor investing in a portfolio of securities and the venture capital (VC) doing so.

The VC model works on the explicit assumption that most of their investments will go down to zero. The ratio goes something like this: 60–70 per cent of their investments will go to zero/near zero. Maybe 25 per cent will make some money and 5–10 will be multibaggers, which is where they hope to invest in the next Google or Facebook. *Essentially, VCs are there for the outlier multibagger and know fully well that most of their investee companies will go bust.*

They are not betting that the bulk of their investments will even survive. So, their analysis is from a totally different perspective from yours.

You are deciding whether or not to buy a single security. They buy that security as one of a basket of securities.

And, as we have seen in a host of companies, from WeWork in the US to Housing.com and Byju's in India, big, marquee VC names often do not even catch explicit frauds, let alone lack of execution by their investee companies on business plans. Therefore, even relying on them for having done their due diligence may not work at all.

Are you and the fund buying at the same price?

There is usually a difference between the price at which you buy and the price or valuation at which large institutions have invested in a firm.

In almost every case, the IPO is at a premium to the price at which these investors have bought shares, even if the last round was as close as three or six months ago.

For instance, the big new-age IPOs that were launched in 2021 in the Indian market, from Zomato to PolicyBazaar to Nykaa, were all in this basket. The IPO valuations were several times the last round of money raised by these companies in the private markets. The IPOs were at twice, thrice or four times that price.

Is your entry price the exit price for the institution?

If the issue involves an offer for sale of shares, the IPO price is an exit price for the institutional or VC investors and an entry price for you.

The big names are SELLING at this price, not BUYING at this price.

That is a very fundamental difference!

You, the common investor, are providing them the exit.

The learning from this is to never be blinded by the list of the entities recommending a stock or having invested in it. Always, and especially in the financial markets, remember the dictum: Caveat emptor—i.e., Buyer Beware!

Buying stocks large institutions are recommending or have bought?

- If large institutional investors, including mutual funds, well-known venture capital funds, foreign institutions, etc., are holding a stock, or large or foreign securities firms are recommending a stock, many investors take it as a cue that they can buy those stocks with their eyes closed.

- But the institutions may have their own agendas, which is also evident from the fact that 90 per cent of recommendations by securities houses are buy recommendations.
- Even when venture capital firms have themselves invested in a firm, remember:
  - They invest on a basket basis and expect most of their investments to go to zero
  - They may have invested at a lower price
  - They may even be exiting at the price you are entering at
- Therefore, do your own analysis. You cannot use institutional recommendations or investments as a signal to buy.

Scan the QR code to learn more

Heads, I Was Right; Tails, the World Was Wrong[25]

Sometime ago, I was watching an interview of Rajiv Bajaj where he mentions going to the village where his grandfather, Jamnalal Bajaj, was born, to shoot a documentary.

His grandfather was born into a poor family. Once, while he was playing outside, he was spotted by a wealthy Sethji, who adopted him.

On that trip, Rajiv Bajaj also met an employee—a security guard at Bajaj Auto—whose home was also in the same village. It then struck Rajiv Bajaj that he had made up so many stories in his head about the reasons for his own success, like his hard work, skills as an engineer and a manager, and so on, but really, if it had been that guard's grandfather playing outside on that fateful day, and not his own grandfather, maybe that guard would have been the owner of Bajaj Auto and Rajiv would have been the guard!

This was a moment of epiphany for him and showed him the fallacy of attributing success to his personal qualities and efforts when luck or destiny had played a crucial role too.

This is a lesson that is awfully hard for human beings to learn, as it is related to one of our inbuilt cognitive biases: the self-attribution bias.

We attribute outcomes to ourselves . . . but only if they're successes!

This self-attribution is not symmetrical in nature. It is not as if we attribute our success and failures equally to ourselves. *Our tendency is to attribute our successes to our personal skills and failures to factors beyond our control.* This, in fact, is the classical definition of self-attribution bias.

Most of us can think of things that we've done and determined where, when everything is going according to plan, it's clearly due to our skill. Then, when things don't go according to plan, then just as obviously we had bad luck or some outside agency or person conspired against us.

If we ace an exam, it is because of our intelligence, talent and hard work. But if we don't do well in it, it is because the rating was unfair, or the professor did not teach the course properly.

When we are selected for a job, we believe that we have been hired for our achievements, qualifications and excellent interview skills. But if we aren't hired, it is because the interviewer was prejudiced or there was some other hanky-panky afoot. That is how the human mind works.

In investing, self-attribution shows up like this: If I pick a stock and that does well, it's because I'm a genius. But if the stock doesn't do well, then it's because of external factors—the economy, central bankers, politicians, company management, stock operators, and so on. In short, there are plenty of factors that can be blamed for my failure.

Almost always, success is because of my skill. Failure is because of some risk that could not be foreseen.

> Every time there is a bull market, you see geniuses abound.

For example, many who opened accounts in the likes of the US brokerage, Robinhood, post the COVID lockdown began to think of themselves as accomplished traders—that too in a foreign market!

They didn't stop to analyse and think that maybe they were just lucky to enter the US market at a good time. Similarly, those who dabbled in crypto-currencies and NFTs in 2021 thought of themselves as extremely savvy about digital assets when they made money and cursed everyone from various governments to Elon Musk to shady crypto exchanges when some news made their holdings crash.

Investing is a game of luck and skill

Investing, like most things in the world, is a game of luck and skill, but investors weigh the two differently, depending on how well they have done recently.

Several studies have shown that this is a real phenomenon.

Therefore if in the past year you've done very well, and then you are asked what percentage of your investment performance you attribute to skill, you are likely to mention a much higher number than you would if you had not done well. Then the luck factor would have been rated higher.

We never stop and think that good luck is just the mirror image of the well-known risk of a market/stock price fall, which we all recognize.

Why does the self-attribution bias exist?

As with most cognitive biases, the apparent 'mistake' in our thinking has a positive evolutionary role.

This cognitive bias allows you to protect your self-esteem. By attributing positive events to yourself, you get a boost in confidence.

By blaming outside forces for your failures, you protect your self-esteem and absolve yourself of personal responsibility.

One advantage of this bias is that it causes people to persevere even after failure—whether it was a failed hunt or a lost race.

When you can blame luck/ outside forces for it, you're more likely to again try what you failed at. For instance, an unemployed person may feel more motivated to keep looking for work if she attributes her joblessness to a weak economy or discrimination rather than some personal failing.

Why this can be a road to disaster in investing (or trading)

Anything that boosts your confidence and self-esteem should be good, right? Only if you are in school!

In the market it can be a disaster.

Taking credit for successes and blaming external factors for failures underlies and reinforces investor overconfidence. Every success is attributed to great analysis and skill, whereas every failure is because of 'bad luck'.

The result? Taking on inappropriate degree of financial risk, trading too aggressively, increasing the downside probability, overtrading . . . are all known results. Self-attribution bias often leads investors to trade too much and take on too much risk—all signs of overconfidence.

It can also result in concentrated positions because you're so convinced of the brilliance of your analysis. This bias leads investors to 'hear what they want to hear'.

All these are things to be avoided!

As an aside, studies show that men are much more prone to this overconfidence and overtrading than women.

Equally important, not taking responsibility for your errors means that mistakes in thinking, the frameworks used, ways of analysis, etc., continue unchecked because you refuse to admit that there was anything wrong with your decision-making process in the first place.

Thus, you're doomed to repeat your mistakes over and over again.

'Don't confuse brains with a bull market'

As this quote says, the first step in the attempt to side-step this bias is to know how much of your gains are due to your luck that you were in a certain market at the right time. When profits pour in during a bull run, it is easy to congratulate yourself and your outstanding analytical skills.

> Always remember that in both success and failure, there is a combination of skill and luck involved.

This happens not just with lay investors but with even professional fund managers, who arguably have even greater incentives to do this in order to justify their fees.

Your mind should not skew your thinking such you believe every one of your decisions that went well was because of your skill, and if not then, '*Poor me! I could not have foreseen that. Bad luck.*'

In real-life investing, both failure and success involve the elements of both skill and luck, but in the investors' mind their success is all skill and their failure all ill-luck.

What to do about this trick your brain plays?

One trick that helps reduce the impact of this bias is writing down your logic for why you are making a certain investment decision. Later on, whether it turns out well or not, you can go back to your notes and check whether your logic was correct. This is important even if your decision turns out right. Even if you make money on an investment, your logic for taking the position may have been totally wrong and the 'right' outcome may've been only a lucky fluke.

If you do not write down your logic down BEFORE you make the investment, you can rest assured that your mind will play tricks and tell you that you always knew what would really happen, which is another cognitive bias altogether!

Of course, when the outcome is not as per your liking or estimates, go back and study your decision-making to see what your mistake or error was.

Another important thought: ***A positive outcome does not mean your decision was correct, just as a negative outcome does not mean your decision was incorrect.*** More on this in the chapter on investing mistakes.

In investing, your decisions are always made with many unknown factors and hence there is always an element of chance that will influence the outcome.

Luck or skill: What determines your portfolio returns?

- Investing outcomes depend on both luck and skill. But the way we attribute our performance to both changes depending on how well our portfolio is doing.
- When we do well, we think it is because of our skill, but when things go wrong, we find many villains or factors to blame.
- We think of the risk in investing, but its mirror image is good luck, which accounts for part of our success. In other words, 'Don't confuse brains with a bull market.'
- Write down your logic when you make a decision. A right outcome does not mean the decision was right.

The Bias That Can Be Almost Invisible[26]

In a previous chapter we talked about how trying to follow the strategies used by the most successful investors can take you totally off track.

This is not a phenomenon confined to only evaluation of successful investment strategies. It can appear whether you are looking for the strongest buildings or great companies.

It is a bias that is all but invisible, because it provides neat explanations to make sense of the world as it appears today. There is no visible hole that draws your attention to the part that is missing. You have to actually go digging for the part that is missing.

Are you evaluating only the survivors?

Let us say you are looking for the best mutual fund schemes, maybe to assess which category of schemes have performed the best. The question then becomes:

Have you accounted for the mutual fund schemes that have been merged into other schemes or folded up altogether?

Survivorship bias not only distorts evaluation of investment styles and methods but also many other things.

For example, an analysis of mutual funds often looks at mutual fund schemes as they exist today and then analyses their past data but does not take into account fund schemes that have gone out of business or have been merged with other schemes as a result of non-performance.

Many losing funds are closed and merged into other funds to hide their poor performance.

For example, a study in the US showed that small-cap funds had outperformed significantly on average.

However, when the study was adjusted for the small-cap funds that no longer existed, the picture was different, because many more small-cap funds had gone out of business than large-cap funds.

Adjusted for survivorship bias, there was actually no outperformance by the small-cap funds. Even in India, many small-cap fund schemes have shut shop whereas people talking about small-cap performance usually consider only the surviving schemes.

Could your parents have left you a better legacy?

Similarly, we get caught up with anecdotes of people who became rich because their parents or grandparents had bought shares of Hindustan Unilever, HDFC Bank, Titan or even Siemens or Tata Elxsi. Because that small investments have now grown into a nice little nest egg.

We then start to rue the fact that our parents did not start investing in the share market a few decades ago instead of sticking to fixed deposits, as that would have provided us with 'early retirement' money. In reality, it would have helped us far less than we think!

This was brought home to me recently when a client shared his mother's portfolio, which had remained nearly untouched for twenty years. And what did I find in there: no HUL, no HDFC Bank, not even an ITC . . . instead there were DSQ Software, Silverline Technologies, NEPC Micon, etc.

You may say these were purchases made during a particular boom in the market, but the issue is not as narrow as that. ***Even the Sensex companies of decades ago were weighted towards textiles, shipping, paper and pulp, the car companies of the time, etc.***

Scindia Steamships, Hindustan Motors, Premier Automobiles, Ballarpur Paper, Zenith, etc., were the blue chips of the day that your parents would have likely bought. These companies have largely faded into oblivion.

Groups such as the Mafatlals, JK, Thapars, etc., dominated the landscape, and these were not fly-by-night groups or companies. They had been around for decades. Yet they are largely irrelevant now.

How not to back-test

Even if you are studying an index or back-testing a strategy, it is wrong to use the current index membership set rather than the actual constituent changes over time.

All the major market indexes, like the Sensex, Nifty, S&P 500, FTSE, etc., aim to maintain an index of healthy companies, removing companies that no longer meet their criteria.

Consider a test to find the average performance of the Sensex or the S&P 500 going back three decades. Or a test for a particular ratio, like the dividend yield.

To use the current composition of the index and then test these companies historically, either for returns or any financial ratio, would be adding survivorship bias to the results.

Companies that had healthy growth on their way to inclusion in the index would be counted in the analysis as if they were in the index during that growth period, which they were not.

Similarly, companies that fell out of favour for some reason and went out of the index would not be included in the analysis.

The only way to actually calculate what happened to the index or its constituents would be to go back in time and apply the entry and exit dates of the stocks that were in the index at every point in time and then calculate the appropriate return for the period for which the security being researched was actually included in the index. That is the only bias-free way to do this analysis.

Be extremely wary when someone is talking up a sector or a category of stocks, because there is often a conscious or unconscious filter sieving their conclusions. For example, in 2020, fund managers extolling the virtues of branded businesses with low capital requirements, high cash flows and moats around their business often talked about Nestle but not about a Gillette India or an ITC, both of which met the criteria but whose stocks hadn't performed for years.

The discussion is only about the 'survivors', i.e., those that have performed of late.

Similarly, someone analysing banks or NBFCs will leave out the ones that have gone out of business or which have had to be bailed out, even as they go into raptures over the returns from HDFC Bank and Kotak Mahindra. In India, the failed or bailed-out ones would include names like Centurion Bank, Global Trust Bank, Times Bank, etc. This seriously overstates the returns from the sector.

How to fix this bias

Of all the biases, this is a relatively simple one to fix.

Like meditation, it only requires you to be conscious, to pause and think. **Look at whether you are analysing the results for every entity that used a particular strategy, or every entity that met the criteria at the beginning of the study . . . or are you analysing only the survivors that used the strategy or met the criteria you are examining?**

This approach will hold, whether you are analysing companies, sectors, indexes, investing styles or fund schemes.

Until now we have dealt with survivorship bias as if it is something exclusive to investing, but of course it is not. It is found in every field of human activity in the world. Here are a few other examples:

Was everything better built in the past?

When we look at a building that is a few hundred years old or a piece of furniture at our grandparents' place or even a machine that is a century old, we often sigh and say, 'Wasn't everything more beautiful, stronger and better built in the past?'

But this is also a survivorship fallacy. **As old buildings are constantly being torn down and new structures built, a city's skyline keeps changing.**

Only the most beautiful, useful and structurally sound buildings survive. The ugly, crumbling, badly built buildings are long gone, and what remains leaves the visible impression, seemingly correct but factually flawed, that all buildings in the past were both more beautiful and better built.

What you see is not all there was

- When you analyse stocks, funds or strategies that exist today, you miss out a critical element—the ones in that category that no longer exist or are no longer included in the list/index.
- The correct analysis of anything requires starting with the total universe of that category, not just those constituents that exist or survive today.
- This will hold whether you are analysing types of companies, sectors, indexes, investing styles or fund schemes.
- Without this, your analysis will be distorted, incomplete and usually completely incorrect too.

Investing Mistakes: How They Occur and What to Learn from Them

Let me tell you of two instances from my investing life:

I made an outsized investment which went down 60 per cent and then went up a hundred-fold, which meant a 40x return for me.

On the other hand, I had an opportunity to invest in Tesla a couple of years after its IPO and I did not. And as everyone and their kid knows, it went on to be a multibagger.

Now the question is, which one of these do I consider a mistake? You'd be surprised to know that it is the first.

What are the mistakes you have made in your investing career? This is a predictable question when looking back over a long innings in the market.

When I think about the mistakes in my investment career, there are three aspects to consider.

One involves the evolution of the investment analysis and process to come to better decisions.

The second has to do with a better understanding of very hardwired human biases and thinking fallacies, and the devising of methods and strategies to get rid of those.

The third is even more fundamental. It is about the definition of a mistake.

What is the definition of a mistake?

This third aspect, which actually dawns on one quite late in life, is to realize that some decisions will always go wrong in investing. They are meant to.

Thus, a decision or rather an outcome going wrong is not necessarily a mistake.

As they say in software, it is a feature, not a bug!

Hence, **the very definition of a mistake changes when you realize this.**

It completely inverts the lens from the outcome to the process.

> Now you are no longer looking at a mistake as defined as a wrong outcome or loss or an opportunity loss, but whether the process of your decision-making was incorrect, given the information you could have had at that point in time.

Is lack of exposure a positive or a negative?

As to whether mistakes are related to levels of education, exposure, etc., yes, they are. By education, etc., I don't just mean the degrees you may have, but how much you have studied finance, investment methods and, most important, your own thinking.

As I have said elsewhere in the book, I came from a background where nobody had any interest in or exposure to investing. Till I started on my MBA, I did not even know what a share was.

It meant that I started from a clean slate, compared with some people I know who grew up in families where the stock market was the daily talk at the dining table.

The question is whether it was an advantage or a disadvantage. *On balance, while I did not know even the basics, it also meant that I did not have any preconceived notions about the subject.*

Let me draw a parallel with the time I was running my own business. At First Global, I hired only freshers as they did not have any unlearning to do, which would have been the case if I had hired from competing firms. On balance, the fact that I entered the field without a background in investing may have been an advantage after all.

And even when I went into equities research or securities research, that discipline itself did not exist in India at all. Nobody knew what equity research was. No listed company had an investor relations department. This was, of course, both good and bad, because you could then start from first principles rather than fit into an existing mode of doing things.

Initially, I thought of learning from foreign securities firms from the developed markets which had decades of institutional experience, but when I looked at their reports, I found that they had neither real substance (due to problems of both competence and integrity explained in earlier chapters) nor great style, and I never considered that route of learning thereafter.

Living through crises brings you a different perspective

We are very much the product of our experiences.

For example, Americans who grew up during the Great Depression avoided debt all their lives, not only personally but even in companies that they led.

For people in the markets, having lived through market cycles gives you a very different kind of experience and understanding, which does not come from and cannot come from just looking at past charts, where it is very easy to see the bottoms and tops, and then say that this is where one would have bought and this is where one would have sold.

It is only when you live through multiple crises—from the 1987 Black Monday Crash to the Asian crisis of 1998, the 2000 tech crash, 9/11, the 2008–09 Great Financial Crisis, COVID in 2020 or the Russia–Ukraine war of 2022—can you actually learn from those experiences. Closer home, the crises would be some of the political change-related falls that helped you learn perspective.

For instance, the market's immediate reaction after an election result may be turned upside down in a matter of days, as happened in India in 2004. On the day of the election results, the markets crashed 11 per cent (even higher intra-day) but soon recovered and were up almost 24 per cent in a year's time. For those too young to remember this, 2004 is when, unexpectedly, the BJP-led National Democratic Alliance government was thrown out of power and the Congress-led United Progressive Alliance headed by Dr Manmohan Singh came in.

> You need the hard miles of understanding financials, reading the investing books, etc., but you also need to live through the school of hard knocks.

That is why most of the great investors, or even traders, have really come into their own in their fifties. Whether it is Warren Buffett, George Soros or Jim Simons, the pattern is pretty much the same.

The difference between mistakes made in crises and in the normal market

There is a big difference between mistakes made in normal market conditions and in times of crises. In normal market conditions, mistakes are often the result of missing out some component of the analysis, inability to foresee certain changes that are coming, and so on. Basically, they are errors of analysis of business or finances or, occasionally, the economy.

During a crisis, mistakes are additionally to do with discipline and control over your own mind. Do you panic? Or are you able to remain disciplined? Because at a time of crisis the concern is not about individual stock movements but the direction of the market as a whole.

So, your mistake was recommending or buying a stock that didn't do well?

In the early phase of career, in my mind, and also in the minds of my clients, a mistake means a decision with a wrong outcome. For example, when you are a research and broking house, your recommending a stock that did not gain, or a sell recommendation on a stock that did not decline, would be counted as mistakes.

For me the problem was particularly acute as many institutional clients expected a 100 per cent hit rate from First Global! A different story from the poor track record of some of our competitors.

It often happened that a foreign institutional client would say that the xyz stock we had recommended did not do well. We would say that it was but one of the ten stocks we had recommended over the last six months and the only one which had declined, and that for most other securities firms, the ratio was almost the other way around, but our clients would cryptically respond: 'We expect better from you.'

Earlier, a mistake meant a wrong outcome, but now the benchmark is different. What you are evaluating now is whether the framework for and the process of decision-making was right or wrong, rather than whether the outcome turns out to be favourable or not. The two can be very different.

What I did not understand well, or at least did not articulate at that time, was that this was actually a mistake of framework. Even though I saw this theoretical concept of outcomes being probabilistic in reports I wrote in as far back as 1996 and 1997, at the time I somehow did not connect it to what the clients were saying.

The concepts of uncertainty in the stock market; of investing being a game of probability, and of quality of the outcome not being the same as the quality of decisions made, have been incorporated into one's thinking only much later in investing and in life. That totally changes the framework of what constitutes a mistake in the first place.

A wrong decision can have a right outcome, and vice versa.

Coming back to where I started the chapter, almost the largest amount of money that I made from my investments was in a stock (or actually a convertible) where I put in an outsized investment. The stock went down about 60 per cent at a time when I was unable to sell because of a lock-in. And from that beaten-down level, it went up a hundred times! So I made forty times my original investment. But that decision was definitely a mistake! *The reason why it went up was totally extraneous to the analysis done at the time of investment when it could not have been foreseen. And taking an outsized risk on it was not right either.*

On the other hand, one may have passed up opportunities to buy stocks like Tesla, which went up several times, but the decision may not have been wrong as the company had come close to bankruptcy several times between 2017 and 2019.

In the 1990s, the effort at First Global was to keep refining the financial analysis techniques and also add on other statistical techniques to refine things like demand forecasts. In other words, every effort was to learn more so that fewer mistakes were made.

Refining financial analysis

While in the very initial phase of my journey in the markets, I started off with regular analysis of profit and loss accounts, margins, growth, valuation multiples, etc., I realized very quickly that this analysis was missing out on a great deal.

Then came the process of understanding traditional cash flow and discounted cash flow methods, along with drivers of return ratios.

And even in financial modelling, one learnt not to resort to shortcut methods of forecasting but to estimate every line item separately, with the understanding that not all of them vary as a percentage of revenues. Basically, we learnt to let the financial estimates emerge rather than try to shoe-horn them into the hypotheses one had in mind.

For instance, this meant not to start with assuming that if a company's profit margin last year was 12 per cent, then this year it will go up to 14 per cent or will be down to 10 per cent. Instead we began to really understand, debate and then forecast every revenue and expense item.

Then onwards it was a process of evolution and analysis. For a time, the discounted cash flow (DCF) method (the sort in books by Prof. Damodaran and Tom Copeland) seemed to make sense, until one realized how sensitive this was to assumptions, especially terminal-value assumptions. This is something that has been dealt with in detail in the chapter on cashflows and financial ratios in Section I of this book.

By tweaking the growth rate or the cost of capital even a bit, one could dramatically change the 'fair value' of the stock and basically come up with whatever value one wanted.

That led me to devise measures to capture near-term cash flows, which are dealt with elsewhere in the book.

The gaps in what you can foresee

Even then there were gaps in what you could foresee. *The whole rise of Indian IT services in the 1990s is something that comes to mind as a mistake or a misreading of the situation.*

At a time when even a PE of 25 or 30 was considered high, these companies were trading at multiples of 60–70, and one thought they were far too expensive and recommended a sell, but they kept soaring past every target you could have had in mind.

This was in spite of the fact that on another dimension I did see the potential of these companies and the sector. First Global had done a report in the late 1990s on the employee strengths of these companies.

At that time, the largest private-sector employer was Tata Steel, with about 65,000 employees. The IT services companies had less than 10,000 employees each. And I projected that in the not-too-distant future, each of these companies would employ more people than Tata Steel. At the time, everyone else thought that this was an absurd forecast. But it did turn out to be true. The forecast was simply based on the revenue model—that if they had to grow at a certain rate, they would need those many employees.

And yet, in spite of seeing that growth, I could not relate it well to what looked like off-the-charts PE multiples.

There are also calls that appear like errors for a short time and turn out to be correct eventually. Satyam Computers comes to mind. I remember meeting the company and its founder, Ramalinga Raju in the very early days, just a year or two after the company's IPO.

I came away and told our institutional clients that I was not impressed with the management at all. I could understand that an entrepreneur may not be a technology expert and may not be able to talk tech, but to be unable to give a sense of the different market segments they were targeting and what could be expected from each I thought was a red flag. The stock price was just about Rs 40 and it had a multi-year bull run from there . . . till the whole house of cards eventually collapsed and the promoter/management were found to be right in the centre of it all.

I would not have counted it as a win in my account if the stock had eventually crashed because of a business problem that arose years later, but in this case the issue was exactly in the area that I had identified as the red flag—i.e., management quality.

Some understanding comes only with time

Here we are talking of specific errors, but there are also things you have to live through in order to really understand them at a deep level.

While I believe in the prescription of 10,000 hours of study to master a subject, the fact is, in investing, just the reading and studying part is not enough; you also have to live through the markets to have the experience to implement the knowledge you have gathered.

And it is not even just learnings from market cycles.

For example, the fact that asset allocation determines 85 per cent to 90 per cent of your returns is there on page 1 of every investment book, but like most others in this field, one will almost invariably start off still looking for the best security that one can get, chasing the golden trail of the multibagger.

It certainly took me a long time to really assimilate the importance of asset allocation and implement it as a key part of investment strategy. And also to realize that multibaggers are always going to be only a few out of the stocks you identify through your process. You also learn that you will not know in advance which specific stocks are going to be multibaggers.

It is a process of evolution

Then there are the errors and mistakes that help you evolve into a better investor because you realize what the parts missing in the whole picture are.

For example, one saw in the 1990s that you could recommend a buy on a stock, but it would fall some more before starting its move up, or that you thought something was overvalued but it kept running up before falling.

Even though your basic premise was correct, you missed out on part of the move. So, while in the 1990s I concentrated only on financials and fundamentals and did a lot of refinements on that, I eventually realized that some part of the picture was missing.

That was when we added some techniques on timing and momentum—and fairly elaborate systems at that. But even as the systems were refined more and more over the decades, I also realized—from the errors I made in the market—that these technical/timing/trading/momentum–whatever systems you call them were too noisy on their own. ***Their real value was only to better time an investment or trade that had been identified based on* fundamentals**, and what I have seen since has not changed my mind on this.

Mind you, the systems I am talking about are much more rigorous and complex than the technical analyses of the sort featured every day on television. Even so, they will not give additional returns without the core being fundamental analysis.

Where they do help is in cases like this one: At one point we had identified a good fundamental switch—a move from Dell to Motorola. Thereafter, we put this data into our system to better time our call. And the Motorola share price actually fell, from US$22 when we had identified the trade, to US$18, and that's when the timing system signalled that it was a buy. This kind of input can be the additional value-add one gets from such systems.

Don't let mistakes become fatal

As for not allowing mistakes to become fatal, that again is something you get to after making a few crippling losses in the market.

That is the reason why *we have a very rigid stop-loss system, and while human fund managers can override on the buy/ investment side, they are not allowed to override our stop-loss because human beings are not good at acknowledging mistakes and taking losses.* Therefore, it is very important to be disciplined and systematic on the stop-loss side.

On the whole, the big change at First Global to prevent mistakes has been to codify its expertise into a system, which then can be applied on a bias-free, noise-free basis on the entire universe of stocks. That is really the only way to get rid of noise in a system, as it is simply not possible to do it humanly. Realization and implementation of this has been the biggest step we have taken in eliminating mistakes at our firm.

Errors of omission and errors of commission

Ultimately, *I am really only bothered about errors of commission.*

> You should never get caught up in the errors of omission because there are always going to be some of those, at least in hindsight.

> Very many mistakes in the market are made because of FOMO, when people jump on to a trend too late.

And the last thing you want is to make transactions driven by FOMO, or fear of missing out.

Fund managers like to launch thematic funds on themes that are running, whether it is a particular industry like IT or pharma or small caps or Nasdaq, but usually, almost all thematic funds underperform the market from the time of their launch, which is usually close to the peak for that theme.

One of my favourite quotes in this context is by Richard Branson, '*Opportunities are like buses, there is always another one coming along.*'

And since investing is a Loser's game, the emphasis is on avoiding errors of commission. *I do not bother about The One that Got Away.*

The simple ways to improve portfolio returns

Over time, you realize that investing is a game of both luck and skill. Hence you are going to lose some, no matter how skilled you are. If you accept that and are actually geared towards it, it makes your life simple and your portfolio better.

I often say that the simplest way to improve your portfolio returns is to say every time you are buying a security that you may be making a mistake.

And if you are aware of this fact, you avoid falling into the trap of attributing the good runs or profits to your skill and the declines in your portfolio to bad luck and unforeseeable risks—the classic attribution bias.

> If you can acknowledge mistakes and get out immediately, that is a superpower.

Getting swayed by your mood if you have a fight in traffic, if you are hungry, and so on, is a human trait. This is part of what is called noise. Over time, I have overcome this simply by coding our investment expertise into an artificial intelligence and machine learning system so that this noise is eliminated and the entire universe of stocks can be ranked based on the objective criteria. There is no other way to eliminate noise, no matter how experienced and expert you are. This phenomenon is dealt with in detail in the book Noise *by Daniel Kahneman, Olivier Sibony and Cass R. Sunstein.*

The real superpower of a machine system is that unlike human beings, it has no mental barriers to acknowledging a mistake and therefore can learn from both positive and negative outcomes.

More on this in the later chapters.

As far as public money is concerned, in principle, I do not believe in charging any entry or exit load because I think an investor must have ready access to their own money on demand, whenever they need it. However, at times I feel an exit load would help when you see investors withdrawing at absolutely the wrong time. Even mutual fund flows peak near the peak of the market, and less than half the investors are invested for more than even two years in a single scheme

A break-up of mutual fund flows shows that investors tend to go towards themes which have performed well in the recent past, whether they are industry themes or small-cap-versus-large-cap kind of divisions. In all these instances, the investor will make sub-optimal returns on average. You can say this is a mistake on part of the investor, but it is one that is encouraged by the fund management industry, which also launches these thematic funds towards the peak of the cycle because they are easy to sell at that point in time and get them AUM.

Learning to reduce mistakes

In my view, books are the best teachers. But you can make a mistake even in this area.

A category of books that people love to read are those that describe the journeys and processes of successful investors and traders. While these stories might have insights, it is important to keep in mind that asking the question why someone succeeded is not really the right question, as in order to evaluate a strategy you have to consider everyone who has used that strategy and find out the probability distribution of the outcome.

Of course, it makes sense to learn from people's mistakes, like from the LTCM (long term capital management) collapse in 1998, where Nobel laureates could not see the limitations of their process, which was essentially the assumptions that were behind their models.

Another was the junk bond boom of the 1980s and the subsequent collapse when the action of the market participants of chasing this category meant that far larger quantities of junk bonds were issued than was the case in the past. This itself changed the quality of the bond pool and the default rates that were being assumed by the marker participants.

But even more important than understanding the mistakes of famous investors or famous people in other fields is to understand the drivers or causes of their success.

As I have written earlier, someone investing in the US markets at the beginning of 1960 would have only seen their money go to 2.3 times in twenty years, whereas anyone investing in 1980 would have seen their portfolio go up ten times in the same time period from just investing in the broad index.

That is why so many success stories of the most well-documented market, which is the US, relate to the 1980s and 1990s.

To my mind the real genius of Peter Lynch, the legendary fund manager at Fidelity, lay in not just his creating alpha (excess returns) over fourteen years but in his decision to quit at the end of those fourteen years, when he was still relatively young. While he has never spoken about it explicitly, it is clear that he realized that what he had made were extraordinary returns and related to a particular period of time and that he could not hope to replicate those gains in the future.

The books which tell you about the fallacies of your own thinking and the hard-coded biases of the human brain are very valuable. More on that in the chapter on books.

The process of refining your decision-making and eliminating your mistakes is

What is also valuable is the understanding that these biases are hard-coded, and very few can be eliminated by your understanding of them. Most cannot be eliminated without the use of a system, even if you intellectually understand them.

endless. That is also the fun part of the market. Even the smartest and most diligent investor or fund manager cannot have a perfect track record.

What I have learned about investing mistakes

- A mistake is not an investing decision that has a bad outcome. Mistakes lie in incorrect processes and reasoning.
- Thus, you can make a lot of money, as I did once, from a decision that was not the right one.
- On the other hand, a certain number of your portfolio picks may not do as well as expected. That is in the inherent nature of the game and may not owe to a mistake at all.
- Certain things are understood only with time and experience. Even if you read the right theories, sometimes you have to live through a variety of markets to understand and implement the lessons in it.
- The important part is not to let mistakes become fatal. Stop losses and other risk management techniques are key.
- The simplest way to improve your portfolio returns is to say every time you are buying a security that you may be making a mistake. Acknowledge errors and get out at the earliest.
- Intellectual understanding of biases alone may not remove errors. Following even a simple system acts as a check.

Why Half-Truths Can Be More Dangerous than Outright Lies[27]

It is normal to think that having at least a grain of truth in what is being said would be better than outright lies, but you would be mistaken.

Why?

'Something that's true but incomplete might be more dangerous than something that's wrong, as a little truth is a fuel for a lot of overconfidence,' said Morgan Housel.

That's why storification misleads; you have to watch out for survivorship bias.

At times, it may be laziness at work, with the mind looking for shortcuts, and at other times a careful 'economical with the truth' decision, even on your own part.

What were the blue chips back then?

We have all seen statements like the following in interviews, on social media etc.

If you, your parents or grandparents had invested $1,000 or Rs 10,000 in Apple, Microsoft, Tesla, HDFC Bank, ITC, Hindustan Lever, twenty, thirty, forty years back, or maybe Tata

Elxsi, Deepak Nitrites, etc., drum roll . . . this is how much you would be worth now.

Now, there are several nuances to this.

One, in the real world, you would not have only bought what turned out to be blue chips or great stocks in hindsight but may well have bought a whole lot of hot stocks of the season, as this real-life example below illustrates.

We've all heard stories of kids who became rich because their parents bought stocks and never sold them as they forgot about them.

As mentioned earlier, this is a real Indian parent's portfolio, which had remained untouched for about two decades. It included hot stocks of their time: DSQ, NEPC, Silverline, Apple Credit, etc.

Worthless now!

Thanks to survivorship bias, by now you had all but forgotten about the hot stocks of two decades ago.

Even if you didn't chase the flavour of the season, all these stocks were in the Nifty50 at some point: Satyam, Idea, Reliance Power, Reliance Capital, Yes Bank, Cairn, Zee, Unitech, JP, Suzlon, Indiabulls Housing and many others that went nowhere.

A few decades back, your parents, buying the blue chips of the day, would have stocked up on the JK group, Thapar group, Mafatlal group, and perhaps shares of the likes of Hindustan Motors and Premier Automobiles.

No one thought at the time that these companies were headed to oblivion.

Even the survivors didn't do well all the time

I have mentioned before that Hindustan Unilever did practically nothing for those who owned the stock from about 1999 to 2010, and Bata brought zero returns for fifteen long years.

Then there's is the data for Apple.

Apple itself remained at its listing price in 1997, eighteen years after its listing. It only doubled from this level in 2000, after twenty years of its listing. That meant a compounding of only 3.5 per cent for twenty years after

> There is yet another nuance: even stocks that are the poster boys for great compounding had long periods of going nowhere.

its IPO, with many steep drawdowns. Remember, this was at a time when interest rates were at or near double digits in the US. Hardly the best investment in decades—until that story turned.

Tesla gave zero returns for ten years till a two-year rally made the CAGR look suddenly spectacular.

To add to the fun, it also nearly went bust in the interim!

These are classic examples of how the eventual result is not a good pointer to whether one's decision to invest in something was correct or not.

The stories may be technically true, but. . .

All those stories of grand compounding successes are technically 'true' and drive a lot of FOMO, but what they leave out is vital.

Many of you would have seen long videos explaining how paints are delivered twice a day from the Asian Paints plant to each dealer.

> And half-truths are not the domain of only survivorship bias either; the same can hold for stories about the businesses of companies.

The truth? Every paint shade is mixed at the dealership itself.

There *is* no twice-a-day delivery. It is just storification.

What's more, it'd be extremely cost-inefficient to have this type of delivery schedule.

The half-truth part of the story? Asian Paints *was* a pioneer in professionalization of management by an Indian-owned company and early adoption of technology.

But this kernel of truth has been used to spin fantastical stories that sound just plausible enough, given the track record of the company.

Of course, a single visit to a paints dealer reveals the truth, but then some of the people can be fooled some of the time.

Add a wide-angle lens and the picture often changes.

Therefore when looking at information presented by someone else or by yourself, check to see not just whether it is technically correct (for example, if the calculations match) but also what it leaves out.

Dangerous half-truths

- It is normal to think that something with even a grain of truth to it would be better than outright lies, but you would be mistaken. Half-truths may mislead even more.
- You may not have become rich even if your parents or grandparents had bought blue chips or hot stocks. The reason? Many blue chips of that vintage are no longer around or relevant. We only look at the survivor blue chips or successes.
- Even stocks that have done well had long periods, even decades, of underperformance or even flat-to-declining prices.
- All those stories of grand compounding successes are technically 'true' and drive a lot of FOMO, but what they leave out is vital.

Are the Crowds Wise or Are They Mindless?

Is the crowd better and wiser than the individual? Or is it somewhere on the craziness scale?

This question arises because you hear of both the wisdom as well as the madness of crowds.

After all, both these books with contrary titles are considered classics, especially for those interested in investing: *Extraordinary Popular Delusions and the Madness of Crowds* by Charles Mackay, and *The Wisdom of Crowds: Why the Many are Smarter than the Few and How Collective Wisdom Shapes Business, Economies, Societies and Nations* by James Surowiecki.

Where does the truth lie?

There is actually a simple answer to this question.

The key insight

Here's the key insight: ***Averaging INDEPENDENT estimates improves estimates or forecast accuracy.***

If, for instance, hundreds of people estimate, essentially guess, the number of marbles in a jar, the average is often remarkably close to the actual number, even if individual estimates are way off.

The results are similar when you try to estimate or predict more nuanced stuff, like company profits.

Why is this so? Because aggregation of independent responses reduces noise, or random variation.

But this holds if and only if the estimates are made independently.

Does the quality of decisions improve with discussion?

Juries, corporate decision-making, etc., get derailed by group dynamics.

Contrary to our general impression, an exchange of ideas and discussions reduce accuracy as people get influenced by each other.

As Cass R. Sunstein, Daniel Kahneman, and Olivier Sibony write in the book *Noise: A Flaw in Human Judgment:*

> Groups can go in all sorts of directions, depending in part on factors that should be irrelevant. Who speaks first, who speaks last, who speaks with confidence, who is wearing black, who is seated next to whom, who smiles or frowns or gestures at the right moment, all these factors and many more affect outcomes.

The net result is that many similar corporate groups faced with the same facts and data can come up with very different decisions in all sorts of matters, from recruitment, retrenchment, expansion and communication to environmental policy, product launches and more.

There is also the human need to belong to a group and not rock the boat. This prevents participants with contrary views from speaking out at a later stage in discussions. Also, persons with no clear position either way are likely to go along with the initial or important speakers.

Basically, as the book further says, '. . . *aggregating the judgements of multiple individuals reduces noise, but because of group dynamics groups can add noise too*'.

You will find almost everyone agreeing vehemently with and supporting the course of action that has been decided on.

Deciding on a corporate initiative or on compensation in the case of a jury?
You're likely to end up with a deadly combination of extreme results and misplaced confidence!

At times groups may come up with the right or wise decision, but at times groups can also follow tyrants or cult leaders under the sway of a shared illusion.

Groups that appear very alike in composition can come up with very different decisions on the same matter, depending on the dynamics among the group members.

What does all of this have to do with investing?

You may well ask this question.

In the markets, do you spend a lot of time tracking what your friends are doing, what 'experts' or institutions are saying and doing? Are you a member of WhatsApp or Telegram chat groups, or spend time on certain websites where investors and traders share ideas, tips and analyses?

First, you may not get from these groups an actual or clear picture of what the individual or institutional investors are really doing. For example, you might get to know only part of an institution's or big-name investor's portfolio or strategy.

But there is another important point: ***This sharing and exchanging of ideas and tips contaminates your thinking.*** More often than not, over the course of discussions in these groups, more and more people buy into the dominant thought or idea.

After a while it appears that there is only one logical course of action as far as the stock or trade being discussed is concerned.

This is risky. ***Without your being consciously aware of it your mind has been hijacked by group dynamics. Paradoxically, you will likely have more confidence in this decision reached by the group after discussions than in your own initial hypothesis, whether both are the same or diametrically opposite.***

To engage in group discussions for your investment decisions is not just a waste of time, it is actually likely to lead you off track and you will end up worse off in terms of decision-making.

Therefore, it is very important to maintain the sanctity and independence of your analysis and not get into an exchange of ideas, which, counter-intuitively, will diminish the quality of decisions.

This is an important point to ponder, because it goes against our general tendency and thinking.

The dangers of being plugged into market news

Even most fund managers spend time talking to brokers and other market participants about what everyone else is thinking or doing in the markets.

Back during the time when I used to be active on the sell side (i.e., as a stockbroker), I remember a mutual fund investment team proudly say that they had a day in the week to do their own work and not talk to brokers.

My question (not articulated to them, as they were clients): Why only ONE day?

Talking to brokers, or to anyone, about what everyone else is doing is a waste of time at best and, as we saw above, can actively mislead you at worst.

This holds true whether you are investing for yourself or for others.

And the opinions of many analysts across many broking houses may not be truly independent at all, as most analysts like to sit in the consensus, if for no other reason than that it is the safest strategy to keep their jobs.

> While pooling of independent opinions improves the quality of decisions, 'talking' reduces it.

This is besides the fact that most brokerage analysts will not say anything negative about any stock held by their major clients. And in any case, only a very small percentage of their ratings will ever be 'sell'.

At best you can look at brokerage research reports to collect facts about a company, but do not give weightage to the opinions they express. The issue is, consciously or not, you may be influenced by their opinions anyway.

I, for one, minimize not just market gossip but even internal meetings unless there is a proper agenda for discussion. It is better to get everyone's opinion separately via email or WhatsApp.

Daniel Kahneman's studies have only proven that this is the right strategy.

There is only one way to invest well: Do the work!

Or outsource it.

For a more nuanced understanding of this (and much else), read *Noise*, by Kahneman, Sibony and Sunstein.

Are groups wise or crazy?

- Averaging INDEPENDENT estimates improves estimates or forecast accuracy. But this holds if and only if the estimates are made independently.

- Deciding on a corporate initiative or on compensation in a jury? You're likely to end up with a deadly combination of extreme results and misplaced confidence!
- In investing, discussing your ideas with friends and chat groups, listening to opinions in the media, finding out what everyone in the market is doing, brings DOWN the quality of your decisions.
- While pooling of independent opinions improves the quality of decisions, 'talking' reduces it.

Scan the QR code to learn more

Hiding in Plain Sight

The least questioned assumptions are often the most questionable.
                                                          – Paul Broca

Although this is an old quote, I came across it only recently and it set me thinking of how much we take for granted as background in our lives, which, when seen with fresh eyes, looks very different.

As we know, ***something that is too close can be as out of focus as something that is too far from us.***

The fish is the last one to know what water is!

For example, when somebody from the West came to India or a developing country for the first time, especially in the days before the world was so connected, they would be surprised that pavement dwellers, beggars or kids selling things at the traffic lights appeared invisible to the privileged local citizens. It was something they spent little or no conscious thought on.

This worked in reverse too. When I first started travelling to the US in the mid-1990s, a few things appeared glaring to me but were not noticed by the residents.

One was the level of waste, which appeared unconscionable to someone from a frugal/scarcity economy. Walking around the major US cities at night, you would notice that the huge office towers around had every light on all night. They were never switched off!

Then there were working lunches at client offices, after which stacks of unused plastic cutlery, paper napkins and 200-ml water bottles were all swept into the dustbin. You'd be screaming inwardly—*all these can be used.*

Even at a more subtle level, it struck me that African American professional women never wore their natural hair. Think about it: from Condoleezza Rice to Michelle Obama, only straightened hair seemed to be acceptable in a professional setting. Only women lower down in the hierarchy, like in cleaning jobs, ever had natural hair.

> In your work life and investments, think of what you're taking for granted.

To me it seemed remarkable that no one noticed that looking like a white woman to the extent possible was what was required to look 'professional'.

The growth assumption: What is invisible

This is a favourite example of mine. In the investment world, reports are written and stock recommendations made every day. Pick up any of these reports and look at the projections or estimates.

> In a running company (not a start-up), there is rarely if ever any discussion as to WHETHER there will be growth in earnings and cash flows. Almost all discussions are about tweaking the growth rates a little up or down.

This is what you will find: nearly 100 per cent of earnings or discounted cash flow (DCF) valuation models assume perpetual growth.

It is assumed that companies will show earnings and cash flow growth in the next five years. That is the way the explicit-period cash flows are calculated. Then the terminal value calculation assumes that the cash flows will keep growing in perpetuity.

The reality thrown up by data: less than *1 per cent* of companies show profit growth every single year for even ten years! This number has remained within the same range whenever we have checked it over the last three decades.

As I have pointed out earlier, in India, for instance, there is precisely one listed company that has shown earnings growth every single year for twenty years: HDFC Bank.

Those showing cash flow growth are even fewer, as usually managements try to show earnings growth, if possible, even at the cost of balance-sheet strain.

But this truth is invisible to nearly 100 per cent of the analysts making fancy earnings and DCF models on their Excel spreadsheets.

Extrapolating the immediate past

Another blind spot leads to extrapolation of the immediate past. *In cyclical industries, it may mean expecting either good times or bad times to continue, even though a zoom-out into a twenty-year picture might show something very different.*

When it is boom time or bust time in let us say a steel, cement or shipping industry, company managements, let alone analysts, are often not able to envisage a different reality.

Let me recount an anecdote. Back in the 1990s, Tata Motors used to be exclusively a commercial vehicles (CV) company, making heavy and light trucks. The passenger vehicles business and the global acquisitions were still to happen. And CVs is a cyclical business. Around 1998-99, there was a trough in the CV business. At the time, we did a regression analysis relating certain macroeconomic parameters to CV sales in the economy.

Based on our analysis, we estimated a 25 per cent growth in the number of CVs sold by Tata Motors that year. When we released our report, we got a call from Ratan Tata's office saying our estimates were too aggressive and they did not expect more than a 10–15 per cent volume growth.

We rechecked our numbers and decided to stick to our estimates. And yes, Tata Motors did register a 25 per cent growth in numbers that year!

It just goes to show that the most experienced and well-intentioned managements can be too close to the action to see the reality.

Think about where the blind spots in your industry are!

When you're too close, you cannot see properly

- Some assumptions are like the air surrounding you—invisible to the normal eye. Unless you make an effort, you cannot see them.
- For example, almost all company financial projections assume that earnings will grow every year out into perpetuity, whereas hardly any company manages to achieve this for even ten years at a stretch.
- Another blind spot leads to simply extrapolating the immediate past.
- In cyclical industries, it may mean expecting either good times or bad times to continue, even though a zoom-out into a twenty-year picture may show something very different.
- When it is boom time or bust time in let us say a steel, cement or shipping industry, often company managements, let alone analysts, are not able to envisage a different reality.
- Always think about possible blind spots.

What Do Self-Driving Cars Have to Do with Investing?

India has more than 1.5 lakh people dying each year in road accidents, among the highest in the world, even on the basis of percentage of population.

Now suppose, from tomorrow, all vehicles are changed to self-driving ones and let us say the death toll drops to 50,000.

What will the newspaper headlines be?

Think carefully before you read further.

Will the headlines be, '*Self-driving vehicles reduce death toll by two-thirds*'?

Or will it be, '*Self-driving vehicles kill 50,000 Indians every year?*'

My guess is, it will be the latter.

Or let me give you another example. **Currently, some cricketing umpiring decisions are outsourced to a system. And every time the machine's decisions go wrong, there is a clamour to scrap it. As I explain later, there is something fundamentally wrong with thinking this way.**

Although they do not deal with these specific examples, in concept this is a paradox that Daniel Kahneman, Cass R. Sunstein and Olivier Sibony talk about in their book, *Noise*.

Systems outperform human beings, but. . .

The authors give example after example of various areas of human endeavour, even those far away from the conventional number crunching like judicial decisions, where well-constructed algorithms consistently outperform human beings—that too human beings with considerable experience and expertise.

For example, whether an accused should be granted bail or not appears to be a problem that only a human being with great judgement (pun intended) can tackle. The test is whether a person out on bail will commit another crime.

Actual studies show that even a very simple algorithm, which may consider only one or two factors, like the age of the accused and their previous crime record, outperforms skilled judges. Here the parameter being measured is whether the accused commits another crime while being out on bail.

Even in activities like corporate recruitment or deciding on insurance premiums, simple, at times even simplistic, algorithms outperform experienced human beings.

Why does this happen?

One of the reasons is that while we think humans bring expertise and nuanced judgement to decision-making, what we forget is that they also bring in 'noise' into the mix.

What is noise? In simple terms, noise is undesirable variability, over and above variability which may be due to bias (e.g., a judge being biased for or against a gender, race or caste).

Bias is easily understood, but even without bias, various judges or insurance professionals or financial analysts will come up with different answers to the same problem.

Even worse, the same human being will come up with different answers depending on variables that are totally unrelated to the matter under consideration—like whether they are hungry, what the weather is like, what their mood is like, and so on. We all understand this phenomenon individually, having noticed that our performance is impacted by our own daily mental make-up. This noise is both across different individuals in the same profession or category as well as how a particular individual performs or makes decisions in various instances.

It is this noise that algorithms or machine-led systems reduce, and that is what accounts for their superior performance.

While the machine-led systems do not have all aspects of the expertise of a human professional, they also do not have this random variability or noise in decision-making. The net impact is that the machine-led systems perform better. Just as in our example, the self-driving cars performed better than human drivers.

Why don't we outsource more to systems?

If systems are so good, why don't we outsource more functions to machines or computer-led systems?

The anomaly lies is how we judge the competing systems against human decision-making.

We intuitively know that human beings will make errors, but consciously or not, we expect a machine-led system, say an artificial intelligence-based system, to be error free.

We are willing to ditch it at the first mistake it makes— the first wrong diagnosis based on a mammogram or the first accused out on bail who commits a crime or the first wrong umpiring decision. Never mind that doctors, judges and cricket umpires are also error prone.

In short, *instead of evaluating whether the machine works better than the human being, we expect the machine system to be perfect.*

This is completely irrational, as the rational thing to do is to test whether the machine system is an improvement on the alternative or the existing system rather than whether it is completely error free on a standalone basis.

This type of thinking leads to wrong choices, as we may abandon an algo/machine even if it does better than what was being done earlier.

That's why we started with the example of self-driving cars, where we aren't willing to live with a single fatality involving them, even when human drivers make many more errors and cause more deaths.

Moral of the story: when evaluating alternative processes or systems, always pause and think—especially to see whether you are using the same yardstick to evaluate all the systems or you have unrealistic expectations of just one.

What does it have to do with investing?

What does it have to do with investing?

In investing as well, human beings are prone to many limitations, like the amount of data they can process plus a huge variety of cognitive biases, like recency bias, survivorship bias, loss-aversion bias and endowment bias. These biases tend to drag down human performance over a period of time, and then there is the element of noise too, when it comes to humans.

Try giving the same company details and financials to five experienced analysts and see if all of them come up with the same analysis. That is almost impossible!

That is where a systematic approach helps.

Even if the system does in a mechanical fashion what the analyst or fund manager say they are doing, and even if its work is somewhat more simplified than what the fund manager claims to be doing, the very fact that it is being done in a systematic manner with no random moves or noise makes it likely to outperform the human being over a period of time.

However, will the system never make mistakes or not underperform at any time? No.

But that is the wrong criterion to use to judge whether an artificial intelligence or a machine learning system is good.

As in anything, if you ask the wrong question, you can never get the right answer!

If your question is whether switching to an artificial intelligence system will eliminate mistakes, then if the answer is no, will you not use that system?

What you need to do is to change the question and *ask whether the system is an improvement on the earlier or existing systems? That is when you will get the right answer.*

The right way to find out which alternative is better is to evaluate whether the systematic approach works better than the human approach over a period of time rather than expect the non-human approach to be perfect and to have all the answers all the time, which is anyway never possible in the market as there are factors that cannot be known in advance, no matter how much information you gather and how well you analyse it.

For example, we at First Global use a human–plus–machine model where most of the heavy lifting is done by the machine.

Does that have a perfect track record? No, but the answer to the question as to whether it is working a lot better than human fund managers, especially on a risk–adjusted basis, is an unequivocal YES.

If you ask the wrong question, you can be led astray. Hence, always stop and think about what your end objective is and whether you are asking the right question to get to that.

Later in the book I have written more about how human-plus-machine systems work.

Systems vs humans: Are you asking the right questions?

- Well-constructed algorithms consistently outperform human beings—that too human beings with considerable experience and expertise in areas like insurance, judicial decisions or cricket umpiring.
- Yet we don't like to use systems and want to discard them as soon as they make a mistake.
- The reason? We are using the wrong criteria to judge them.
- We expect systems to be perfect. Whereas they only need to be better than the alternatives. Thus, the umpiring system may also make mistakes, but as long as it makes fewer mistakes than the human umpire, we should logically prefer it.
- At First Global, we use a human-plus-machine model where most of the heavy lifting is done by the machine. Does the model have a perfect track record? No, but the answer to the question as to whether it is working a lot better than human fund managers, especially on a risk-adjusted basis, is an unequivocal YES.

Why Is Your Brain Out to Sabotage Your Investment Journey?

One of my favourite topics of interest is to do with cognitive biases or fallacies in our thinking which derail our judgements in all areas of life in general, and our investment journey in particular.

Throughout the book I have written about and explained several specific biases, but have you thought about *why these biases exist?*

And why it is so hard to get rid of them?

In short, why is your brain out to sabotage your investment journey?

The answer? These biases arise out of human evolution, so they are hard-coded into you.

Human evolution wired you for survival . . . not investing

If you look at storification bias, for example, all human beings tell stories and are influenced by stories. In fact, that is the one of the things common across all civilizations across time and

265

across geographies, and from the most primitive to the most sophisticated.

Human beings convey information to each other and convince each other by means of stories.

If you look at loss aversion bias, aversion to loss and pain is an integral part of evolution to keep you alive.

In our hunter-gatherer days, if you saw what you thought was a sabre-toothed tiger in the bushes, it was better that you took action to save yourself, even if it later turned out that there was no tiger and it was a false alarm.

That's the reason why, in your investment journey, you are so reluctant to admit to a mistake or take a loss.

The bandwagon effect, where you want to rush where everyone else is, also comes out of the fact that for much of history the cost of not belonging in a group meant not being able to procreate to not surviving at all. We are all the progeny of people who chose to stay on with the tribe. Hence, we are wired to want to belong to groups. That was the characteristic evolution selected for. That is why it is so very uncomfortable to go against what 'everyone else' is doing.

All these biases have been hardwired into us for thousands of years because their purpose was to keep us alive with the minimum use of resources.

It is the same with most other biases.

The human brain doesn't really care at the core level about what happens to your investment portfolio!

That is the reason why it is so difficult to get rid of biases.

Can you un-see an optical illusion?

Think of optical illusions: many are of the form where two lines or objects appear to be of different sizes.

However, if you take a measuring tape and you measure them, you will find they are of the same size.

But even after knowing this for a fact, your eyes and brains still see them being of different lengths. This is because the brain takes many shortcuts in interpreting what our eyes see.

For example, many optical illusions with images that alternately look concave and convex rely on the fact that our brain assumes that light always comes from the top, because that was a good enough thumb rule to work with when almost all the light came from celestial bodies in the sky most of the time.

The brain goes with good enough, not with the best or the true

The brain uses shortcuts even in instances that have nothing to do with optical matters. It does not care for precision or for the absolute best result, given a huge amount of data it is fed. It does not even care for the truth.

What is 'good enough to keep us alive without using too many resources' is what the brain goes with.

That is the real reason why our biases are that hard-coded. In fact, Daniel Kahneman whose life work has been on biases, and who won a Nobel Prize on biases, has said that in spite of intellectually understanding biases, he still could not get rid of them in his own decisions. His decision-making had essentially not changed at all!

That is the key thing—that your brain will continue to have those biases. There are certain systems you can put in place, you can try to sidestep the biases and overcome them, and that is why we depend on a Human-plus-Machine model that we talk about, because a human-only model can never be bias free.

Why your brain systematically sabotages you

- Biases derail your judgement. And hence your investment journey.
- Why do they exist? Most biases served a purpose during human evolution. That is why they are so hardwired into you and near impossible to get rid of.
- Evolution was concerned with survival and procreation. It didn't care about the best solution or even the truth. Therefore it has zero concern about your portfolio.
- Like optical illusions, biases are hardwired into our brains. Intellectually understanding them doesn't remove them from our decision-making. Only a system can help get rid of them.

Scan the QR code to learn more

SECTION IV

The Future Is Here: The Changing Nature of Investing

Thus far in the book we have discussed how to get started in the investment business, what are the generally touted myths that don't really hold up to scrutiny, what mantras to use and, most importantly, how to see the fallacies of your own thinking which can derail the best calculations.

Now comes a critical part. Most of what has been discussed earlier in the book is, in a sense, about the unchanging part of investing and human nature.

But now there is a fundamental change in the nature of investing, which will shake up the way investment management is done.

Most professionals in the business have not yet realized it or find it too difficult to implement. They are still playing the game the way it was done twenty or thirty years ago. And it is simply not working!

In this section, I will talk about what has changed, what has not, and how to tackle this new world.

269

How the Playing Field in Investing Is Changing, and Why You Can't Afford to Be Left Behind

All of us have heard of the term 'changing the playing field', and while this is normally used as a metaphor, it actually refers to something that we can see in the real world, at times literally.

For example, in cricket, whether you are playing in a dust bowl or on textbook greens, the mix of players and skills you need are very different for each. Of course, occasionally the field on which you play literally changes, as happened with our national game, hockey.

What happened to hockey when the field changed

Ever heard of Major Dhyan Chand?

For the sake of the Gen Z readers, let's do a quick bio of Dhyan Chand, the hockey equivalent of cricketing legend Sir Donald Bradman.

Dhyan Chand scored fourteen goals at the 1928 Amsterdam Olympics. He was hailed as a 'magician of hockey' by newspapers. So astonishing was his stick work that the Netherlands hockey authorities are believed to have broken his hockey stick to investigate whether there was a magnet inside it. After India's win at the 1936 Berlin Olympics, Hitler offered Dhyan Chand German citizenship!

And, of course, India and Pakistan were kings of the field hockey heap, from the 1920s to the 1970s. *From 1928 to 1960, the Indian men's hockey team remained unbeaten in the Olympics, winning six golds in a row. They were also the only team ever to win in the Olympics twice without conceding a single goal in the whole tournament. In 1960, they won the silver as Pakistan lifted the gold. Both India and Pakistan continued to win medals in hockey in the global arena in the 1960s and 1970s.*

The subcontinent teams' fluid passes, superb dribbling and bewitching stick work ran circles around the Western and Australian teams, enthralling crowds worldwide.

And then, one sudden day, India and Pakistan became part of the also-rans for decades.

Why?

The developed nations struck back: they changed the field of play. Literally. By introducing Astroturf, or artificial grass technology.

This technological innovation changed hockey forever.

Astroturf offered a flat terrain, allowing fast passes with precise ball control. Because the speed of ball travel went up enormously, reaching the ball in time to convert passes became critical. Therefore, fast sprinting speed became absolutely essential. This meant extreme fitness.

No prizes for guessing which players were fitter: those from the developed nations! There were Western hockey players who could run the 100 m in under eleven seconds!

To add to this, their superb fitness was the result of superior training and nutrition tech. Precise video recordings, unheard of in India, were brought to play. Kinesiology, the science of movement, came in (Sydney University led in this); time-release nutrition became the order of the day.

At all levels of the game, from grass to training to nutrition, deep science and tech took away the edge that the 'traditional' players had enjoyed. They were simply out-muscled and out-gunned in this tech arms race. They didn't stand a chance.

The Traditionals became history.

Sport after sport has gone that way. Remember tennis legend Bjorn Borg making a comeback to Wimbledon with his comfort wooden racket, in face of titanium rackets, and beating a retreat, never to be seen again on a tennis court? And this was a man who had won the championship five times in a row in the previous era.

Today, sensors in active wear allow players to measure their breathing, heart rate, temperature and hydration in real time.

Then there are GPS and lasers that measure the players' exact positions, acceleration, distance from each other and velocity, moulding their movements and speed to the desired targets. An elite cyclist only needs a pair of heads-up display glasses to record cycling information and make adjustments mid-ride. Swimmers utilize sensors to capture dive angle, leg movement, rotational speed and hydrodynamics.

Being faster by a few milliseconds can mean winning the Olympic gold.

It is the same as an auto company saying today that they will stick to the traditional combustion engine and not look at electric vehicles or other green technologies.

> Once the playing field changes, the option of continuing to play by the old rules and with the old skill sets is gone. If you choose to do that you will be left far, far behind.

We all know how that story will end for any manufacturer who says/does that.

The playing field is changing in investment management . . . and how!

Advanced tech is doing to investment management what it did to sport.

Traditionally, investment decisions were made only by the human mind. There was only one way to do things.

If you put your money in a mutual fund or PMS scheme, your 'human' fund manager painstakingly analysed company and industry data in order to decide where to invest.

Think Warren Buffett and Peter Lynch.

> Almost all investment management practices today remain frozen in a 1940s–1990s time warp.

They still do this. They attend conference calls. They read annual reports (at least you hope they do!).

It's all touchy-feely old school . . . still.

But there is seismic change afoot . . . already.

Why the human-only model of investment management no longer works

For one, a large part of what made the traditional model work lay in getting additional or unique information by meeting companies and their management. It was a game of information arbitrage. This was true not just of India but of all markets around the world, where large fund managers could sit in a closed room with company officials and get information.

I have done plenty of that myself. For decades I met company managements, went around the countryside to visit steel manufacturers in Jamshedpur and Tarapore or aluminium plants in Renukoot, auto-ancillary units on the outskirts of Chennai and the NCR and pharma companies around Hyderabad. I visited umpteen company offices and plants, trying to glean that extra bit of information or insight that would give me an edge.

Hand on heart, I would say that it was the most fun part of my job as an equity researcher!

However, the finest output is not about what is most fun for you individually but about what works the best . . . in this case, what results in an optimized portfolio.

Information arbitrage is gone!

Just as an example, earlier, conference calls after an earnings announcement used to be accessible only to a handful of professionals. Now all call transcripts have to be out in the public domain, by law.

> The edge that the securities industry or fund managers had in getting information from companies has been regulated away across the world—information availability has been made largely uniform.

In fact, now the problem is something quite different, which is that there is an absolute surfeit of data which is humanly unmanageable.

And this is where the machines come in . . .

To handle tonnes of data, you need advanced computing power for extreme data-crunching prowess.

Most important, they can do this consistently and without bias—something that is impossible for human beings to do.

Machines do the thinking for you. Machines 'learn' quicker and better than humans ever can.

> There are mathematical models that dispense insights at speeds unimaginable in the past. They can analyse more securities AND more data points in each of those securities than is possible even for large teams of humans.

Adaptive learning systems can replicate human inventiveness, only much better.

Artificial intelligence (AI) and machine learning (ML) are set to transform portfolio management. Truly forward-thinking portfolio management services companies are training ML models to automate various aspects of trading and investing.

An expertly constructed quant ML model can do bewildering things: it can read millions of research papers, balance sheets, conference-call transcripts and social media feeds!

It can analyse a company's auditor's reports and management commentary. It can distinguish between good accounting policies and bad.

It can granularly analyse ratios, in time series as well as in cross section, across thousands of companies.

A well-developed machine can expertly analyse reams of data, discern patterns and linkages among stocks and securities across the world. No set of humans is equipped to cast an eye so wide and narrow, contemporaneously, on data.

More on the nuances of this in the coming chapters.

The playing field has changed in investing

- When the playing field changed in hockey from grass to astroturf, a different set of skills became critical for the players. The same happened in sport after sport and industry after industry.
- The investment field has also transformed, with information arbitrage going away. Now what is required is the ability to deal with huge amounts of data, where machines have an advantage.

- Still, most of the fund management industry is using obsolete methods, which is why they cannot outperform the markets.
- Systems can analyse more securities, a larger number of factors for each and do it without bias or noise, which is impossible for human beings to do.

Scan the QR code to learn more

Why Machines Work, and Where Do You Still Need Humans?

In the previous chapter, we were talking about all the work that machines can do to help investment management.

Let us break this down a bit, on why 'machines' work and where you still need human beings.

More securities and more factors per security

The first reason—machines can analyse a very large number of securities.

Globally, we analyse almost 25,000 securities in order to pick our final portfolios. In India, we analyse all companies that meet our liquidity and market capitalization criteria—which is roughly 750 stocks.

No traditional research team, no matter how large, will be able to analyse so many securities.

Secondly, it is not just the number of securities, but how many factors we can analyse for each security.

As a human being, I can analyse only handful of factors. As for a machine, it can analyse hundreds or even thousands of factors.

Even more difficult, or rather impossible, for a human being to match, is **the machine's ability to analyse not just hundreds of factors but even the interactions between those factors.**

For example, our systems look not just at growth—which is the first derivative of earnings or sales (like velocity)—but can additionally analyse the second derivative, which is the acceleration, and the third derivative, which is the jerk.

At First Global, we have developed, in addition, a system called FG-Agreement in Motion. This system, which is part of our larger investment tech stack called ExoTech, looks for areas of maximum 'agreement' or consensus, across the world. By knowing that, one can find out if world's opinion on various matters is converging or diverging. This sets up very interesting trades.

> Very few humans, if any, have the compound skills that being a successful investor needs.

Can any human ever be able do this?

The machine is consistent—it has no biases or noise

Number three is very important: The machine, or rather the AI and ML-based system, is very consistent. Even if I had a thousand analysts analysing twenty-five securities each, they will not be consistent because different human beings faced with the same set of data will come up with different analyses, different conclusions.

The book Noise, which I have quoted from earlier, talks about how even well-qualified and experienced professionals, say a set of doctors, judges or insurance professionals, presented with the same data and facts will come up with highly varied conclusions and judgements.

And this they do with a very limited and well-defined set of variables, like medical reports. The chaos will be even more

in the case of a stock market with its many disparate pieces of information.

Surprisingly, or maybe not, this variation is not consistent even when it comes to the individual. The same person may decide the same matter differently, depending on all kinds of factors, from their mood to the weather.

Human beings are many things, but they are almost never consistent. Their world view keeps changing depending on their own circumstances.

> Whether we are angry, hungry or have had a fight . . . all impact our performance and judgement.

Besides this random variation across people, human beings are also prone to a very large number of cognitive biases, which I've written about elsewhere. Storification, recency, hindsight, endowment and loss-aversion biases and many more are hardwired into us as part of our evolutionary process.

For example, Endowment bias tends to make us overvalue stocks we already hold compared with those we do not hold.

Loss aversion bias makes us unwilling to admit we have made a mistake and therefore must exit a position and make losses as a result.

Of course, the list of biases goes on and on.

Even more disturbing is the fact that *just an understanding of these biases makes little or no difference to how we make our decisions.* This is because, as mentioned earlier, the biases are hardwired into us for evolutionary reasons.

> The machine has no biases. This is the big advantage of the machine approach.

The great Daniel Kahneman has said that while he has spent a lifetime analysing human biases, he has not been able to eliminate them from his own thinking and decision-making.

The machine ages well, humans don't!

Finally, there is the question of how human and machine-based systems evolve over time. Human beings decline with age, and they also do not like to admit mistakes.

> The machine improves with age. It learns from its successes. It learns from its failures. It has no problem admitting its mistakes and modifying its system. Hence, it keeps evolving, keeps getting better.

Then why do we need humans?

Since machines work so well, it begs the question: Do we need humans at all in the whole process, along with the machines?

First, let me tell you an anecdote. Most of you would have heard of the time when the IBM supercomputer—the Deep Blue—was pitted against the then chess world champion Gary Kasparov in the 1990s. In that match, the computer won. This was sensational news at the time.

What most people don't know is that in 2005 the same experiment was repeated, with the supercomputer playing against not the world champion but against reasonably good chess players armed with laptops. And who won? The chess players with the laptops.

> The human+machine system worked better than the best human, and it worked better than the best machine.

Therefore, in the investment management context too, *you need human beings with those decades of market experience in order to code the machine correctly. Which is why when only techies do it, it usually doesn't work because they rely solely on machines.*

Machines look at thousands of factors, do tonnes of computations and find some factors that appear to explain what happened in the past. Essentially, they find some factors which had a correlation with market movements in the past, but there are many spurious correlations in the world.

For example, if you plot a graph between, let's say, nuclear energy and total cheese consumption, the correlation can be nearly one, but they have nothing to do with each other. When people with only a technology background start building investing or trading systems, they are likely to get sidetracked by these spurious correlations.

Essentially, for any artificial intelligence and machine learning system to make sense, the factors fed into it must be logical. There are many areas where coding human market expertise is required. Only then will the output of the machine make sense.

In any case, I do not believe in using black boxes where one doesn't know why the machine is recommending a particular course of action. In the systems we use, we can always go back and check why they are recommending a buy or a sell. That is as far as machine output goes.

You need an overlay of human expertise once again. Because the machine relies on past data, there could be some things not captured by it.

Let us say a pandemic is on the horizon, or there are geopolitical tensions on certain international borders, or there is an announcement by OPEC on crude production. All these things have to be overlaid on the machine model by the human being.

Here are a couple of real-world examples of developments that needed to be overlaid on our machine system: In the beginning of March 2020, Italy and Japan were hit by COVID and began to shut down. Schools were closed and all tourist attractions deserted. At the time, we at First Global took a call to be very conservative, increasing cash and non-equity assets, buying insurance, etc.

In 2022, we steered clear of some stocks that our systems had recommended based on their past performance, because among the companies' main markets was Europe, where we saw a slow down on the horizon.

To summarize this chapter, *human inputs are required, first to direct coding and programming of the system, which essentially codifies human expertise; and thereafter to provide an overlay of human wisdom that may not have been captured after the machine has given its output.*

This is how a human–plus–machine system, as we call it, comes to maturity.

Why a human-plus-machine model?

- The machine can analyse thousands of securities and hundreds of factors for each stock.
- It can do so on a consistent, bias-free basis, without random variation.
- The systems also learn with experience and become better.
- Human inputs are required, first to direct coding and programming of the system, which essentially codifies human expertise.
- Thereafter, they are required to provide an overlay of human wisdom that may not be captured after the machine has given its output.

Scan the QR code to learn more

Do Quant Methods Work in Investing?

This is a question I get sometimes: Do quant methods work in investing?

Let me ask you another question: Do you think financial models and estimates made on Microsoft Excel are accurate?

So, the question now changes to: How do you ensure that the quant methods work?

I'm sure you'd say this is an absurd question because everybody makes their estimates for company financials on Excel, and accuracy depends on what they are putting into the model.

It is exactly the same thing when it comes to quant methods, artificial intelligence or machine learning. They are only tools: How good those systems are or the quality of their output depends on how well you use those tools.

I will tell you some things that we do differently when using quant methods to ensure quality output:

Quality data is number one

The first requirement is quality of data. One must collect data, correct it and comb through tons of it to ensure it is accurate, because otherwise it would be garbage in, garbage out. That is the first step.

I can tell you that a very large amount of time goes in cleaning data. *As per our internal estimates something like 60 to 70 per cent of the total time of our quant team goes in ensuring data quality.*

To give only one example, the data has to be survivorship-bias free. So, the test cannot start with the listed securities and look at their history, because other securities which are no longer traded may have been listed in the past. The test has to be on all listed securities in that set as they existed back in time to wherever our tests are starting—usually about twenty-five years at least.

Factors have to be defined FIRST

Secondly, *when we test factors that can impact stock price or market movements, we start with those that make sense and ensure that there is logic behind them*. Otherwise, if you are just going to randomly test a large number of factors, you will find correlations which have worked in the past, but which actually have no logical basis. If you base your systems on those factors, the results will go haywire.

As I have written elsewhere, if you randomly test a large number of factors, some are certain to have a high correlation with market movements, even if the correlation is spurious.

Therefore, we only test factors where the logic behind them can be easily explained.

Third, *the system itself has to be extremely robust and rigorous. We say we have systems with over a million lines of code, and that is no exaggeration.*

These are very complex, rigorous systems.

The testing process

Four: *The testing has to be extremely meticulous. Because otherwise you cannot rely on the systems.*

Let me tell you that my quant team doesn't allow me to override any of the parameters they have set, because they say that once you violate anything in the system then you can't rely on the results.

For example, we may try out different systems/factors for a twenty-year period, 1998–2018, which is called the sample period. The choice of system will be made after these trials. Only then do we test for 2018–23, the out-of-sample period, to see how the selected system performs. You cannot 'cheat' by looking at what happened in the last five years from 2018 to 2023 first.

But I often hear people say they have back-tested a system based on the last twenty years' data and are now using it to trade in live markets. This approach is fundamentally flawed.

Human-led investing has a large component of chance

Investing, the way it has been done so far, is nothing but luck masquerading as skill, with most gains coming from just a handful of stocks from the scores that may have been invested in. As Charlie Munger says: 'If you take away our few big winners, Berkshire's record is very mediocre.'

This, in mathematical terms, is luck. Not skill.

Machines reduce the role of luck hugely, bringing skill to the fore.

This is exactly why the traditional investment management business worldwide has been in a crisis for years, because traditional fund management simply cannot beat the markets owing to their severe cognitive limitations.

Properly devised systems outperform Humans because of their capabilities

Done well (the last word is key) quant systems translate into consistent market beating performance which the traditional fund managers simply cannot match, because of their biases, and inherent inability to process and comprehend vast amounts of data.

One of the more interesting aspects of quantitative investing is that *the more the data fed into the machines, the more accurate predictions they generate. This is absolutely the opposite in humans!* Most human brains decline in capabilities with age and with load.

This increases correlation in the portfolio, leading to very volatile returns. The statement 'I will invest only within my circle of competence' is just a fancy way of saying that I will only invest within my comfort zone. And, as an investor, why should your investment be constrained by your fund manager's comfort zone? This is something dealt with in greater detail earlier in the book.

Because humans can process only limited data, they tend to build more concentrated, clustered portfolios, largely around their comfort zones.

In contrast, machines can build far larger, more carefully diversified portfolios across a wide spectrum of securities. This approach reduces correlation within a portfolio, thereby reducing risk while not sacrificing returns.

Dealing with a deluge of data and learning from mistakes

Another important difference between humans and machines is that the latter are clinical about acknowledging and analysing mistakes as well as correcting the process that led to these mistakes. Each of these steps is extremely difficult for a human being to take, as we are hardwired to defend our decisions and stories.

The reality: ***humans have limited capacity to absorb data, and when confronted with vast amounts of data the human brain simply shuts down and resorts to 'armchair thinking',*** forming reliance on under-analysed, oversimplified, lazy opinions and simple stories.

Quantitative investing is free from behavioural biases and emotions. The human mind, no matter how intellectually sound, cannot be emotionless.

The machines are now entering the investing game. The playing field is changing. Sticking to the old way of doing things will only mean that you will be out of the game.

Don't become obsolete, like the combustion engine will in an era of electric and other green vehicles.

Do quant methods do better than humans?

- Quant methods are just a tool. The results depend on what you do with them.
- Used well, they outperform human beings because they can deal with volumes of data without getting overwhelmed, learn from mistakes, improve over time and reduce the impact of luck in investing.
- Among the things to take care of is data quality, ensuring rigour in testing, defining factors in advance rather than testing random factors, and so on.

- Artificial intelligence and machine learning systems are being developed and used not just because they are available but because the current market structure is such that humans cannot consistently outperform without the use of systems.

Scan the QR code to learn more

Acknowledgements

This book is an amalgamation of learnings, and for these I am indebted to all my teachers—those who formally taught me in school, at university, IIM-A and the numerous authors whose writings sparked so many thoughts in my head—even if at times these were to refute what I had read.

Prakash Iyer, whom I had pushed to write his first book, returned the compliment by chasing me to get going on this project.

The friends who read through the drafts and gave comments, including Shailendra (Shail) Bhatnagar, Jayant Krishna, Pradeep Mane and, most of all, Rohit Tandon, who read through every word and did the first proofing of the book. Given that this is not a fun job, to do it shows the depth of the friendship we share and the goodness of his heart.

To my colleagues, past and present, including Hitesh Kuvelkar, Kavita Thomas, Achin Agarwal and many others, discussions with whom have enhanced my understanding of investing.

Most of all, my marvellous assistant, Santosh Kadam, who runs the hard drive of my life. Even with half-baked instructions, locating a quarter-century-old report is a matter of minutes for him. He also helped coordinate the tables, images, QR codes, etc.—the nuts and bolts of this book.

My apologies to any teachers, friends and colleagues I have missed. Heartfelt thanks to you all.

Thanks also to Manish and Saba at Penguin who helped edit this book.

I am grateful to the loves of my life, my mother and my daughter Precia, as writing this book took time away from them.

Suggested Reading

First Global started over thirty years ago with practically no capital to speak of. We did not take any outside capital either.

So, what was it built on? There is only one answer to that: intellectual capital.

Let me share the only path I personally know of to riches: feeding your mind and building your tool box.

Presenting how to be a great, and hopefully wealthy, investor . . .

The bad news: It requires some work.

The good news: Here's the blueprint.

The Ultimate Booklist.

Some new. Some old.

In the markets, there is no lasting wealth without knowledge, which usually comes from reading. Of course resources such as videos, podcasts and even online courses are available today. But I have personally done it the old-fashioned way, via books.

Here are some books that you may enjoy, whether you are just starting on your investment journey or are already further along the way. Obviously, the list is far from comprehensive. It is just meant to get you started!

I have split them into six categories:

I. Books to understand the way our own mind works (including our own biases, blind spots and fallacies in thinking)

Before you can conquer the world, you must conquer your own mind and, more importantly, understand it!

In some senses, it is easier to learn the tools of the trade in terms of accounting, finance, how markets work, etc., than to manage your mind through the ups and downs of the market.

It always looks very simple when you look at charts in hindsight. It is obvious as to where you would have bought and where you would have sold. It is not quite so straightforward when you are living through the market gyrations in real time.

As a starting point, I would recommend these few books, starting with *Thinking Fast and Slow*, by the Nobel laureate Daniel Kahneman.

It is a comprehensive look at how your own thinking can mislead you; how the automatic, fast, intuitive, 'natural' thinking that you rely on for most things in life—the one that feels right—may be actually completely wrong in objective terms. It talks about the many human biases, like endowment bias, recency bias, loss-aversion bias, anchoring bias, and many more (most have been explained in earlier chapters of this book)—all of which can derail not just your regular life but also your investing and trading career.

The caveat, of course, is that just because you understand what investing, or rather cognitive, biases are, does not mean that you will be able to eliminate them from your thinking.

A second important book, co-authored by Kahneman is *Noise*, which goes beyond biases into how random variations between supposedly equally skilled and experienced people (like judges, insurance valuers, etc.) can cause big variations in their decisions on the same matter. Even worse, the same person may make widely varying judgements depending on all sorts of factors, from their hunger levels to the weather outside.

The Invisible Gorilla: And Other Ways Our Intuitions Deceive Us by Christopher Chabris talks about the illusions of our mind, about how our minds are finite resources and hence, from our attention to our memory, our performance is far below what we think it is.

It deals with some of the reasons why human beings make bad witnesses, and how confidence is no proxy for competence. A very useful book to make you aware of the several illusions you carry as you go about the world.

Even if elimination of these illusions is not possible, awareness of their existence changes the lens through which you see the world.

Misbehaving: The Makings of Behavioral Economics, by Richard Thaler, also illustrates with many examples how we human beings are not as rational as what we think we are, and how changes that should not make a difference to a rational person do make a difference in the real world.

The Halo Effect, by Phil Rosenzweig, talks of how several characteristics that we attribute to successful companies and corporate leaders (great strategy, customer focus, outstanding human resource practices, etc.) are all mostly due to the halo cast by the current performance of these companies. As their performance changes, the same characteristics that were called their 'secrets of success' appear to become liabilities.

Some recent book recommendations on thinking frameworks that added totally new dimensions for me were: *Anthro-Vision: How Anthropology Can Explain Business and Life* by Gillian Tett. Unlike what we usually think, anthropologists can study not just remote tribes but also groups like copier salespeople, computer buyers in India or stock traders.

Everything Is Obvious: Once You Know the Answer, by Duncan J. Watts, is about how so-called common sense can totally mislead us. Our rationalizing something that has happened is mostly equivalent to saying it happened because it had to happen. Unfortunately, if the opposite outcome had been the reality, we would have come up with an equally good explanation as to why that was inevitable. The negative of reading this book has been that it makes glib explanations for the past as well as estimates for the future much more difficult.

Alchemy: The Surprising Power of Ideas that don't Make Sense, by Rory Sutherland, says that humans are less 'rational' than we think, and that is why 'illogical' advertising and marketing ideas can work brilliantly. The recommendation is to see what works rather than try to justify it.

I call *The Art of Thinking Clearly*, by Rolf Dobelli, the kunji or CliffsNotes version of the relatively heavy books on biases, like the ones by Daniel Kahneman. It deals with each bias or thinking quirk in easy language in just three pages each.

II. The Nitty-Gritties of Investing

This is distinctly unsexy stuff but if you want to make a serious effort in investing or trading, you need to have the building blocks.

If you have already done a structured course in finance, like CFA, MBA or a post-graduation in finance, you may be familiar with much of this. Otherwise, it is worthwhile to spend your time and effort on some books like *Damodaran on Valuation*, by Aswath Damodaran, and *Valuation, Measuring and Managing the Value of Companies*, by Tom Copeland, which will give you an idea as to how to go about analysing the financials of a company and make an attempt to value it.

This does not mean that you should apply all the techniques in these books exactly, but as in art, even to break the rules you should know the rules.

If you are a beginner in this field, basic books on accounting and finance may also be required, but you definitely need to have this in your toolbox in order to make sense of your investments.

If the investing business is something you want to get into full time, it might be worthwhile doing the CFA course too.

III. Stories of Great Investors and Traders

These have to be read from the point of view of not getting a final how-to prescription, but of understanding the many different approaches that are there to heaven . . . or hell.

Ideally, you should read about many different strategies and tactics used by investors before you can evolve your own. Do this widely. From reading *Berkshire Hathaway Letters to Shareholders*, which is about patiently buying businesses and holding on to them (whether Berkshire itself stuck to this prescription is something else altogether) to *The Man Who Solved the Market: How Jim Simons Launched the Quant Revolution*, by Gregory Zuckerman, which is about Jim Simons and the totally different approach of taking millions of bets with a small edge and a lot of computing power.

Then there are books like *Market Wizards, The New Market Wizards* and *The New Money Masters* and others of the kind that have interviews of (or analysis of the strategies of) many well-known traders and investors. Even some of the older, out-of-date books in this category are worth reading, simply from the point of view of knowing that what appeared like the holy grail at one point in time stopped working thereafter.

There are also investing practitioners, like George Soros, who have written about their theories and techniques, and others like

Nassim Taleb and Peter Bernstein, who have written about risk
and markets in more general terms. As always, not everything
written in their books is right or correct. Taleb, in particular, has
a lot of ideas, some good, some bad, some indifferent, and you
need to sift through them.

To understand how to structure your thoughts about
investing, *The Psychology of Money* and *Same as Ever* by Morgan
Housel also provide some food for thought, more in terms of
how to think about money rather than about specific investing
techniques. They are especially recommended for young people.

IV. The History of Markets

We may think that our times are different when it comes to the
financial markets, but much of what is happening at any point
in time has parallels in the past. For instance, IPO frenzies go
back centuries.

Bubbles of many sorts have come and gone in the markets.
A good investment education would involve reading about some
of these past bubbles. A couple of recommendations, which are
good starting points, are:

Manias, Panics and Crashes: A History of Financial Crises by
Charles P. Kindleberger and *A Short History of Financial Euphoria*
by John Kenneth Galbraith.

Then there are accounts of people who have worked in
the markets, mostly Wall Street, such as *Where are the Customers'
Yachts?* by Fred Schwed and *Reminiscences of a Stock Operator* by
Edwin Lefèvre.

These are decades old but tell you that markets and market
participants don't change quite as much as you would think.

In addition, there are books on specific crises, the following
being some of them:

*When Genius Failed: The Rise and Fall of Long-Term Capital
Management* by Roger Lowenstein; *The Big Short: Inside the*

Doomsday Machine (on the 2008 crisis) by Michael Lewis; and *The Great Crash 1929* by John Kenneth Galbraith

There have been many ups and downs in the Indian stock and commodity markets too but few authoritative books describing them. Even business history is still a relatively nascent field in India.

V. Autobiographies and Biographies of Businesspeople and Businesses

There is an ocean of these. Since investing is mostly about investing in securities of corporations, it is important to understand how businesses are built and run.

You will often find that the one-line story or impression you have of a business is very different from how it is actually built-up step by step.

For example, reading *The Everything Store: Jeff Bezos and the Age of Amazon*, by Brad Stone, you realize that while the public impression of Jeff Bezos is that of a great leader and of Amazon as a company with linear growth, the reality was very different. At every step of the way, Amazon took dozens of bets, lost a great deal of money in many of them with only one or two of them at every stage paying off.

Similarly, Nike appears like a great success story from the word GO, but when you read *Shoe Dog: A Memoir by the Creator of Nike*, by Phil Knight, you realize that this was a company that was started in the sixties and took a very long time to even come to take-off stage. And also, contrary to the general impression, it was not a very marketing-oriented company, neither in the beginning nor for a long time afterwards.

There are some businesspeople who have led very interesting lives, and their stories can make for fun reading. A couple of books on them that I can recommend are Richard Branson's

Losing My Virginity, which proceeds at breakneck speed, and Subhash Chandra's *The Z Factor*, which is as candid an account as you can get of what it means to run a business in India.

There are also interviews, investor letters and so on by business veterans like Jeff Bezos, Steve Jobs, etc., that can give you different perspectives on business and markets.

As with the books about great investors and traders, read every one of them but don't swallow everything whole. Evaluate what people are saying and see whether it makes sense to you.

Also account for the fact that what someone did or succeeded with may have worked in a particular country or market at a particular time and may not be something that can be extrapolated to other environments and other times.

VI. Books on technicals/derivatives/trading techniques

This category may not be relevant for everyone, but if you do plan to trade rather than invest, or trade in derivatives, please ensure that you read multiple books on your chosen methods and techniques.

Indeed, textbooks are probably what you should start with to understand the instruments properly. Otherwise, don't venture here at all.

While the books recommended here broadly have something to do with the markets, actually reading across history, science and many other disciplines also gives you insights about how markets, businesses or even people work.

The more you feed your mind, the more agile it will become. My own reading is very eclectic, and sometimes insights come from totally unrelated fields, including fiction.

It is an ocean of books out there. What I have talked about in this chapter is only about how to get started.

Annexure: Financial Ratios

While I have tried to avoid using too many formulas or equations in the book, you cannot talk about financials in valuation without bringing in some ratios.

Here is a quick primer on these.

All of these may not have been used in the book, but it is helpful to have a ready reckoner when you come across certain terms in other books or in the financial press.

Hence there is no need to read this section line by line unless you wish to. It may be more useful as a reference table to come back to if you are not sure of what a particular term or ratio means.

Income statement and income statement ratios
Gross sales
Less: Excise
Net sales
Other operating income
Total revenue = net sales + other operating income
Less:
Cost of raw material

Less: Increase/(decrease) in stocks

Net cost of goods sold (COGS)

Gross profit = total revenue – net COGS

Gross profit margin = gross profit / total revenue

Other operating expenditure:

Employee benefits expense

Power and fuel expenses

Other operating expenses

Total other operating expenditure

EBITDA = gross profit – total other operating expenditure

EBITDA margin = EBITDA / total revenue

Less : Depreciation

EBIT = EBITDA – depreciation

EBIT margin = EBIT / total revenue

Interest paid

Non-operating income

Profit before tax (PBT) = EBIT – interest paid + non-operating income

PBT margin = PBT / total revenue

Tax

Deferred tax

Fringe benefit tax

Total taxes

Effective tax rate = total taxes / PBT

Profit after tax = PBT – total taxes

PAT margin = PAT / total revenue

Net operating profit less adjusted taxes (NOPLAT) = EBITDA – depreciation – adjusted taxes)

Interest coverage ratio = EBITDA / interest paid

Balance Sheet

Liabilities:

Equity capital

Equity share application money pending allotment

Reserves and surplus:

General reserves

Revaluation reserves

Profit & loss account

Other reserves

Share premium

Total reserves

Total equity = equity capital + equity share application money pending allotment + total reserves

Preference share capital

Net worth = total equity + preference share capital

Minority interest

Total loans

Deferred tax liability (DTL) (net)

Other long-term liabilities

Capital employed = net worth + minority interest + total loans + DTL + other long-term liabilities

Assets

Gross block

Less: depreciation

Add: lease adjustment account

Net block

Capital WIP (CWIP)

Investments in subsidiaries (strategic)

Investments – others

Total investment

Intangible assets

Others – A
Current assets:
Inventories
Sundry debtors
Cash and bank balance
Normal cash (1% of cash and bank balance)
Excess cash
Loans and advances:
Operating loans and advances
Non-operating loans & advances
Others:
Others – operating current assets
Others – non-operating current assets
Total current assets = inventory + debtors + cash + loans and advances + others
Less: Current liabilities & provisions
Sundry creditors
Provisions:
Provision for tax and others
Provision for dividend
Others
Operating other current liabilities
Non-operating other current liabilities
Total current liabilities & provisions = creditors + provisions + other current liabilities
Current ratio = total current assets / total current liabilities and provisions
Net current assets = total current assets – total current liabilities and provisions
Miscellaneous assets

Capital applied = net block + capital WIP + total investments + intangible assets + net current assets+ miscellaneous assets

Balance sheet ratios

Return on equity (ROE) = ((profit after tax – preference share dividend) / (average equity – revaluation reserve –miscellaneous asset + dividend + preference share dividend + dividend tax))

Return on capital employed (ROCE) = ((profit after tax before minority interest + interest paid) * (1 – effective tax rate)) / (average capital employed – revaluation reserve + dividend + preference share dividend + dividend tax)

Debt to equity ratio = total loans / (net worth – revaluation reserve – miscellaneous asset)

Interest to debt ratio = interest paid / average total loans

Net operating assets = net block + CWIP + investment in subsidiaries + inventories + debtors + normal cash + loans and advances + other current assets - creditors-provision for tax and others - operating other current liabilities

Total assets = capital employed + total current liabilities & provisions

Asset turnover ratio = total revenue / total assets

Working capital = inventories + debtors + normal cash + operating loans and advances + other current assets - provision for tax and others - operating other current liabilities - creditors

Working capital turnover days = revenue / average working capital

Net operating profit less adjusted taxes (NOPLAT) = (EBITDA – depreciation – adjusted taxes)

Return on operating assets (ROA) = NOPLAT / (average net operating assets)

Return on incremental capital (ROIC) = (change in NOPLAT) / net investment

Free cash flow (FCF) = operating cash flows - capital expenditure

Free Cash Flow Analysis

EBITDA

Less: Adjusted taxes

NOPLAT

Plus: Depreciation

Gross cash flow

Less: Increase in working capital

Operating cash flow

Less: Net capex

Less: Increase in net other assets

FCF from operation

Less: Increase/(decrease) in investment

FCF after investment

Plus: Gain/(loss) on extraordinary items

Plus: Foreign currency translation effect

Total FCF

FCF to equity= FCF - interest paid

Income Statement Ratios

1) **Gross profit margin** = (revenue − cost of sales) / revenue
   The gross profit measures the revenue the company retains after deducting basic operating costs like raw material and other direct production costs.

This, as a percentage of the revenues, gives you the gross profit margin.

2) **Earnings before interest, tax, depreciation/ amortization (EBITDA) margin** = (revenue − total operating expenditure, including cost of sales) / revenue

Depreciation and amortization are non-cash expenses. When you buy an asset it is assumed that its value will go down over time and it will eventually need to be replaced. Depreciation is a way to account for this.

While interest and tax are cash expenses, these may depend on management decisions external to the quality of the business − for example, how much debt is used to fund the business.

The EBITDA margin measures, in a sense, the 'pure' cash profit the business made in a given year.

While it may make some sense to compare EBITDA margins within an industry, it usually makes little sense to compare it across sectors or countries, as the amount of capital required to run a business can vary very dramatically between different industries.

3) **Effective tax rate** = taxes paid*/ profit before taxes

Effective tax rate can be defined as the average rate at which a corporation is taxed on pre-tax profits.

*The actual numerator used is (current tax + deferred tax + fringe benefit tax)

4) **Net profit margin** = profit after taxes (net profits) / revenue

Net profit margin measures the amount of profit a company obtains per rupee/dollar of revenues.

Unlike the EBITDA, it includes all expenses of the business.

5) Earnings per share (EPS) = profit after taxes (net profits) / number of equity shares

This is a measure of how much profit has been earned for each equity share issued. This is important, allowing one to relate to the price that is being paid per equity share in the market. More on this in the valuation ratios.

Balance-sheet ratios

1) **Return on equity (RoE)** = profit after tax /average net worth

   This is also sometimes called return on net worth (RoNW).

   RoE represents the total return on equity capital. It gives you the return the business is making on the equity investments made to run the business.

   The detailed formula we use for our calculations is the following, but unless you are a finance professional there is no need to get into this.

   ((Profit after tax − preference share dividend) /(average equity/ net worth − revaluation reserve −miscellaneous asset + dividend + preference share dividend + dividend tax))

2) **Return on capital employed (RoCE)** = (profit after tax + interest paid) $\star$ (1 − effective tax rate) / average capital employed

   Where capital employed = net worth + debt

   RoCE is a ratio that measures how efficiently a company is using its capital to generate profits.

   This is viewed in conjunction with the return on equity, or RoE. The reason to see this additionally is because RoE can sometimes be improved by simply taking on more debt.

   The RoCE is the number that is more comparable across companies. It shows the operational efficiency of companies before the capital or financing structure comes into the picture.

The detailed formula we use for our calculations is the following, but unless you are a finance professional, the one given above is good enough for an understanding of the ratio.

(Profit after tax before minority interest + interest paid) * (1 – effective tax rate) / (average capital employed– revaluation reserve + dividend + preference share dividend + dividend tax)

A more precise formula for capital employed is.

Capital employed = net worth + minority interest + total loans + deferred tax liabilities (net) + other long term liabilities.

3) **Return on incremental capital (ROIC)** = increase in NOPLAT during the year / net investment

NOPLAT is an acronym for net operating profits less adjusted taxes. It is derived as earnings before interest and taxes but after depreciation (EBIT), less adjusted taxes. Adjusted taxes are calculated as actual tax paid less tax on other income plus tax shelter on interest.

ROIC measures not just the efficiency of total capital but also whether the additional or incremental capital being employed is being used efficiently.

4) **Debt to equity ratio** = total loans / (net worth – revaluation reserve – miscellaneous assets)

The debt-to-equity ratio is a leverage ratio that indicates the proportion of a company's assets that are being funded through debt.

5) **Interest coverage ratio** = EBITDA / interest paid

The interest coverage ratio is a debt and profitability ratio used to determine how easily a company can pay the interest on its outstanding debt.

6) **Asset turnover ratio** = sales / total assets

Asset turnover ratio measures the company's sales or revenues generated relative to the value of its assets. The ratio measures the efficiency in the company's use of its assets to generate revenues.

7) **Book value per share** = net worth/ number of equity shares Net worth is a company's equity plus reserves.

This, in a sense, is the per-share value of all the equity that is currently invested in the business. This includes the initial investment and also the profits retained in the business and not paid out as dividend.

There are adjustments to be made if there are preference shares and revaluation reserves, but that is a nuance you can learn about later.

8) **Working capital** = debtors + inventory - creditors

Cash flow statement ratios

1) **Net operating profit less adjusted taxes (NOPLAT)** = (EBITDA – depreciation – adjusted taxes)

NOPLAT represents a company's operating profit after adjusting to normalize for the impact of capital structure and deferred taxes. This metric is a profit measurement that includes the costs and tax benefits of debt financing.

2) **Operating cash flows** = NOPLAT+ depreciation - change in working capital

This represents the cash a company generates from its normal business operations.

3) **Free cash flows (FCF)** = operating cash flows - capital expenditure

FCF is the money a company is left with after paying its operating expenses (OpEx) and capital expenditures (CapEx).

4) **Free cash flow (FCF) to equity** = Total FCF – interest paid – debt repayment

FCF to equity is a measure of how much cash is available to the equity shareholders of a company after all expenses, reinvestment and debt repayment.

Valuation ratios

5) **Price to earnings (P/E)** = current market price / fully diluted EPS

The P/E ratio indicates what the market is willing to pay today for a stock for each rupee or dollar of its past or future earnings.

6) **Price to book value (P/BV)** = current market price / book value

The P/B ratio considers how a stock is priced relative to the book value of its asset.

Now, remember that the return on equity is calculated on the book value. A company may have a high return on equity or return on capital employed, but if you are buying it at an elevated price to its book value, that higher return ratio is probably already priced in.

7) **Enterprise value (EV) to EBITDA** = EV[1] / EBITDA

This is a ratio that measures how much you are paying to purchase a company, or its value relative to its EBITDA. The PE ratio measures this only for equity. This ratio measures it for the entire company or firm, which means it is for equity and debt holders.

And, since it is measuring it for equity and debt holders, the relevant number from the income statement has to the profits before the payment of interest.

This multiple can be used to compare companies with different levels of debt.

---

[1] EV = market cap + preference share capital + total loans − cash and bank balance

Notes

1 'The Changemaker at First Global: Most Powerful Women 2022', *Fortune India*, available at https://www.fortuneindia.com/mpw/devina-mehra?year=2022.

2 Based on Bloomberg data.

3 First Global research calculations based on Bloomberg data.

4 First Global research calculations based on Bloomberg data.

5 First Global research calculations based on Bloomberg data.

6 Ibbotson, Roger G. and Paul D. Kaplanvol, 'Does Asset Allocation Policy Explain 40, 90, or 100 Percent of Performance?', *Financial Analyst Journal* 56, no. 1 (Jan–Feb 2000): 26–33.

7 Ashutosh Shyam, 'Another feather in India's m-cap: D-Street turns 5th biggest market with 3.8% share of global market cap', *Economic Times*, 27 December 2023, available at https://economictimes.indiatimes.com/markets/stocks/news/another-feather-in-indias-m-cap-d-street-turns-5th-biggest-market-with-3-8-share-of-global-market-cap/articleshow/106306260.cms?utm_source=contentofinterest&utm_medium=text&utm_campaign=cppst.

8 Based on Bloomberg data.

9 First Global research calculations based on Bloomberg data.

10 First Global research calculations based on Bloomberg data.

11 First Global research report based on Bloomberg data.

12 Bejamin Graham, *The Intelligent Investor* (HarperCollins, 2009).

13 John Kenneth Galbraith, *A Short History of Financial Euphoria* (New York: Penguin Books, 1994).

14 Rolf Dobelli, *The Art of Thinking Clearly* (New York: HarperCollins, 2013).

15 A version of this chapter appeared as 'What do past stock market returns tell us about the future?', Moneycontrol, 7 September 2023, available at https://www.moneycontrol.com/news/business/markets/what-do-past-stock-market-returns-tell-us-about-thefuture-11326981.html.

16 'What works on Dalal Street', First Global, May 1997, available at https://www.firstglobalsec.com/vintage-reports.

17 A version of this chapter appeared as 'This Diwali let's get rid of some investing myths and junk lying in portfolios', *Economic Times*, 7 November 2023, available at https://economictimes.indiatimes.com/markets/stocks/news/this-diwali-lets-get-rid-of-some-investing-myths-and-junkslying-in-portfolios/articleshow/105030559.cms.

18 Ellis, Charles D., 'The Loser's Game', *Financial Analysts Journal* 31, no. 4 (July/August 1975): 19–26.

19 'The Race', Tata, available at https://www.tata.com/newsroom/heritage/jrd-tata-aga-khan-race-aspy-engineer.

20 A version of this chapter appeared as: 'Why following successful investors may set you up for failure – Part 1', *Economic Times*, 16 April 2024, available at https://economictimes.indiatimes.com/markets/stocks/news/why-following-successful-investors-may-set-you-up-for-failure/articleshow/109153477.cms?from=mdr and 'Why following successful investors may set you up for failure – Part 2', *Economic Times*, 17 April 2024, available at https://economictimes.indiatimes.com/markets/stocks/news/

following-your-stock-market-heroes-may-not-always-pay-off-heres-why/articleshow/109340551.cms.

21 Hughes, John S., Liu, Jing and Zhang, Mingshan, Overconfidence, Under-Reaction, and Warren Buffett's Investments (July 5, 2010). Available at SSRN: https://ssrn.com/abstract=1635061 or http://dx.doi.org/10.2139/ssrn.1635061.

22 Kahneman, Daniel, Knetsch, Jack L., and Thaler, Richard H., 'Experimental Tests of the Endowment Effect and the Coase Theorem', *Journal of Political Economy* 98, no. 6 (1990): 1325–48.

23 Morgan Housel, 'Lots of Things Happening At Once', Collaborative Fund, 8 July 2020, available at https://collabfund.com/blog/lots-of-things-happening-at-once/.

24 A version of this chapter appeared as 'The story behind our high-conviction stock ideas', *Economic Times*, 21 November 2023, available at https://economictimes.indiatimes.com/markets/stocks/news/the-story-behind-our-high-conviction-stock-ideas/articleshow/105377475.cms?from=mdr.

25 A version of this has appeared as 'Heads - I was right, Tails - world was wrong. Devina Mehra explains self-attribution bias in stock investing', Moneycontrol, 16 August 2021, available at https://www.moneycontrol.com/news/business/markets/heads-i-was-right-tails-world-was-wrong-devina-mehra-explains-self-attribution-bias-in-stock-investing-7339631.html.

26 A version of this has appeared as 'Why following successful investors sets you up for failure, Devina Mehra of First Global explains', Moneycontrol, 5 July 2021, available at https://www.moneycontrol.com/news/business/markets/why-following-successful-investors-sets-you-up-for-failure-devina-mehra-of-first-global-explains-7123041.html.

27 A version of this has appeared as 'Why half-truths can be more dangerous than outright lies, argues Devina Mehra', Moneycontrol, 27 December 2022, available at https://www.moneycontrol.com/news/business/markets/devina-mehra-on-why-half-truths-can-be-more-dangerous-than-outright-lies-9772831.html.

Scan QR code to access the
Penguin Random House India website